CHRISTINA STEAD

Christina Stead

Joan Lidoff

FREDERICK UNGAR PUBLISHING CO.
NEW YORK

Acknowledgments:

I would like to express my gratitude to some of the thoughtful and encouraging readers who have helped this manuscript along its way: William Alfred, Morton Bloomfield,
Mary Kate Bluestein, Monroe Engel, Mary Anne Ferguson,
James Garrison, Anthony Hilfer, Jean Humez, Paul Starr,
William Sutherland, and to Max Bluestone, in grateful
memory. My admiration and special thanks to Christina
Stead, for a generous share of her time and spirit. This
book was completed with the aid of summer grants from
the University Research Institute of the University of Texas
at Austin and from the National Endowment for the
Humanities.

Portions of this work have appeared in *Aphra*, *New Boston Review*, *Southerly*, and *Studies in the Novel*.

Library of Congress Cataloging in Publication Data

Lidoff, Joan.
   Christina Stead.

823
S799zb

   (Literature and life series)
   Bibliography: p.
   Includes index.
   1. Stead, Christina, 1902–   —Criticism and
interpretation. I. Title. II. Series.
PR9619.3.S75Z7 1982   823   82-40283
ISBN 0-8044-2520-5   AACR2

Contents

To my family

Chronology

1935	Returns to London, pays first visit to the United States, attends the First International Congress of Writers for the Defense of Culture in Paris
1936	*The Beauties and Furies* published. In Spain, but leaves at start of Spanish Civil War for France
1937	Moves to the United States for the next nine years
1938	*House of All Nations* published
1940	*The Man Who Loved Children* published
1943	Goes to Hollywood as screenwriter for MGM. Returns to New York. Teaches a workshop in the novel at New York University
1944	*For Love Alone* published
1945	*Modern Women in Love*, anthology edited by Stead and Blake, published
1946	*Letty Fox: Her Luck* published. Stead and Blake leave U.S. for Antwerp
1947–1953	Live in Europe: Montreaux, Bologna, Basle, Brussels, Lausanne, London, Paris, the Hague, before settling in Surbiton, England, near London in 1953
1948	*A Little Tea, A Little Chat* published
1952	*The People with the Dogs* published
1955	Published an edition and a translation: *Great Stories of the South Sea Islands*, and *Colour of Asia* by Fernand Gignon
1956	Two translations published: Jean Giltène, *The Candid Killer* and Auguste Piccard, *In Balloon and Bathyscaphe*
1965	*The Man Who Loved Children* reissued
1966	*Dark Places of the Heart* (*Cotter's England*) published
1967	*The Puzzleheaded Girl* published. Recommended but refused for Britannica Australia Award
1968	William Blake dies in London
1969	Visits Australia as a Fellow in the Creative Arts at the Australian National University, Canberra

1

Always Original: The Shape of a Career

Who is Christina Stead? When Saul Bellow received the Nobel Prize in 1976, he proclaimed Stead deserving of that award.[1] Lillian Hellman seconds his faith.[2] Stead's fervent admirers include poets, novelists, and critics: Randall Jarrell, Robert Lowell, Tillie Olsen, John Updike, Elizabeth Hardwick, Stanley Burnshaw, Denis Donoghue, Christopher Ricks. Susan Sontag ranks Stead's novel *The Man Who Loved Children* with *Anna Karenina* and *The Great Gatsby* as one of the few masterpieces of literature that will endure.[3] Yet Stead's thirteen volumes, novels and tales, from the first in 1934 to the most recent in 1976, have been irregularly received and preserved. Her early works were hailed for their originality and abundance of invention. After the peak achievement of two autobiographical novels in the 1940s, her writing diminished in power; then, for nearly fourteen years, she ceased publishing. With the reissue of *The Man Who Loved Children* in 1965, Stead, in her sixties, resumed what seemed almost a second career. Throughout her seventies, she continued to publish new work. Some of her early fiction, out of print, is being reissued in the United States, England, and her native Australia.

Stead has often baffled reviewers, who are drawn to her power and originality, yet disturbed by the excesses that both define and frequently short-circuit

1

her genius. The major criticism of her has yet to be written. She is said to be "impervious to literary fashions"[4] and her place in literary history is difficult to determine. The passion and range of arguments on her behalf reveal conflicts in understanding every aspect of her work. Hortense Calisher sees in Stead a "strange blend of outmoded interest in character and avant-garde sensibility."[5] Writing about her greatest novel, *The Man Who Loved Children*, Randall Jarrell and Elizabeth Hardwick, who ardently admire her, and Mary McCarthy, who does not, find Stead an original, and this novel unique. Both Christopher Ricks and José Yglesias see its continuities with fiction of the last century. Though Stead differs from the nineteenth-century novelists in offering no comforting resolutions, "she has not diminished the proper canvas of the novelist,"[6] but addresses concerns political, sociological, and psychological. "In its sense of growth and of generations," writes Ricks, "in its generality and specificity, above all in the central place it accords to feelings of indignation and embarrassment, *The Man Who Loved Children* is in the best tradition of the nineteenth-century novel."[7]

Standing in sympathies between eras, her novels keep the nineteenth-century's devotion to realism, its scope of social concern, texture of observed detail, interest in character. Yet her understanding of these is informed by Marx and Freud, by a material social critique and by depth analysis of individual fantasy life and family relations. José Yglesias,[8] a Marxist critic, claims that her Leftist politics have kept her from consistent public favor, but Stead denies taking a formal political position; rhetoricians of the Left are targets of some of her harshest satire, as are followers of Freud. Her 1970s revival has been sparked by the interest of feminist readers. Stead adamantly disowns feminism, but her fiction traces with profound attention and understanding the constriction of women's lives by social circumstances, and individual women's rebellion in a search for independence. Even Stead's national identity is a matter of some uncertainty. Australian born, she spent most of her adult years in England, the United States, and Europe; her writing belongs to no one national tradition.

Like her work, Stead's life is distinctive, defined with unusual independence. Born on July 17, 1902, in Rockdale, a suburb of Sydney, Australia, Christina was the only child of David and Ellen Butters Stead. Her mother died when Stead was two, and Christina lived with her father, his sister Florence, and Florence's baby, Gwendolyn, until David married Ada Gibbons in 1907. David and Ada Stead eventually had six children. Christina's father was an ardent naturalist; their home was filled with his creatures and collections, and the endless tales he told his daughter, until, she reports, the younger children were born and she became "the cradle rocker and message runner and the one who sang the sleep [sic] and told tales."[9] "Eldest, a girl, I had plenty of work with the young children," Stead writes, "but was attached to them, and whenever I could, told them stories, partly from Grimm and Andersen, partly invented."[10]

While Stead's stepmother was one of many children of a wealthy Australian family, her father was the son of a British immigrant, Samuel Stead. According to family legend, Samuel had left England in 1864, inspired by the success of Magwitch's Australian venture in Dickens's new novel, *Great Expectations*.[11] Stead reports that the family was "full of Dickens" while her grandfather was alive;[12] her style shows that influence.

The characters and events of Stead's childhood seem familiar to the reader of her autobiographical masterpiece, *The Man Who Loved Children*. Her father, David, worked for several Fisheries agencies of the Australian government and wrote natural history monographs on Australia's fish life. In 1922–23 he went on a government trip to Malaya, and was prominent enough to appear in *Who's Who in Australia* from 1922 to 1950, before he died at eighty years of age in 1957. After the death of his second wife, Ada Gibbons, in 1951, David married a young botanist the age of his daughter Christina—Thistle Harris, who survives him. Her father's delight in the natural world and his long-term belief in socialism permanently shaped Stead's interests.

In a eulogy of her father, Stead writes, "He never went to the theatre or to concerts; he abhorred dancing, because of the contact of bodies; he did not allow kissing or embracing in the home, nor endearments, nor cajoling, which he thought led to degrading habits of mind. The home was, however, because of his own gaiety and talent for entertainment, and endless invention, gay and lively. He liked to lecture, he liked meetings and he did not miss the arts; . . . He believed in himself so strongly that, sure of his innocence, pure intentions, he felt he was a favored son of Fate (which to him was progress and therefore good), that he was Good and could not do anything but good. Those who opposed him, a simple reasoning, were evil."[13]

The Stead family moved from Rockdale to Lydham Hall, Bexley, in 1907, and, in 1917, with all seven children, to Watson's Bay, near the entrance to Sydney Harbor (the setting for Stead's second autobiographical novel, *For Love Alone*). After the last move, Stead went to Sydney High School, where she edited and wrote poetry and prose for the school magazine, *The Chronicle*. Her first extended writing project was a sonnet cycle celebrating an English teacher there.

Stead won a scholarship at Sydney Teachers' College in 1919. Until 1924, she worked on and off as a

teacher, but did not like teaching and suffered peri-
odically from voice strain. In these years, she taught
a class of retarded and emotionally disturbed children, taught in the Correspondence School of the
New South Wales Department of Education, was a
Demonstrator in Experimental Psychology at the
Teachers' College, and worked with psychological
testing in the schools.

Inspired by reading George Henry Lewes's biography of Goethe, Stead was determined to go to a
European university where she imagined a "whole
life, howling with philosophical arguments."[14] Like
Teresa Hawkins, the heroine of *For Love Alone*, she
went to business school at night and found employment, first working for an architect, then as a secretary in a hat factory. For five years, she lived at
home, contributing money to her family and painfully saving the rest of her earnings for her passage.
On March 28, 1928, she set sail from Sydney for London: she would not return to Australia for the next
forty years.

In London, Stead found a job as a secretary for a
firm of grain merchants, the manager of which was
an American, William Blake (born Blech). Blake was
a Marxist economist and writer, a man of great learning and eloquence. Stead was to live with him for the
next four decades, until his death in 1968.[15] In 1929,
she went with him from London to Paris to work at
the bank that provided the material for her grand
scale exposé of international banking and bankers,
House of All Nations (1938).

Blake was a devoted supporter of Stead and her
writing career and was partly responsible for her first
publication. "I wrote my first novel, *Seven Poor Men
of Sydney*," Stead writes, "in a London winter, when
I got home from work and was in poor health: . . . I
must have mentioned it to William J. Blake, for
whom I was working. . . . He read it over a weekend

and returned it, rather surprised. 'It has mountain peaks,' he said."[16] Blake took the manuscript to Sylvia Beach, of the bookstore Shakespeare and Co. in Paris, who brought it to the attention of the publisher Peter Davies. Davies asked Stead for another book to publish first. Working in between her secretarial duties at the bank, Stead dashed off the forty-odd stories of *The Salzburg Tales*, which was published in 1934. *Seven Poor Men of Sydney* (1934) is a sad, and only partially successful exposition of the thwarted lives of working class Australians during the Depression years in Sydney. Always interested in obscure men, Stead combines social realism with a gift for lyric prose. In the frequently gothic short stories of the *Tales*, Stead's fantasy finds open expression and this brilliant collection of stories reveals many of the themes and preoccupations of her later work, as well as displaying her extensive literary knowledge.

Living in Paris from 1929 to 1935, Stead traveled around Europe and spent six weeks in 1931 at the Mozart festival in Salzburg, the setting for her *Tales*. In 1936, she returned to London, paid her first visit to the United States, and attended the First International Congress of Writers for the Defense of Culture, in Paris, for which she wrote the English *compte rendu*. She went to live in Spain, but left for France after the outbreak of the Civil War. In 1936, her third book, *The Beauties and Furies*, was published. The story of an introspective, sensual heroine who tries to leave her English husband to find love and freedom with a young lover in Paris, this is Stead's first attempt at treating a tale she will tell more successfully in *For Love Alone* (1944). In 1937, Stead and Blake came to the United States, where they remained for nine years.

In New York, they were part of a circle of radical writers, some of whom were to become part of the persecuted Hollywood Ten. Stead read manuscripts for the Leftist journal *New Masses*, and wrote occasional book reviews. In 1943, she went to Hollywood, to work as a screenwriter for MGM; the experience was short-lived. Returning to New York, Stead taught a "Workshop in the Novel" at New York University in 1943. Stead tells how she and Blake also spent some months living in Washington, D.C., and Annapolis, gathering the details of setting necessary to transpose her family story there. During her time in America, Stead wrote *The Man Who Loved Children* (1940); *For Love Alone* (1944); *Letty Fox: Her Luck* (1946), a satire on the American way of life, especially the institution of marriage; *A Little Tea, A Little Chat* (1948), her most bitter exposé of ruthless moneymakers; and *The People with the Dogs* (1952), a more gentle critique of a large communal family and one of its listless sons, also set in and around New York. Her work had been declining in power and after this novel, Stead was not to publish anything for fourteen years.

In the increasingly anti-Communist climate of 1946, Stead and Blake left the United States for Antwerp. They had little money as they traveled around Europe for seven years (living in Montreaux, Bologna, Basle, Brussels, Lausanne, London, Paris, the Hague) before settling again in England in 1953. They lived in Surbiton, a southern suburb of London, not far from Blake's daughter from a previous marriage. There Stead stayed until, in 1974, she went back to Australia to live with her brother Gilbert in Hurtsville, a suburb of Sydney.

The years of travel in the 1940s and 1950s were apparently not productive ones for Stead, though some of the trunkful of fragments she says she has stored from that period have come into print in the 1970s. In this time she did some translations from the French and edited two anthologies of short fiction.[17]

A new wave of writing started for her after the reissue of *The Man Who Loved Children* in 1965, assisted by her friend and mentor, Stanley Burnshaw. A major novel, *Dark Places of the Heart* (*Cotter's England* in its English edition) was published in 1966. That has been followed by a fine collection of novellas, *The Puzzleheaded Girl* (1967), three about shallow, greedy American girls wandering rootlessly around Europe; and a fourth which revives her gothic mode of revealing the violence in human nature. In 1975, a reweaving of two earlier stories was published as *The Little Hotel*, a slight but accomplished account of an odd collection of expatriates who shelter in a small Swiss hotel after the Second World War. Her 1976 novel, *Miss Herbert* (*The Suburban Wife*), though marketed as a novel about a "liberated" woman, belongs more to the particular Stead genre which dissects the character of a likable egotist who lives on the optimism growing out of self-delusion. Through her seventies, Stead has continued to publish novels and short stories.

Stead's expatriate status has made her nationality a matter of ambiguity, at least to her native Australia. In 1967, she was recommended by its literary committee to the General Council of Australia for a $10,000 Britannica Australia Award. After wide public debate, Stead was rejected on the grounds that "her long residence abroad (since 1928) rendered her ineligible" although she had never given up her Australian citizenship. However, in 1969, Stead was made a Fellow in the Creative Arts at the Australian National University, Canberra. Her reputation and renown in Australia has grown; in 1974, she became the first recipient of the Patrick White prize, which White has designated to be given annually from his Nobel Prize money to an Australian writer of mature years. Australia now recognizes her as one of its major writers.

Stead still has a large unfinished work about the thirties, part of which was published in 1962 as the first chapter of a novel to be called *I'm Dying Laughing*.[18] One reader has suggested that, if finished, it might match in intensity and range *The Man Who Loved Children*, the novel for which she will be remembered.

Stead's life has been spent in many cities and countries; her novels, equally variously set, enthusiastically observe a wide range of creatures, places, and things. Often written in hotel rooms, they treat poor working-class characters in Australia, rich businessmen in Paris and New York, radical American journalists and European expatriates, printers and lace makers. Though she started writing stories and poems as a child, Stead claims that she does not think of herself as a writer. "I don't associate with writers. They're nice people. I was associated with them in New York . . . but what can you learn from each other? I learn from human beings, or even a cat, a hedgehog."[19] "I think I have remained out of it to have a quiet life," she writes. "I know the literary life is just what some people need, it helps many; but my life has been spent in different places, in touch with businessmen and people interested in economics—and even medicine . . . those businessmen—they are good raconteurs; for some reason they will tell a writer anything, even business secrets."[20]

While Stead's fiction is perceived as political, there are continuing conflicts about just what her politics are. Stead herself proclaims, "I am not puritan nor party [sic], like to know every sort of person, nor political, but on the side of those who have suffered from oppression, injustice, coercion, prejudice, and have been harried from birth."[21] In our interview, she insists, "I had no feeling about women when I wrote. I *am* a woman, therefore I write a certain way about women. It wasn't Women's Lib, any more than I suppose a writer who writes about man's sorrows is writing about men's liberation. It's what he sees, the tragedy of people."[22]

At the core of Stead's vision of the tragedy of people is a quintessentially political perception of the omnipresent workings of power. Those who have it exert it to compel those who do not to serve the needs of the powerful rather than their own. The rights and integrity of the individual are everywhere threatened by the unbridled demands of others. This dynamic pervades personal and family relationships and is reflected in the social, economic, and political arrangements of the state.

All individuals are capable of this devouring egotism; all social, political, theological, psychological, and philosophical systems can be used in its service. Tyrants are as enslaved as victims by their selfish desires, and victims are as capable as their oppressors of manipulating others for their own gratification. Socialist orators and sick old women have strategems of oppression as adept as those of patriarchs and bankers.

Language itself reveals what it tries to disguise: the dominating drive to dominate. Stead persistently unmasks the languages of self-deception: fully blown personal systems of rhetoric used to deceive the self and others in the pervasive human attempt to wrest others to one's will. Whenever doctrinaire political statements—socialist, feminist, humanist—appear in her fiction, they are invariably in the mouth of a character whose tone of delivery is whining or bombastic or in some way self-serving; they are ironically undercut by the narrative. Stead is fascinated not by what words express, but by the way words are used in power relations.

Stead understands people to be not primarily the rational beings their discursive language and logic would have us believe them to be, but more deeply determined creatures of primitive feeling and fantasy, of urgent needs and unmet desires, of a whole rich and dark being that their language at once reveals and disguises. Behavior is neither controlled nor expressed accurately by the language of reason. The rhetoric of logical abstraction in particular is, in her characters' hands, a weapon of egotistical domination: a tool for imposing one's vision on others.

What makes such deceptive and deceiving exercises of power reprehensible to Stead is a moral system grounded in one central affirmative tenet. Her own vision rests on a faith in the vitality of the individual human spirit struggling for expression and fulfillment, capable of flourishing within whatever constraints and distortions are imposed upon it. She believes in the miracle of human growth: the unfolding of energy, capacity, potential in creative development. Her caveats against egotism express her systematic opposition to all that thwarts and represses that unfolding. That includes all the structures of human and material production and reproduction; structures of individual, family, gender and class organization, economic and political structures; the functional structure of language itself.

Stead's vision draws on both Freud and Marx. The integration of conscious and unconscious thought and feeling is crucial to her idea of personality—and therefore of literary characterization. But private, individual consciousness is not just private; it is shaped as well by the forces of the particular society in which the individual lives, and whose forms are understood as they manifest themselves within individual consciousness. An acute sense of natural and social milieu balances the relentless introspection of her novels and tales. In her refusal to split the individual from the social, the personal from the economic, Stead is most deeply political. Without being

ideological, her thought is deeply grounded in Marxist and feminist perception. *The Man Who Loved
Children* brilliantly shows the family as the social
microcosm which mediates between the individual
and the culture. Each of her novels continues to be
rooted in this firm assumption of the reciprocal interconnection of personal and social structures of
experience.

Both her choice of subjects and the structure of
her fiction show her commitment to expressing what
has not been expressed of this conception of human
nature and society. She planned early to leave accounts of those who did not find a voice in history:
"At Sydney Girls' High School, I had my first serious
project, based on a footnote in a textbook of European history we used. The footnote referred to the
Lives of Obscure Men and this appealed to me
markedly. I planned to do that. . . . It came back to
me later, when I returned to England, after the war.
. . . I began to collect notes for an Encyclopedia (of
Obscure People) to have another title; a sort of coun-
ter *Who's Who*. By this time I knew something about
official reference books and I knew some very able
people who would never appear there, because of
their beliefs. Anyone I approached was willing to
help with his life-story. . . . I did eventually do
something of that sort. My first novel was called
Seven Poor Men of Sydney (title taken from Dickens'
Seven Poor Travellers) and one of my most recent,
Cotter's England (the working class north of England) has this subject."[23]

Seven Poor Men of Sydney is but the first of a
number of Stead's novels with collective protagonists. While *The Man Who Loved Children* most
brilliantly makes an entire family its center, this
novel, *House of All Nations, The People with the
Dogs,* and *The Little Hotel* all explicitly extend their

primary focus to a group of characters rather than subordinating everyone else to a single individual hero. This structural choice itself indicates a faith in the equivalent interest of all individuals.

Stead's writing attends to the secrets that fascinate her in the concealed lives of individuals of every classification. Especially concerned with "these thousand and thousand grains of sand of individual lives" that have been only partly recorded,[24] she makes literary record of many such lives. In spite of her persistent disclaimer of particular interest or origins in feminism, many of the unrecorded lives whose stories she tells are those of women; and the unrecorded story she tells best is her own. Stead's most coherently powerful fictions are her two autobiographical novels, *The Man Who Loved Children* (1940) and *For Love Alone* (1944). In them, Australian critic Dorothy Green finds "one of the most remarkable accounts . . . written of what it feels like to be a creative artist who is also a woman, a woman of intellect and passion, to whom both are equally necessary, growing from childhood through adolescence to the threshold of full adulthood."[25] To those two novels we must turn for the inner truths Stead herself would find most important about her life and, even more significantly, for the original fiction she makes of them.

2

Family Fictions:
The Man Who Loved Children

At the heart of Christina Stead's fiction echoes the persistent moral issue: egotism. She sees everyone striving by subtle or overt manipulations to subordinate others to his or her own needs and desires, trying to take as much while giving as little as possible. In her 1940 masterpiece, *The Man Who Loved Children*, Stead criticizes this ongoing struggle between competing egotisms, not only in her characterization and analysis, but in the very form of her fiction. This novel takes as protagonist no single hero, but an entire family. The animating conflicts from which Stead has constructed her story are the manifold tensions of family life. She shows each of her characters from his or her own point of view, but also as seen by the others. Creating all of her characters as they affect and are affected by each other, Stead achieves a multiple layering of distinct and fully developed perspectives. The world of the novel is an ironic suspension of the constantly colliding visions of the distinct personalities within the family, through which the family as a whole comes to life as a dynamic organism with its own personality and vitality. This interlayering of views is the objective correlative of Stead's moral stance against egotism. Through her imaginative generosity, she achieves in this novel what none of her characters do, a vision broader than the egotistical one, which admits the claim to life, space, and integrity of more than a single sensibility.

Shaped by the autobiographical family of Stead's adolescence, *The Man Who Loved Children* stands out from her other work as a masterpiece. Critic Susan Sontag compares it to *Anna Karenina*; like Tolstoy's, Stead's novel is about an unhappy family— unhappy in its own way, but at the same time in a way that is paradigmatic. One of Stead's special skills is to render with profuse particularity individual characters and dynamics so as to make clear their universal significance. This novel, writes Randall Jarrell, in his adulatory introduction, "makes you part of one family's immediate existence as no other book quite does." It penetrates the surfaces of personal sentiment and social pretense to expose an ongoing battle of domination, humiliation, and resistance that goes by the name of family love. Family relationships become psychological struggles in which female and male, young and old, the powerless and the powerful, are locked in relentless opposition. "*Little Women* rewritten by a demon," one critic calls it.[1] And Stead shows with special brilliance the connection between the politics of the family and those of the larger world. In spite of this relentless analysis, however, Stead takes zestful delight in the very range of personal differences that such struggles seek to deny. With little of her characters' need to reduce the variety of experience to simple abstractions, she not only tolerates but enjoys multiplicity. The abundance of Stead's imagination is manifest in her exuberantly inventive imagery and in the vast range of human and natural detail she draws within her fiction's net.

With vivid intimacy we come to know Samuel and Henrietta Pollit, Louisa, the oldest daughter, and the six younger children. Each child has a dis-

tinctive personality, especially Ernie, canny in adult
ways of money and power; and Evie, the manipulative "little woman." Tommy, the baby, plays affectionate ritualized kissing games with Henny. Unlike
his twin, Little Sam, Saul strikes out against his
father in sporadic outbursts of big Sam's own grotesque ribaldry. But it is Louisa, Sam's daughter
from a previous marriage and Stead's autobiographical counterpart, who grows to dominate the latter
half of the novel. Louie's determination impels her
out of the enmeshed tangle of her family; in the
course of the novel she begins to develop an independent way of seeing, and as the family declines, she
grows.

Seen in the context of grandparents, aunts and
uncles on both sides, the Pollits emerge for us from a
detailed accounting of their daily experience. The
social texture of their world is extended for us by
knowing Henny's rich, decaying family, the Collyers;
and the rowdy Pollits, especially Sam's sisters, Jo and
Bonnie. In one scene Jo arrives, "boiling with self-
respect" to reprimand the "butter-hearted" Bonnie
for her behavior with a married man. We overhear
not only their interchange, but also Evie playing
mother; Sam on the roof egging the boys on to fight
with each other; Louie intervening and bringing tea;
while Henny is off downtown complaining to her
lover Bert Anderson about Louie and life with Sam.
All these voices rise at once, to give a sense of full and
variegated family life. Within any one scene of this
novel, half a dozen characters go about the small particulars of their daily lives and conversations, rendered with a density of detail that is sometimes
overwhelming.

The moral strength of a novel or a family may be
measured by its capacity to tolerate difference. Like
every novel, every family has a collective world view
of its own; each shapes experience so as to define a

social world in which its characters live. Both fiction
and family construct their own universe of discourse,
defining the norms of emotional interaction, deter-
mining the parameters within which individual
character can take shape. Theory that describes the
functioning of family dynamics can also illuminate
that of the world of the novel, especially of this
novel.

A microcosm of the larger society, the family inculcates patterns, both cultural and idiosyncratic,
that perpetuate themselves in its children's psyches.
Its world view is synthesized from accepted cultural
norms and from its members' distinctive personalities. Like any social unit, the family mediates, more
or less adequately, between the needs of the individual and those of the group. It creates a system in
which a slighter or larger number of individuals are
given latitude for self-expression and independence.
Conflicts are governed by structural rules of age, sex,
and hierarchical power to balance the bonds of affection and eroticism that make for cohesion against
disorganizing incestuous impulses. Families try to
modulate the unifying and the divisive forces of love.
Maintaining an equilibrium of the tensions generated by disparate and divergent needs, a family is
generative to the degree that it allows different personalities room for growth.

Like an individual, a family establishes a self-
image, a family myth, which allots each individual a
characterization and a place within the working
whole. The myth functions smoothly to the degree
that each member accepts it and its commonly held
explanation of the tenor of experience and of individual behavior. Significant deviation from its silently agreed-upon system of explanations and tacit
rules upsets the finely integrated balance of family
dynamics.

With ruthless persistence, Stead's narrative unmasks mechanics that the family mythology conceals, undercutting family fictions with unyielding revelations of the least graceful or generous of motives. Like fiction, the family myth lends coherence and meaning to experience; when it is shattered (before it gradually reforms), chaos ensues. Stead's special art, always, is to render this chaos in aesthetic form, to find a shape for shapelessness.

Stead captures the family organism in the process of change and growth. She does so by giving us a young heroine painfully probing, dissecting and discarding the family myth. Thirteen-year-old Louisa Pollit starts to question her parents' versions of reality. She begins to develop an independent vision, which changes her perception of the family, and ours.

The real development in the novel is found in the multiple, changing visions and re-visions of the same core of family experience. The actual story of *The Man Who Loved Children* is rather melodramatic; more interested in the psychological exploration of character than in event, Stead is not an architect of well-built plots. She works, rather, as critic Graham Burns has demonstrated, by compiling scenes of emotional and moral climax.[2] *The Man Who Loved Children*, however, has a firmer structure than any of Stead's other novels, its unities lent by the family it describes.

In the two years of family life the novel explores, the struggles of Sam and Henny Pollit are counterpointed by the progress of Louisa's adolescence. Though Sam makes a trip to Malaya, where he enacts his domestic imperialism in a more public context, most of the dramatic force of the novel comes from the dialogues, dinners, and gatherings of just a few days of family life. When Sam loses the government job his father-in-law's influence had secured for him, and the Pollits are forced to move from their old

Georgetown mansion in Washington, D.C. to a tum-
bledown house near Annapolis, Henny, as battered
as the house is, broken by her loss of status, gives in
to despair and loses force in her continual battle
with Sam.[3]

As Henny and family life deteriorate, the oldest
child, Louie, gains strength. School begins to assume
emotional importance for her. She forms close attachments to her teacher, Miss Aiden, and to Claire,
another student. As she develops her own conception
of the family, she ceases to believe in Sam's and finally reaches the point of strength and desperation
at which she defies her father to assert her claim to
independence. Louie begins to assume responsibility
for the course of events, and the climax of the book is
of her making. Deciding that she must poison her
parents to free herself and the other children from
their destructive tyranny, she puts cyanide in a cup
of tea that Henny knowingly drinks. At the novel's
end, Louie is starting out on a "walk around the
world," finally freed from the oppressive intricacies
of family life, or so she thinks.

The power of vision and of language to shape vision is one of Stead's central subjects. Each of Stead's
characters is determined by a different rhetoric, and
each is extreme. While they are all acting on the same
stage, the Pollits are reading scripts from different
plays. Though both are characters of commanding
imaginative and rhetorical power, Sam and Henny
are so different that they scarcely speak the same
language. Stead profoundly understands the way the
primary gender division is a metaphor for the strife
of otherness, the constant tension caused by the need
to live with the existence of other wills and souls
than our own. In Sam and Henny Pollit, Stead dis-
tinguishes a masculine and a feminine vision, at such
irreconcilable poles that communication is almost
impossible. Sam is a charming orator, full of games

and play, overflowing with humanitarian, vaguely
Socialist rhetoric. Sam loves, in all-encompassing abstraction; Henny hates, with vile particularity. Her
wild, helpless tirades against her foolish husband,
poverty, womanhood, and the demands of a large
family abound in grotesque and acute perceptions of
the dark underside of life—which doesn't exist in
Sam's universe. Their children are amazed at

this world of tragic faery in which [adults] lived. Sam, their
father, had endless tales of friends, enemies, but most
often they were good citizens, married to good wives, with
good children (though untaught), but never did Sam meet
anyone out of Henny's world, grotesque, foul, loud-voiced,
rude, uneducated and insinuating, full of scandal, slander,
and filth, financially deplorable and physically revolting,
dubiously born, and going awry to a desquamating end.

Yet their incompatible world views are meshed
in their continuing marriage. Henny and Sam are
locked into an ongoing though destructive arrangement that sustains both of them, if unhappily. Each
uses the other as a target for his or her angers and
disappointments; they continue to produce children,
and to maintain daily life, however full of strife and
bitterness.

Setting her novel at the beginning of Louie's adolescence, Stead chooses a moment of crisis at which
old family structures and mythologies are challenged.
Louie's awakening sexuality evokes Henny's negative
feelings about her own femininity, as well as her conflicts with her stepdaughter. Sex becomes an overt
issue, and subtle shifts in the balance of power of the
family configuration occur. Louie moves away from
her strong attachment to her father and her acceptance of his point of view as absolute, into a new alliance with Henny (the coalition of the oppressed
that unites the women of this novel). As she grows
older, Louie begins to assume adult prerogatives.

Her rejection of the powerlessness of childhood rip-
ples through the family to erupt in rebellion against
Sam, the figurehead of authority. Louie's gradual
dissent from the received family mythology promul-
gated by her father causes a massive imbalance in the
psychic equilibrium of the family system, stirring
waves of implication and reaction throughout the
entire family. As her power-wise brother Ernie perceives, "Now Louie had her own right and wrong, she
was already entering their world of power."

The battle for control between Sam and Louie is
fought in and over language, as Louie insists on the
right to articulate her altered perceptions. The dramatic world views of Sam and Henny Pollit clash and
collide to create a world for their children. As
Louie's developing vision recasts the old family mythologies, it lends ironic perspective to the closed
systems of her parents' thought and behavior. The
tension of the conflict of Louie's vision with those
from which it was derived generates the field of force
of this novel, which frames all of these smaller visions in a wise if dark understanding.

To embody her own complex vision, Stead creates
a style I call the Domestic Gothic, one which draws
on a distinctive kind of grotesque imagery. Stead
does what Louie wished to do: "invent an extensive
language to express every shade of her ideas." "I
never told any one what it is like at home . . .
because no one would believe me!" cries thirteen-
year-old Louisa; and indeed, the situations and conversations Stead reports, while not impossible, are
extreme. The imagery and action of Stead's fiction
are true not so much to ordinary behavior as to the
workings of the inner life. Stead turns what Christopher Ricks describes as the "false . . . overblown,
indiscriminately theatrical" rhetoric we use when
"we speak to ourselves in the privacy of our skulls"[4]
into external speech that exceeds the cadences of

normal conversation in order to expose fantasies or-
dinarily kept hidden and reveal the characters' personal ways of seeing.

Stead recasts words into new associations which,
disjointed and dislocated, create painful new perceptions. While she never cedes her fiction to the forms
of inner consciousness—like Joyce or Woolf or
Kafka—she exploits the psychological fluidity of grotesque techniques. In her prose, unexpected analogies juxtapose the animate and the inanimate, animal
and human, confounding the distinctions between
them. Though people may be described in cockroach
imagery, however, they do not become cockroaches,
as they would in Kafka. Stead creates no logical or
even psychological impossibilities; her grotesque
metaphors are used to give visible shape to her characters' distress. With realism more psychological than
behavioral, Stead turns fantasies into fictional events
and uses metaphor and dialogue to expose the emotional distortions of her characters' private realities.
When, at the novel's end, for example, Louie poisons
her stepmother, she acts out an Oedipal fantasy of
murder and liberation.

In Stead's distortions, paradoxically, is her
story's realism. The family Stead recreates for us in
The Man Who Loved Children is not quite like any
we might see. It is closer to that internalized version
of family experience that an individual reshapes to
accord with his or her fears and desires, resentments,
angers, and wishes. Stead and her characters create a
world of language that penetrates by its very excesses
to this psychological core of intensified experience.

While everything in Stead's fiction is intensified,
stained with the violent colors of fantasy, the texture
of her prose is nevertheless dense with naturalistic
renderings of the material world and acute observations of the human. For all the extremity of language
and feeling, the setting and materials of this novel

are not surreal but ordinary. Though pervasively
colored by the emotional and metaphorical excesses
of gothic fiction, unlike the gothic, Stead's novel operates within the context of nineteenth-century realism. This narrative is set in an (almost) ordinary
house in Washington, D.C., not in a Gothic castle in
an exotic land. Its settings and situations, characters
and events, are realistic, or nearly so, its materials
domestic commonplaces: housework, eating, playing,
shopping, visiting. *The Man Who Loved Children* is
rooted in a real time and place; its characters are
neither stylized villains nor innocent victims, but
complex figures with humanly mixed motivations.
Stead's plotting and characterization, however, draw
from the depths of the subterranean fantasy world
that informs gothic fiction. Her grotesque imagery
projects these violent fantasies onto the physical
world, using ordinary domestic vehicles to release
the emotional forces that seethe beneath ordinary
events. This Domestic Gothic style with its capacity
to encompass fantasy in the quotidian world, balances profound access to the turmoils of the inner
life with equally acute observation of the natural and
political world to express the comprehensive moral
vision of the novel, one of depth and breadth of understanding greater than that of any of its characters.

Sam

At the center of this novel's manifold and shifting visions is Sam Pollit; Stead's title gives him
ironic prominence. In one sense, the whole novel is a
redefinition of the way Sam "loves" children. "Mother
earth," whispers Sam, "I love you, I love men and
women, I love little children and all innocent things,
I love, I feel I am love itself." Yet Sam, the man who
loved children, is of all the Pollits, the least willing

to admit the reality of others, to give credence to their separate existence, distinct from his own. While unmasking Sam with surgical precision, Stead nevertheless loves him in exactly the way he is incapable of loving: she allows him the integrity of his own vision. She sees how he sees and creates his system of perception in full vitality of detail. Critics have called Stead the woman who loved the man who loved children. While her novel will question, and undermine, the controlling assumptions of Sam's behavior, and show the underside of his most exalted ideals and self-conceptions, she also reinvents this character as a high-energy charmer. With wonder and attention she recreates his exuberant spirits and imaginative fertility as well as his narcissistic feeding on the children he "loves."

Like all of Stead's best characters, Sam is a creator as well as a creation. When Sam designs a project, everyone gets involved. He keeps a menagerie of animals, and constantly mobilizes his children into animal energy. On his "Sunday Funday," he marshals everyone to participate in his schemes. While he orchestrates fights among the boys as well as projects to paint the roof, he keeps everyone moving, circling around his center. Like a not so benevolent Prospero, or like the novelist herself, he has a distinctive imaginative vision and the power to impose it on others, who enact the world his mind invents. While his rhetoric is self-deluded, it is powerful. In another of Stead's novels, *Dark Places of the Heart*, it is observed of the central character that the light emanating from her father keeps her dazzled, blinded to all else as long as he lives. Louie breaks out of that charming circle of light, and Stead is able to let Sam keep that illumination, while herself standing beyond it.

While each of Stead's adult characters has a fixed and idiosyncratic world view, Sam's is distinguished

by its monolithic abstraction and blindness. His
speech is full of large abstractions. He believes in
Love and Goodness and Truth and Reason. "I wish I
had a man," Henny cries in despair, "and not a dish-
rag printed over with big words like 'constitutional
rights' and 'progress'!" Sam lacks Henny's one re-
deeming virtue—irony—the perspective of self-
awareness. He is uniquely innocent of self-knowledge.
Like Meredith's Egotist, Sam is compounded of
words; because he knows himself so little, his words
are not honest. All that he preaches is distorted by
the blind glass of his desires. There is a greater discrepancy between Sam's conceptions, and reality as
seen by the narrator and by the others than there is
for any other character. An overgrown child, with a
child's greedy needs and lack of realistic controls,
Sam has an adult's power to impose his will. He is the
most closed and damaging of all Stead's characters. It
is his vision against which the others struggle.

Sam insists, "I know men love their children, but
mine are bound up in me, part of me," making no
distinction between egotism and love. "I understand
him because he is myself," he says of Little Sam.
Stead's profound and persistent interest in individual and collective narcissism begins with her perceptions of Sam. Even when he believes he is giving his
children what they need, Sam is making them recep-
tacles for what he needs to give. When he comes
home from Malaya, he floods them with his experiences. "Already he was beginning to slop over, drown
them with his new knowledge, bubbling, gurgling as
he poured into them as quickly as possible all that he
had learned." Stead's metaphor evokes the grotesque
meal in which Sam decides to feed his children as
birds do their young, by chewing food and then forcing it from his mouth into theirs. After kissing
chewed banana into Tommy's mouth, he tries to do
the same to Louie, but she runs away, repelled. The

erotic undertones of Sam's play emphasize his violation of the taboos of parental behavior toward children, trespassing across boundary lines that should be
sacrosanct. Throughout Stead's fiction, the response
to longed for nurturing generally echoes Louie's repulsion at this excessive and unnurturing "giving"
that scarcely disguises the egotistical need from which
it proceeds, that threatens to encompass and absorb,
feeding off that which it pretends to feed.

Operating within a rhetoric of love and goodness, Sam makes emotional demands on his children
that their mother, for all her rages, never makes. In
one of his economizing schemes, he has organized all
the children to boil down a huge marlin to extract its
smelly oil for multiple household uses. One of the
twins, Little Sam, vomits, revolted by the fish offal
he has to clean up. Sam, however, is determined that
his son overcome this weakness, as he himself had
overcome a weak stomach as a boy. "Little Sam
here is the dead spit of his old man, and he got to
have a strong stomach," declares Sam. He pushes his
son towards moral perfection by throwing a dipper-
ful of foul-smelling fish offal all over the miserable
boy. Henny's intervention only eggs him on to assert
his control over the child, who has been reduced to a
pawn in his parents' battle. Sam never acknowledges
committing a cruel act; yet he torments his children
in the name of instruction or in the guise of wit.

Garbed in self-righteousness, Sam never acknowledges his negative emotions or self-interested motives. Punishing Louie, he insists, "I am not angry: I
am not punishing you out of pique. I am just." Com-
partmentalizing his sensibility, Sam uses one moral
rhetoric to preach to his children and expound his
scientific theories, and another, compounded of im-
itations, baby talk and highly aggressive grotesque
jokes, for play. His "humor" cloaks the combative,
selfish elements of his personality that his intellec-

tual posturing denies. The hostility he hides from himself, he releases against his children. His disguised aggression is all the more potent for its displacement.

With a penetrating eye for psychological dynamics, Stead exposes Sam's subtlest manipulations, and shows his emotional mechanisms to work by denial, projection, and repression. He protects his own glorified self-image by projecting all that he holds evil onto others. In his version of the family story, Henny is the violent and angry one, the source of all troubles; while he is patient, forebearing, generous, good, and loving. Henny, indeed, does use the children as objects on which to vent her anger, but for all that, she never violates them as Sam does. If she hurts them, she sees and respects them nevertheless. Sam demands that his sons be extensions of his own ego, marshaling them to his scientific ideas and quelling any deviation from his view of moral order. Simultaneously, he eggs them on to humiliate and abuse each other as he does. Unconsciously seductive with his daughters, he demands from Louie the sympathetic understanding he fails to give to her. With Evie, his "little woman," he teases and flirts, flattered by her submissive, delighted dependence on him.

The awakening sexuality of Louie's adolescence exposes one of Sam's overriding forms of denial: sexual repression. Stead shares Freud's central insights into the building of culture on repression, and the painfulness and power of repressed motives and feelings. In Sam, she paints a strong portrait of the mechanisms of sexual repression and their compensating displacements and distortions.

For all his love of nature, Sam is prudish. Like Henny, he is repelled by voluptuousness. But his revulsion is focused on female sexuality, something dissociated from himself. In Henny these feelings

take the form of self-hatred; for Sam, women become
the scapegoats for his distastes and fears while he
wraps himself in self-elevating piety. "He feared,
with the shrinking of the holily clean, the turpitudes
of adolescence, and although boys might go through
it, he heartily wished that bright pure womanhood
could leap straight from . . . innocence to . . . gentle
sobriety. . . . The swelling thighs and broad hips and
stout breasts and fat cheeks of Louisa's years . . .
were repugnant to Sam: he wanted a slim, recessive
girl whose sex was ashamed."

When Sam goes with a government anthropolog-
ical mission to Malaya, Stead fully exploits the expressive possibilities of the tropical setting to reflect
the threat sexuality holds for Sam. (She characteristically invents the natural environment in its own
concrete, vivid particularity, but also suffused with
human feelings that mirror and intensify the emotions, needs and fears of her characters.) In the hot,
teeming, sensuous climate of Malaya, where human
illusions of control are washed away, "the river of
moisture" drowns and suffocates Sam. Smelling of
mildew and sweat, "destroying and breeding nature
reached in everywhere here, could not be banished,
made man ridiculous." In this atmosphere Sam's
normally contained feelings "rushed in on him and
fastened in his flesh, devoured him, as an invisible
but rapacious creature." Dismayed, he has a moment
of recognition of his lusts. Well practiced in the sub-
terfuges of sublimation and rationalization, however, he transmutes sexual fantasies into idol worship of his dead first wife (romanticized by the
distance of death and time); enjoyment of the admiration of young girls, like his young colleague Gillian
Roebuck, and thoughts of his daughter—all loves he
considers pure.

Louie's adolescence, which threatens to upset his
conception of her, repels Sam, but fascinates him,

and intensifies his psychic devouring of her. "Louisa
was his first adolescent. . . . He poked and pried
into her life . . . with mental lip-licking he followed
her in her most secret moments . . . becoming more
horrified every day as Satan's invisible world was revealed to him." As Louie matures, it becomes more
difficult for Sam to maintain his blocked perceptions of sexuality.

Sam's exploitation of Louie is even more complex, though no less cruel, than his treatment of the
other children. Louie is his confidante; when she
begins to resist his confidences, to insist that she
must leave ("You must let me leave you, you must
give me some freedom" "I want to leave home. . . . I
must leave home"), he fights to keep her attached to
him with weapons ranging from trust and flattery to
humiliation and abuse. A clever manipulator, he
plays on Louie's better feelings of compassion as well
as on her well-reinforced self-doubts. Binding Louie
to him by the flattering insistence that he needs her
support, Sam simultaneously disparages her. Even as
he attempts to make her feel responsible for giving
him the unquestioning feminine adoration he needs,
he shames her, mocking her efforts at dancing, taunt-
ing her about her writing, exposing and ridiculing
whatever cherished fantasies of hers he can ferret
out. When she thwarts him, he insists that she is ugly
and helpless and could never survive without him.
Asserting that they have telepathic communication,
and can read each others' thoughts, Sam means that
Louie thinks and feels just as he does; he cannot believe her when she denies it and says she will never
confide in him. He wants to keep her by him forever;
to keep her, in essence, part of him forever.

The scenes between father and daughter are full
of complex emotional tensions. Louie clearly once
adored Sam, believed in his charades, participated
willingly in his fictions, and she is still susceptible to

him. He can humiliate and torment her. But, in her
adolescent way, between sullen withdrawal and passionate outbursts she begins to pull away from him,
insisting, "You must let me be on my own."

The intensity of Sam's reactions to Louie highlight not only his manipulation and lack of sympathy
for her, but also the intertwined intimacy of family
life, where changes in one person unavoidably affect
the others, upsetting their most fixed ways of dealing
with private issues. As Sam's personality influences
Louie, so her development alters his psychic equilibrium. From the complexity of her apprehension of
this interdependence of character, Stead invents the
world of her novel to mirror the reciprocally inter-
acting world of the family.

Her perception of the dynamics of human interaction is also informed by an acute awareness of the
pervasive importance in them of power. In the hierarchical determination of power, the family reflects
the patriarchal structure of the larger society of
which it is a part and whose values it inculcates.
While Louie does begin to change her relationship
with Sam, forging a new vision of reality, Henny is
locked with him into an unchanging confrontation of
incompatible visions. Louie's growth alters the workings of this network of interlocked feelings, but Sam
and Henny are frozen in stasis, in a self-perpetuating
if destructively consuming pattern of behavior. While
each of them are potent psychological forces, the relations between husband and wife are defined ultimately in terms of power; and in their ongoing struggle, Sam holds the final advantage, superiority not of
spirit, but of socially affirmed status.

Irreconcilable extremes, Sam and Henny are in
perpetual conflict. Henny rants while Sam moralizes.
Sam shapes the world into idealized norms; Henny
invents a realm of animated attacking grotesques.
The difference in their speech represents such a pro-

found difference in their personalities that they have
no common ground for communication. "They had
no words between them intelligible." Fights characterize their entire married life. In the bitter battle
they have just before Sam leaves for Malaya they try
to hurt each other in every way they can, starting
with words and ending with a kitchen knife. Their
differences are never resolved, but afterwards they
are brought together by sex, as is their custom. Polarized forces, their only union is in passion, angry or
sensual; never joyous or loving, their sexuality grows
only out of released aggression and unremitting opposition. The cycle perpetuates itself, as each new
pregnancy creates a new line in the chain that binds
them in unloving dependency. In the lull after the
worst physical violence of their fight, Henny looks
down at the wedding ring on her finger and thinks:

If this plain ugly link meant an eyeless eternity of work
and poverty and an early old age, it also meant that to her
alone this potent breadwinner owed his money, name and
fidelity, to her, his kitchenmaid and body servant. For a
moment, after years of scamping, she felt the dread power
of wifehood; they were locked in each other's grasp till the
end—the end, a mouthful of sunless muck-worms and grass
roots stifling his blare of trumpets and her blasphemies
against love.

Henny continually struggles against Sam, but
her self-hatred ultimately keeps her dependent on
him, and her dependence increases her self-hatred.
Stead brutally reduces their interdependence to its
crudest terms. They are economically and socially
bound together, but their union fills deeper emotional needs as well. Sam and Henny use each other
as targets against which to vent their hostilities and
their disappointments. Each blames the other instead of himself for the diminution of their dreams.
Sam believes he could have been a great man if he

had had a more worshipful wife. Henny, despite her
vituperation, has counted on Sam for strength that is
not his to give. Having grown up the spoiled daughter of a wealthy and indulgent father, Henny has
looked to Sam for the same kind of paternal support.
She has great difficulty in relinquishing the idea that
she is protected by a man who can make everything
turn out all right for her. When she finally realizes
that Sam cannot fill this godlike role (after the Pollits become irredeemably poor and move to Annapolis) she despairs and dies. She is incapable of sustaining herself unsupported once she has seen through
the last of her own mythology to the real Sam.
Within this violent and hurtful marriage Stead makes
clear the self-sustaining dynamics by which two
people can support each other in their mutual
unhappiness.

Yet there is an imbalance in their equilibrium.
Henny's anger, always abundantly expressed, has always been futile—a vast expense of energy directed
towards no positive goal. Finally it is only self-destructive. Sam has the advantage of being a man in a
man's world. It seems to his wife that "life was a rotten deal, with men holding all the aces." Outside the
sphere of his own family, Sam is vulnerable; he
makes a fool of himself, is stained by scandal, loses
his job. He cannot hold his own in the world of men.
But within the shelter of his family, Sam does have
the power to impose his will, however out of touch he
is with human realities. In this Stead sees something
of the patriarchal power structure that mediates the
polarized visions within the family. Sam lives in a
clear daylight world of natural animals and events
that simply denies the dark mysteries of feeling and
fact that inform Henny's world of passionate misery.
His cantish optimism and self-righteousness keep
him above conflicts he refuses to recognize. "He
lives . . . in a golden cloud floating about over a lot

of back alleys he never sees," says Henny, "and I'm a citizen of those back alleys, like a lot of other sick sheep." Henny's means of seeing and coping are destructive to herself; her anger turns inward in a feisty, gnarled, feminine self-hatred. All of Sam's personality defenses are self-protective; he preserves himself at others' expense. However, his vision is functional in the economic and political public world. Even though it is Henny who manages their money so the family can survive, only Sam in his role as bread-winner has access to means of earning money. Though Henny's vision is more emotionally honest, Sam is better able to live in terms of the distortions of his. Henny is ultimately at a disadvantage because Sam's vision and power have social confirmation hers lack. Henny gives in to despair in the end and drowns, while Sam's unseeing egotism keeps him floating above the surface. Sam survives, inflicting more harm on others than himself; he continues, with vitality, energy, and even a certain charm, to thrive.

Henny

For all the potency of her critique, Stead portrays Sam with unusual fullness as an individual, a man, a husband, and especially, as a father. He is seen, in fact, most vividly, in relation to his children. Stead's portrait of Henny as mother of the Pollit family is also unusual. Because they are the most powerful figures of early childhood, mothers are especially vulnerable to subjective distortion through the lenses of a child's own needs and desires. The literary history of their portrayal has been one of idealization or denigration. Images of mothers often divide into the good mother, created from early memories of benevolent nurturing and protection, a fount of oceanic love and perfect sympathy, intuitive, giving, self-

sacrificing and self-effacing; and the inimical oppressor of adolescence, the incarnation of destructive
power and repressive social constrictions against
which the maturing hero rebels. For women writers,
the myth of feminine sympathy is often internalized
and the maternal ideal incorporated in the heroine's
self-image. Stead, notably, throughout her fiction,
resists maternal idealization, just as Louie resists
Sam's attempts to cast her in a nurturing feminine
role. Because her characters refuse to internalize the
demands of the maternal ideal, they have an independence of vision, and the energy and urge for self-
definition thwarted in more motherly characters.

Never an idealized nurturing mother, neither is
Henrietta Pollit an all-powerful evil mother figure, a
stepmother from a fairy tale. Though Sam would like
to cast her as this stylized villain, Louie, moving towards the novel's narrative vision, begins to see her
stepmother more complexly. As Louie comes to understand and Stead seems always to have known,
Henny's rantings grow out of the pains of her own
life:

Louie had passed on to an entirely original train of
thought which was, in part, that Henny was perhaps not
completely guilty toward Sam, that perhaps there was
something to say on Henny's side. . . . Henny was gradually
becoming not a half-mad tyrant, whose fits and maladies
must be cared for by a stern, muscular nurse; not all a hys-
teric, the worthless, degenerate society girl whom Sam had
hoped to reform despite vitiated blood and bad habits of
card playing, alcohol, and tobacco; but she was becoming a
creature of flesh and blood, nearer to Louisa because, like
the little girl, she was guilty, rebellious, and got chastised.
Louie had actually once or twice had moments when she
could listen to Henny's scoldings and (although she
trembled and cried bitterly) could recognize that they
came from some illness, her neuralgias, or cold hands and
feet, or the accumulation of bills, or from Sam's noisy joys
with the children, and perennial humanitarian orations.

While Sam would like to make the family history a romance, with good guys and bad women, Louie resists that vision, and Stead seems never to be tempted by the psychological simplicity of the form. She portrays Henny as both loving and destructive, a complex being whose love and injury proceed from the same sources. Henny rants at her children, but she has little rituals with each of them: kissing Tommy in the mirror, reciting with Ernie the bedtime litany they have repeated since his babyhood; telling riddles. She and her maid Hazel rail at each other, but both acknowledge that between them "the stream ran deep and still." There is a real antagonism between Henny and Louie, but when Henny takes Louie downtown to shop for shoes, they show each other an accustomed mutual respect and a connection in the habitual routines of daily life. Each allows the other to go her own way; when Louie wants to visit a pet store, Henny makes nasty remarks, but she goes, and she protects Louie from the condescending neighbors they encouter.

Stead shows parents as their children experience them, as absolute sources of power, but also as limited humans who themselves do not have absolute resources or strengths. This wisdom makes her stern judgment more compassionate. Stead lets us see Henny as she might see herself. Henny is not only a mother and a wife, but a woman of passions—angry, sensual, selfish; of sharp tastes and sharp words. She is an angry character, but not a character created exclusively from a child's angry perceptions.

Henny's life, however, is shaped largely by her anger. Through her language, Stead shows the alien hellish world, like that of a grotesque Bosch painting, in which Henny wanders. Feeling hopelessly trapped by her unhappy marriage, Henny peoples the world around her with astonishing creatures who reflect her frustrations. When she goes downtown to shop she invariably sees characters like a dirty shrimp of a man with a fishy expression who purposely leaned over me and pressed my bust, and a common vulgar woman beside him, an ogress, big as a hippopotamus, with her bottom sticking out, who grinned like a shark and tried to give him the eye . . . and waitresses smelling like a tannery (or a fish market), who gave her lip, . . . there were . . . creatures like a dying duck in a thunderstorm, filthy old pawers, and YMCA sick chickens, . . . and women with blouses so puffed out that she wanted to stick pins in, and men like coal-heavers, and women like boiled owls and women who had fallen into a flour barrel; and all these wonderful creatures, who swarmed in the streets, stores, and restaurants of Washington.

Henny constantly encounters animated objects and animalized people—weird aggressive creatures who act as angry as she feels. She sees herself as a victim who, though constantly scrapping, has no hope of escaping to clearer air. Her constant tirades express her lack of coherence as a person (though not as an aesthetic creation).

Stead uses for Henny imagery of fragmentation that reveals Henny's defective self-esteem. "Haggard, threadbare, over-rouged," she is a slatternly witch, distinguished by her dark eyes, "the huge eyeball . . . deep-sunk in the wrinkled skullhole, the dark circle round it." Stead's metaphors evoke the decay of aging, but more than that, they tend to fragment and objectify Henny—to portray her in pieces, rather than as a whole, as an inert object rather than as a living being. Henny's appearance reflects her feelings: her skin is wrinkled and her clothes threadbare; to her "life is nothing but rags and tags and filthy rags at that."

In the formative opening metaphors of the novel, Stead introduces the Pollit children as a collective vital force, dashing, tumbling, steaming and popping like a bubbling volcano, as they flow into Henny's room. When they leave, they all rush off like water down the sink, leaving her sitting there, with blackened eyes, a yellow skin, and straining wrinkles: and she would think of the sink and mutter, "A dirty cracked plate; that's just what I am! . . . I'm a greasy old soup plate." Using household items to caricature herself in Dickensian fashion as a ludicrous, passive, defective object, Henny collaborates in her own metaphorical denigration. Her wry deflation, which evinces her imaginative energy and force, nevertheless diminishes her full humanity.

Henny is often confounded with her physical environment by both Stead's imagery and her own. "Toothaches and headaches, the insane anxieties about cancer and t.b." that preoccupy her get confused with "the winds, the rattlings and creaking of the old house" in which she lives. She thinks of her house, in which she feels a prisoner, as her marriage, and of both as a diseased body "full of living cancers of insult, leprosies of disillusion, abscesses of grudge, gangrene of nevermore, quintan fevers of divorce, and all the proliferating miseries, the running sores and thick scabs [of] the flesh of marriage." The physical is so intermingled with the psychological that external realities which intrude on Henny become projections of her inner conflicts and are themselves seen as animate. This loss of boundaries intensifies her misery and imprisonment. All of her life is of a piece, but it is all in pieces. Everything reflects her wretchedness.

Henny's metaphoric failure to distinguish her feelings from the world outside herself derives from a way of perceiving that colors all of a character's environment with the suffocating reflections of her own fantasies. There is an osmotic permeability between Stead's characters' psyches and their surroundings. Objects and scenes are coextensive with feelings and imaginings. Stead uses grotesque metaphors as

objective correlatives of her characters' distress—
pulling all the created universe into the shapes of the
fears, angers, desires of their inner lives.

Like Dickens, Stead releases vivid distortions of
feeling in this grotesque imagery which blurs boundaries to threaten us with recognition of the immanence of chaos.[5] The incongruous combinations and
distortions of the grotesque, the sudden transformations wreaked on what had seemed stable shake our
basic certainties about the constancy of human form,
both physical and psychological. The grotesque
awakens our fear that we are somehow not persever-
ing autonomous entities with enduring shape and
purpose. Threatening us with the violation of our
physical and emotional integrity, this imagery
touches, at the physical extreme, on fears of death, at
the psychological, on fears of dissolution of identity.

Stead's grotesque style provides an appropriate
correlative for the internal conflicts about the boundaries of oneself that we understand to be the result
of Henny's ambivalent and troubled self-conception.
But Henny is not alone in her conflicts. An extreme
character by any standards, Henny Pollit nevertheless emerges from a familiar social context. Stead
embeds her both horizontally and vertically in the
web of her immediate and extended family and of
the larger society the family reflects. Looking at her
mother and daughters, Stead shows the roots of
Henny's fragmentation and angry feminine self-
hatred in the enforced dependency and passive submission to external forces that characterize women's
domestic lives. She represents the vision of the
Domestic Gothic style as one generated from the constraints and the strengths of women's life in the
family. The aesthetically fruitful but personally debilitating habit of confusing oneself with one's surroundings reflects not only Henny's habit of perception, but what psychologists describe as a pervasive

problem in feminine ego development. Women tend
to define themselves not entirely as discrete and autonomous entities, but in a more affiliative fashion
as part of a network of relationships; as continuous
with external presences in their lives. This emotional
pattern results in what is professionally called "weak
ego boundaries" (though contemporary psychologists
suggest this phenomenon might also be described as
a strength, not a weakness). In a culture that primarily values independence and autonomy, such a re-
lational way of perception is disadvantageous and
devalued.

Henny shares with the other women in the novel
the experience of life as dirty and threateningly
chaotic. When she takes Louie and Evie to visit her
mother at Monocacy, the old family estate, Old Ellen
Collyer drolly passes her feminine wisdom on to
Henny's stepdaughter: "'Life's dirty, isn't it Louie,
. . . Don't you worry what they say to you, we're all
dirty. . . . Only it's all over now; I'm clean now.
. . . The worst was when they were all . . . tramp-
ing through the house, dirtying it all up. . . . She
laughed uproariously. . . . Now it's different. I'm, a
decent body, fit to talk to my washerwoman. No
more milk on my bodices, mud on my skirts, only
snuff on my moustache.'"

Old Ellen is a wonderful comic caricature, like
many of the grandmothers in Stead's fiction, and like
the Dickens characters Stead learned to know from
her own grandfather. But her wit expresses serious
wisdom. Old Ellen is beyond the messiness of birth
and child rearing now, by virture of age, and laughs,
as only the very old and the very young in this novel
can. During their reproductive years, the shape of
women's lives is determined by immersion in the dirt
of sustaining daily life. For Henny, the omnipresent
dirt mirrors despair. The sheer messiness of caring
for children and maintaining physical needs, to which

her husband remains oblivious, overwhelms her. Returning home, towards the disastrous climax of the book, she retreats to the babies' room filled with disorder, smelling of babies' dirt. The children's cry, "The baby's eating dirt. . . . He's eating dirt," calls her from this messy refuge. "The baby's eating his own crap—sh! excrement, Mother." "And yesterday he ate a caterpillar." "'Ooh!' cried Evie. 'It's so dirty, it squidged out. . . .' They shrieked with laughter.'" What's funny to the children and their grandmother is tragic to Henny for this mess shapes her whole life. While pre- and postmenstrual women enjoy a certain freedom, life as an adult keeps these women enslaved to their own reproductive biology.

It is not so much the facts of childbearing, however, as it is cultural attitudes and constraints that determine that this life be devalued and destructive. While the realities of domestic and child care immerse women in perpetual messiness, their assignation to that role carries a symbolic weight of social subordination. Anthropologist Mary Douglas, in *Purity and Danger*, explains that to create order from the chaos of experience, a culture determines definitions of dirt and cleanliness which distinguish order from disorder. "Dirt" is essentially disorder, which is to be tamed. The consignment of mundane dirty tasks to women, which is echoed in a cultural derogation of female sexuality, is an indication of women's subordinate social role as bearers of the fearsome elements of chaos that the dominant culture struggles continually to suppress.[6]

Degradation to the role of keeper of rejected values has psychological consequences; women internalize the image of dirt and disorder. A preoccupation with dirt and disease (an internalization of the feeling of being dirty and out of control) characterizes the women in this novel. The Collyer women's discussion is almost exclusively about sickness, dirt, and disaster. Their "gossip" begins with an extensive discussion of various ways of committing suicide, and concludes with a helpless lament about the plight of women: joining them, Louie overhears "the end of a discussion about varicose veins, girls in factories with unwanted babies, and clots in the brain and the heart." "When I see what happens to girls," declares Henny, "I'd like to throttle my two, or send them out on the streets and get it over with."

Henny's feelings of degradation, then, of uncertain identity and lack of control are part of a family heritage, which is itself a product of the culture it expresses (and passes on). By setting her novel at the beginning of Louie's adolescence, Stead uses Louie's puberty to evoke her stepmother's denigrated and denigrating feelings about female sexuality. These are part of Henny's self-hatred; inherited from her mother, she passes them on to her daughters.

Like more contemporary women writers, Stead breaks silently but widely accepted taboos to talk about specific facets of female sexuality such as menstruation, and makes explicit its association with dirt. Henny's sexual ambivalence spills out as in one of her frequent angry tirades to Sam she shouts that

> she wanted to know whether Sam knew that his beautiful genius's clothes were smeared with filth and that most of the time the great big overgrown wretch with her great lolloping breasts looked as if she'd rolled in a pigsty or a slaughterhouse and that she couldn't stand the streams of blood that poured from her fat belly and that he must get someone to look after such an unnatural big beast.

The epithets she hurls at Louie are violent, but the imagery she uses for her own body is also degrading. When she is pregnant, her bloated figure is as grotesque as her normal haggardness. "I feel full as a tick," she says, or, turning the oceanic imagery often associated with motherhood inside out, "I'm so

empty, I feel like a big barrel floating out to sea."
When she is angry, her dehumanization is more violent: "My back's bent in two with the fruit of my
womb. . . . I go about with a body like a football,
fit to be kicked about by a bohunk halfback . . .
such a rotten, helpless, stupid thing . . . I am . . .
going through the bloody mess again."

Sex to Henny is hostile aggression. Passive and
misshapen, she portrays herself as the despicable,
helpless object of someone else's will. Her passivity,
in the endlessly reinforcing cycle of childbearing and
dependency, intensifies both her anger and her helplessness, regenerating the negative feelings her grotesque imagery expresses.

Her reactions to other women also betray sexual
revulsion. Voluptuous women offend her; she insults
them as she does Louie, mocking the features that
emphasize their sexuality. One women "had a breath
like a salt mine and a great belly like a foaling mare,
floating and bloating." Another was "beefier than
ever in the hips . . . and great big shoulders lollop-
ing . . . a ton of beef [with] that great body of hers."
Henny's young daughter Evie reflects her mother's
feelings in her reaction to her Aunt Jo:

She shrank from the long, plump, inhuman thigh, the
glossy, sufficient skirt, from everything powerful, coarse,
and proud about this great unmated mare. . . . "Oh,"
thought Evie to herself, "when I am a lady with a baby, I
won't have all those bumps, I won't be so big and fat, I
won't creak and shout, I will be a little woman, thin like I
am now and not fat in front or in the skirt."

The animality of these big women offends Henny
and her daughter, but Henny's disgust reflects her
own internal contradictions: she is repelled by sex,
but she is actively sexual; she has a lover who is just
such an elephantine character as she finds revolting;
she reviles childbearing but has six children. Her

sensuous metaphors make physical realities repugnant, but it is sensuous things that she notices. In her memoirs, Simone de Beauvoir observes in her mother the same tension that Stead senses in Henny: "She had appetites in plenty; she spent all her strength in repressing them and she underwent this denial in anger. . . . A full-blooded, spirited woman lived on inside her, but a stranger to herself, deformed and mutilated."[7] Henny exposes this deformed and mutilated inner self to public view by her vividly distorted imagery.

While Henny's characterization benefits from the aesthetic resilience of Stead's style, which transforms these constrictions and constraints into comic energy and expressive creativity, as a person Henny is more limited, more frustrated. Unlike Sam, Henny shares Stead's penetrating understanding of the dark crevices of human nature; her apprehension feeds a wildly creative imagination expressed in language full of animal, aggressive energy. But because Henny is unable to see herself as effective or self-determining, all her abundant force is expressed in self-destructive rages and ineffectual flailing about in circumstances she feels she cannot change.

Stead shows how Henny's vision is inherited, and how it is passed on. Henny's young daughter Evie picks up intact many of her attitudes. As we see Evie acting as a willing pawn in Sam's maneuvers of seduction and submission, or orchestrating her own games as Mother, we see in her a perpetuation of the traditional woman's role. Louie, on the other hand, resists as much as she is shaped by Henny's vision. While Henny does not have the strength of her own desires, Louie, like Stead's narrator, will be able to use her desires, however twisted by the very pressures that trap Henny, to transcend her limitations, assert a new vision of herself, and take the action that vision implies.

Louie

Louie's conception of herself is initially shaped by
her father's bullying manipulations of his family to
extract their sympathy, and by her stepmother's
fragmented self-denigration, that spills over onto the
children and pollutes their perceptions as well as her
own. From both Sam and Henny, Louie inherits a
view of herself as gross and clumsy; in the bewilder-
ment of adolescence, she feels like an awkward beast.
Her parents, both experts at insults, build for her a
special collection of epithets. She is a "silly fathead,"
a "mountain of fat," a "great fat lump," a "sack of po-
tatoes," a "boiled owl." Henny rants that she will kill
"that great stinking monster, that white-faced ele-
phant with her green rotting teeth and green rotting
clothes." Louie becomes the physical embodiment of
Henny's vision of the painful mess that is women's
lot.

   Louie struggles with the denigrated image of
femininity handed down by her parents, intensified
by the disturbing violence of the animal feelings she
is beginning to recognize within herself, which also
subject her self-image to monstrous distortions. When
she argues with Evie, seeing the "look of terror on
her sister's face she felt she was a human beast of
some sort. . . . And the worst thing, more terrifying, was the way she villainously held back the
animal in her, while it waited to pounce." The unac-
customed passions of adolescence—sexual stirrings,
newly discovered aggressions—make her feel like an
oddity. Like the twelve-year-old Frankie in Carson
McCullers's *The Member of the Wedding*, she iden-
tifies with freaks, whose grotesque and sexually ambivalent forms embody the stresses of adolescent
self-doubt, and particularly those of female
adolescence.

   Stained with many of the doubts and angers of

Henny's vision, Louie, like her, is weighted down by self-hatred, tormented by the grotesque sensibility that derives from the violent intimacies of family life. But Louie struggles to resist the "frightful sloughs of despondency and doubt and uncleanness which seemed to be sucking her down." She feels mired in the "trivial miseries, self-doubts, indecisions, and all those disgusts of preadolescence, when the body is dirty, the world a misfit, the moral sense qualmish, and the mind a sump of doubt." But in spite of this, she develops a more active sense of herself than her stepmother has. Tormented by her anger and lust for destruction, Louie is like Henny and unlike Sam in acknowledging the primitive violence within herself, but this awareness does not paralyze her. While Henny is the strongest spokesman of the emotional grotesque in the novel, Louie is its agent, and commits wished for acts of violence that the adults cannot quite bring themselves to. (Early, a neighbor talks Louie into drowning a cat she is too pietistic to drown herself. At the end, Louie acts out Henny and Sam's violence.) While Louie will have to struggle with the guilt her actions entail, she does act, and her perception of her capacity for action is crucial to her growth.

Growth is central to Stead's characterization, which is not static but dynamic. She portrays Louie as a developing personality, and is quite clear about the mechanisms of change. In Louie, Stead shows both the profound influence of family life and the individual's resistance to it. She captures that electric interplay between that which the individual is free to influence by her own will, and that which shapes her beyond her conscious control. If Louie is formed by her parents' anger and abuse, she also gains from Henny honest self-awareness, and from Sam energy and imagination, an ability to shape ideas, language, and action. Consolidating strengths neither parent alone has, Louie is able to overcome Henny's essentially passive response to life and move beyond the destructive confines of the family world to a more self-determined existence.

Conceiving of personalities and relationships as organically growing, Stead shows the other influences and attachments that help Louie change. Louie wins her freedom for growth as she learns to perceive new points of view, which necessarily bring into question the absolutism of the original family mythology. As the novel opens, we see Louie begin to question her initial wholehearted trust in Sam and his telling of the family history, which casts Henny as the villain. The first steps of Louie's growth are seen in her movement away from Sam and towards Henny. While Stead never underestimates the antagonism between stepmother and stepdaughter, she shows Louie slowly begin to identify more closely with Henny, a change which starts to free her from her father's absolute influence. Separated first by dislike, they move, through Louie's adolescence, into a strange bond of feminine distress and sympathy, in which their two separate miseries become nearly indistinguishable.

Between Henny and Louie is all the animosity of stepmother and stepdaughter: "Louisa was Henny's stepchild, as everyone knew, and no one, least of all Louie, expected Henny to love this girl as she loved her own." Henny transfers some of her anger at Sam to his daughter, in whom she sees many of the Pollit traits she despises, and she often uses Louie as a convenient object on which to vent her general rage.

In spite of Henny's abuse, she does not provoke the conflict with Louie that Sam does, because she does not make emotional demands on her. "Henny, delicate and anemic, really disliked the powerful, clumsy, healthy child and avoided contact with her as much as she could. It happened that this solitude was exactly what Louie most craved. Like all children, she expected intrusion and impertinence: she very early became grateful to her stepmother for the occasions when Henny most markedly neglected her, refused to instruct her, refused to interpret her to visitors." Although Henny ignores Louie or beats her, she does not manipulate her. She does not ask her for emotional support, as Sam does. Louie, on her part, has minimal expectations of Henny, so she is not as vulnerable to her as she is to her father. The tension between stepmother and daughter is not compounded so much of mutual needs; their relationship is never as intense or manipulative as Louie's and Sam's. When Sam is away, there are actually scenes of regard, almost tenderness, between these two as they spend a day shopping or an evening at home.

As time goes on, both the hostility and indifference between Henny and Louie give way to a feeling of mutual misery. When Henny exclaims to Sam about Louie: "She's over eleven and she's getting to be a woman already. It makes me sick to think I have to tell her what's coming to her, what she has to go through. . . . I couldn't drag her into all the darn muck of existence myself. . . . When I think that whoever she is, she has to do what I have done, and know what I have known . . . ," her general feeling about the oppression of women makes Louie her ally in the pervasive sexual struggle. For Henny, women are drawn together in an alliance of mutual despair. Her "I hate her, but I hate myself" becomes a source, ultimately of compassion. "Although Louisa was on the way to twelve and almost a woman, Sam had not suspected this veering. He went on confiding in her and laying the head of his trouble on her small breast. But Henny, creature of wonderful instinct and old campaigner, had divined almost instantly . . . ." This sexual alliance becomes a dominating force in *The Man Who Loved Children*, a strong determinant of angle of vision.

One night, in despair, Henny starts to strangle

Louie, who looks back at her "in an affinity of misfortune. Henrietta dropped her arms quickly and gripped her own neck with an expression of disgust . . . and cried, 'I ought to put us all out of our misery!'" This scene foreshadows the book's resolution, in which Louie responds to Henny's repeated suggestion and kills Henny, or helps Henny kill herself. Louie poisons a cup of tea, which Henny drinks, knowing that it's poisoned. There is some ambiguity in that act of poisoning as there is in this first confrontation. Who is the attacker? Who is the despairing victim? There is between Henny and Louie some "distorted sympathy" which makes each a reflection of the feelings of the other in spite of their antagonism.

Just as moving closer to Henny's point of view helps Louie become more critical of Sam's, so, as Louie's social experience widens, she gains fresh perspectives to change the shape of her awareness. She develops a fervent schoolgirl crush on her teacher, Miss Aiden. Miss Aiden's visit to the Pollits on Sam's birthday provides the reader with an outsider's view of that family's misery and poverty; and it does the same for Louie, reinterpreting her family's situation through the standards of a new set of values.

Stead has made explicit in interviews her faith in this process of growth. "When I was fifteen," she says, "I thought there was only one writer in the world who told the truth about families, and that was Strindberg." But children survive even the most difficult of families. "Children grow up anyway. . . . On the whole, people are pretty hard to twist. School has an immense influence on children. It's the first valuable break from family. . . . Then comes the playground, then the gang. Then they've got four sets of mores. This is when you grow up. . . . I think on the whole it's a very healthy thing . . . a standard by which to judge the family."[8]

Literature has offered Louie a similar escape and widening of vision. She is an ardent if self-guided reader—of Milton, Melville, Cervantes, Nietzsche, Shelley. Her imagination, formed by her extensive reading as well as by her family experience, manifests itself in literary ways. Her growing independence is expressed as a wordsmith. Louie withdraws, thinks, dreams, imagines, writes. At night, she tells herself and the other children stories drawn from dark fancies and the pounding of her blood, precursors of some of Stead's *Salzburg Tales*, told in Stead's own gothic-grotesque style. In an invented language, Louie (like a female Hamlet) writes a play modeled on Shelley's *Cenci*, of a daughter's rebellion against the strangulation of her tyrannical father—a birthday present for Sam. The plot of this play foreshadows the culmination of the plot of *The Man Who Loved Children* when Louie determines, under the rubric of justice, to free herself and the other children from their parents' debilitating abuse by murdering Sam and Henny. This symbolic act signifies her determination to write the script for her own life. In the brilliantly wrought scenes of psychic warfare, in which Stead specializes, Louie's resistance to Sam takes the form of verbal battles over the definitions of words and situations. At the beginning of the novel, Sam discourses on his definitions of freedom and genius. At the end, Louie redefines those terms. Mastery of language becomes the power which defines values, judgments, and actions. The teller of the tale has the ultimate determination of its shape; the story Louie insists on telling is her own.

If literary creation will be Louie's ultimate source of power in defining her own life and vision, the literary tradition also gives her something to use in her growth toward this freedom—an alternative myth to replace the one she is giving up to help her refashion her concept of herself. As she fixes the family's breakfast, Louie is reading, for the third time, of

Roland and Oliver, in *The Legend of Roncevalles*.
Tacked up on her wall is a motto from Nietzsche,
"Throw not away the hero in thy soul." The play she
writes for Sam's birthday casts herself as a hero re-
belling against a destructive tyrant. Like Henny, she
sees a polarized world of victims and oppressors, but
unlike Henny she has the internal resources to do
something about her plight. More active than her
stepmother, she can turn her internal stresses into a
positive source of energy. She counters her parents'
denigrated image of her and her own monstrous feelings with an equally exaggerated heroic self-image.
By recasting Sam's version of the family story into a
tale of tyrannical power and heroic rebellion, she is
able to create a new myth that will help her to free
herself from that power and define her own center of
force.

Louie tries to free herself from the overwhelming influence of her family and escape its octopus
grip by imagining herself a stoic hero. Infinite in her
expectations of either success or disaster, she casts
the world in dramatic extremes. Stead shows clearly
why such a powerful myth is necessary for Louie, but
she also makes clear the exaggerations and the limits
of this adolescent self-aggrandizement. With others
of Stead's heroines, Louie believes that by sheer
strength of will she can deny her emotional and physical needs and accomplish anything she wishes, alone.
Sympathetic with her heroine's ambitions and fantasies, Stead neither pities Louie nor wholly shares her
dreams. Both conveying and placing Louie's struggle
for self-mastery and personal power, Stead portrays
her from an ironic distance in a larger context than
that in which Louie defines herself.

While the myth of the hero casts the individual
as a solitary, independent being, Stead draws Louie,
as she does all her characters, within the dense social
texture of family life. Stead shows in Louie the access

to fantasy life and the verbal mastery that make us believe in her as a potential artist, but this is no ordinary portrait of the artist as a young girl, from that genre of autobiographical fiction. More typically, the artist sees himself as a unique and special individual whose consciousness is both the central subject of the novel and its defining vision. Stead resists the temptation to place her autobiographical heroine alone in the foreground center of a bildungsroman. She firmly perceives the individual as existing within a web of inevitable social influences and interconnections, and the form of her novel mirrors that belief. We see Louie performing daily household tasks: making tea for Henny or the others, stringing beans, washing dishes, folding laundry, minding the younger children, withdrawing to the shower to read her book. We come to know her from her very different emotional interactions with Henny, with Sam, with each of the children. Like all of Stead's characters, Louie materializes out of the matrix of family life. She exists in the context of other equally large characters, whose inner lives and perspectives are as fully developed as her own. The form of Stead's novel becomes an embodiment of her central moral tenet. Placing her characters in the shared membership of collective family life mitigates the distortion of vision of the pervasive human egotism she continually combats.

This understanding is not incidental, but inherent in Stead's vision of individual growth, and therefore in her own more complex definition of heroism. While Louie does struggle heroically for the power to shape a self-determined vision and to take action, she must also finally struggle against just that egotism that individual heroism is itself prey to. Stead sees each of us trying perpetually to wrest control so we may define the terms of the fiction we live, and place ourself center stage. This becomes not just a matter of shaping our own lives, but of trying to force others to live out our vision. Battling to make our drama our own and ourself the star, we collide with others who are seeking the same power. While the artist can impose his vision on the world of his fiction, when a single vision dominates peoples' lives, it results in predatory narcissism, which reduces all others to serving the needs of one individual or family. The real heroism, for Stead, is to transcend this ossification in a more multiple and supple vision that allows others as well as oneself primary imaginative reality.

Stead shows us Louie imagining herself as an individual hero, acting out this concept and growing through it. At the end, Louie feels she has won the battle for the power of definition, but Stead is more equivocal and ironic about her victory. She supports Louie's idea of her role as tragic hero by giving her the resolving action of the novel—the poisoning. In the psychic life of the family, Louie does move progressively to center stage; she does assume responsibility for her family and for herself. Asserting "I am my own mother," she sets off at the novel's end on a walk around the world, amazed at "how different everything looked." "Things . . . were no longer part of herself but objects that she could freely consider without prejudice." Louie believes she has broken free from the suffocating identification with her family that shadows all of the children with their parents' egos and casts the entire world of *The Man Who Loved Children* into reflected grotesque forms.

As Stead's novel has so profoundly demonstrated, one is never wholly one's own mother; the walk around the world leads back home. If Stead's later heroines will discover how pervasive is their family inheritance, how indelibly their bright new visions are stained with the colors of the old, if they will fight old family battles on new territory—still they will have freedom enough to carve out a different course for themselves, and not repeat exactly the closed circles of their parents' lives.

Louie does grow; but not quite as she thinks. With a last ironic wrench of redefinition, Louie achieves not the literal independence she believes she has won, but a new angle of vision. From this larger perspective, a productive conflict with her parents' fixed mythologies of family life generates the more magnanimous vision of this novel. The complexity of Stead's narrative vision becomes the largest statement of freedom: never an absolute freedom to singularly determine the plot of a life, but a freedom to see more complexly and wisely.

Nor is this aesthetic vision free of the influences Stead has portrayed within the Pollit family. One critic accuses Louie of "thinking Gothic" and having "a tendency to see great patches of life as gothic melodrama."[9] But Louie's Gothic sensibility is also Stead's narrative voice. The violence that permeates life and death, sex and conversation, for the Pollits becomes part of Louie's world view and that of the novel itself. Stead's style is shaped by the conflicts, strains, and tensions of family life, but transcends them. In her fiction, these influences become not inhibiting or destructive constrictions, but materials from which she forges the vehicle of her imaginative freedom.

Dickens

Of all the distinctive linguistic styles of this novel, the most interesting is that of Stead's framing narrative voice. In both style and spirit, Stead shares some of the charm and vitality of Charles Dickens, an author who was a living presence in her family as well as her literary life. Like Sam Pollit's father Charles in *The Man Who Loved Children*, Samuel Stead, Christina's paternal grandfather, "loved Charles Dickens, lived in a Dickensian world," writes his granddaughter.[10] Christina Stead recalls going, as a

child, to meetings of her grandfather's lodge where
recitations from Dickens novels were regularly per-
formed. "When he was alive," she says, "the family
was full of Dickens."[11]

Stead too is full of Dickens, though she is as
plainly part of the twentieth century as Dickens was
of the nineteenth. She has Dickens's comic eye for
significant animating detail, and his ear for the exaggerated rhetoric with which they both define the idiosyncratic characters they delight in. *The Man Who
Loved Children* is full of Dickens allusions. Calling
herself a "lorn, lone crittur," Bonnie echoes Mrs.
Gummidge in *David Copperfield*. Charles Pollit per-
forms the Aged Parent from *Great Expectations*. But
Dickens's direct influence is less striking than their
similarities of vision and technique, most pronounced
in the pervasive use each makes of the grotesque.
Stead's Domestic Gothic style is devoted to the moral
seriousness and specificity of observation of the
quotidian, the concern with character and social relations of nineteenth-century realism. Simultaneously, like Dickens, she uses the grotesque to probe
beneath the surfaces to capture, without entirely
taming, the emotional field she finds in the depths of
the human psyche. Writing in the immediate tradition of the nineteenth-century novel, Stead stands,
however, on this side of Freud. She shuns the nostalgia frequently found in that genre, and the particular form in which it appears in Dickens, as dualism.

Stead's novel is colored by neither yearning for a
lost golden past nor hopes for an idealized future.
While both Stead and Dickens perceive a world of
oppressors and oppressed, built around the core of a
child's feeling of helplessness in the face of adult
power,[12] Dickens mourns the destruction of an innocence Stead believes never existed; nor does Stead see
in simplified black and white moral dimensions.
There are in Stead no refuges in the past or future.

The ideal of the middle-class family that, though remote, suggests for Dickens escape from exploitation
at a cozy fireside is for Stead the crucible of strife.[13]
Dickens characters are "terrifyingly alone and unre-
lated." They meet in "sudden confrontations between persons whose ways of life have no habitual or
logical continuity with each other."[14] Dickens seems
to imply their wistful solitariness and frequent silenc-
es might be dispelled by community. While Stead's
characters collide rather than collaborate, in the
Pollit family there is all too much "togetherness."
Though their emotional interactions are nearly all
conflicts, they are emotionally intertwined. Their intimacy is not satisfying, but they are intimate. The
Pollits are inextricably connected by the habit of
family life, and it does not do for them quite what
Dickens hoped.

   Like *The Man Who Loved Children*, Dickens's
autobiographical novel *David Copperfield* was written when its author was thirty-eight, looking back on
his childhood. But Stead's novel has none of the nostalgia of looking backwards that permeates Dickens's; she writes of the past as a living present. Intrin-
sic to Stead's unsentimental stance is the absence of
idealization in her fiction. She does not divide her
characters into separate good and bad figures: Sam
Pollit is both the tyrannical villain Mr. Murdstone,
and Mr. Micawber, the loving, ineffectual father. In
Stead's novel, there are no disciplined hearts capable
of mature love, the ideal for which Dickens heroes
strive. The Pollit children think adults "unreason-
able, violent beings, the toys of their own monstrous
tempers and egotisms." Yet, an overgrown child himself, Sam does love his children, in his way; and
Henny, with all her vileness and violence, loves them
too. What affection the Pollit children get comes not
from separate idealized parental figures, but from
these mixed characters themselves.

Stead is ruthlessly unsentimental. The restraint she exerts on feeling if not on form keeps her free from self-pity though often from pity as well. Dickens likes his good characters; he approved warmly of them and invites the reader's approval.[15] Stead's sympathy is more tinged with distaste and controlled by ironic distance; it is expressed as acceptance rather than approval.

Like Dickens, Stead delves into fantasy to release energy both comic and aggressive, creative and destructive, and reveals the violence usually suppressed in everyday behavior. In *The Man Who Loved Children*, Stead's fantasy and realism, passionate language and tight ironic control reach their most productive equilibrium, and this, the best of her novels, stands at a height few other novelists achieve and she herself will never reach again.

3

For Love Alone:
A Woman Hero

With *For Love Alone* in 1944,[1] Christina Stead continues the tale she started in *The Man Who Loved Children.* Set in the suburb of Sydney in which Stead grew up, *For Love Alone* follows her autobiographical heroine, renamed Teresa Hawkins, into her twenties and out of Australia. Teresa's father, Andrew, is the next incarnation of Sam; this motherless family could be the Pollits ten years after Henny's death. Unlike *The Man Who Loved Children*, however, this novel soon drops the family to focus on a single protagonist, relinquishing social scope for individual intensity.

For Love Alone traces Teresa's inner development and her changing relation to the outside world. This novel and *The Man Who Loved Children*, read together form a single *bildungsroman*.[2] The task of maturing, and of this genre of fiction that depicts it, is to form a proper relation, on the one hand, with one's past—neither ignoring it nor letting it haunt the present—and on the other, with the present and future, developing relations with other individuals and a social community through love and work. In *The Man Who Loved Children*, Stead recreates her heroine's childhood and shows its shaping influence on Louie's character and vision. *For Love Alone* picks up the next part of the task, starting with adolescence, to concentrate on problems of autonomy

and adult relation. In Teresa Hawkins, the bravado
of Louisa Pollit's heroic self-conception is developed into a determination to leave Australia and
make a better life elsewhere. Capable of acting on
her heroic vision, Teresa can encounter experiences
that will modify the dimensions of her self-idealization along realistic lines. For all its exaggeration,
hers is a vision that determines a heroic plot. The
title notwithstanding, Teresa's quest is not for love
alone, but for identity, for the realization of her intellectual and emotional drives through love and
work in the world.[3]

Initially, *For Love Alone* portrays the Hawkins
family with the same density and subtlety of interaction that revealed the Pollits to us in the previous
novel. Another devouring narcissist, Andrew Hawkins jocularly dominates his two grown sons, sullen
Lance and loving Leo, and daughters, Teresa, the oldest, and the compliant Kitty, who sacrifices herself to
care for the others. Teresa completes the break with
her family that Louie had begun (though family di-
lemmas are avoided rather than resolved). Father,
brothers, sister, aunts and cousins fall abruptly into
the background; the novel belongs to Teresa. Her
passions, ambitions, fantasies and actions are the
novel's compelling concerns.

Teresa teaches school, but scorns the feelings of
helpless entrapment and the terror of isolation that
paralyze the other young women teachers. She goes
to business school at night to learn typing and shorthand, and takes an evening course at the university,
where she begins to discover her undisciplined but
ardent intellectual style. In her Latin teacher, Jonathan Crow, an impoverished student who has won a
traveling scholarship to England, Teresa finds a
focus for her fantasies of escape. Jonathan is almost a
caricature—a cold carrion character who feeds off
others' suffering. Though he is twisted and sadistic,

Teresa endures a prolonged attachment to him. Determined to follow Jonathan to London, she goes to
work as a secretary in a hat factory to earn her passage. She develops a daily regimen of extreme hardship, denying herself the most minimal needs of
food, clothing, and companionship; walking miles to
save pennies. Through this heroic ordeal, which
Stead renders with grueling conviction, Teresa does
save the money she needs, and at twenty-six, sets sail
for London on her odyssey of discovery.

In London, Teresa finds a job in a business firm,
one of whose managers is the eloquent and kindly
James Quick (a glowing, idealized portrait, flooded
with images of warmth and light, modeled on William Blake). Quick falls in love with his strangely serious and haggard secretary, and is finally able to
rescue Teresa from her emotional enslavement to
Crow by unmasking Jonathan's perverted character
to her. Quick discovers the brilliance in a novel
Teresa has been working on and respectfully nur-
tures her writing talent. Instead of marriage, he and
Teresa develop an open though committed arrangement, in which Teresa is free to take a lover, and
does. The conclusion of *For Love Alone* is embued
with Teresa's elation that she has become, at last,
fully herself. At the same time, her joyful awakening
into a sense of her powers is qualified by an acknowledgment of the continuing highs and lows of the
struggle for growth and fullness of being.

At the burning center of this novel is Stead's
characterization of Teresa. Stead treats her heroine
with a distinctive balance of sympathetic identification and ironic distance. Teresa's inner life is portrayed with detailed respect and concentration even
while the fiction as a whole is constructed to show the
limitations of that inner world, and the price Teresa
pays for her fantasies. *For Love Alone* has the intensity of a romance without being one. The fictive world

of romance is coextensive with its hero's inner life;
Stead's novel, rather, in the realistic tradition, sets
her heroine within a larger material and social world,
which is conceived with equal subtlety and density.
In describing the typical structure of romance,
Joseph Campbell discerns three stages—of Separation, Initiation, and Return—in which a developing
hero separates himself from his family and his society,
voyages out into the unknown where he endures
trials that educate him to his strengths and limitations, and finally returns, with newly won maturity,
to reintegrate himself into the social order.[4] This
outer voyage is a symbolic reenactment of an inner
one; the figures the hero meets and trials he endures
are projected fragments of his own psychic world
with which he must learn to come to terms. Stead's
novel follows the tripartite pattern of romance, but
rather than being a fantasy projection, it is a more
distanced examination of the act of projecting. Teresa
makes a literal sea voyage away from home in search
of a larger, more heroic conception of herself, which
after severe trials and necessary modifications, she
does approach. But Teresa's journey is at once physical and psychological, literal and symbolic; it takes
place in a concrete world that exists apart from her
imaginings of it, whose characters are not parts of
herself, but genuinely distinct individuals.

Stead frames Teresa's ocean journey within a
complex narrative structure that shows a more subtle
journey of development. This novel is shaped not by
the wishes, lies, and dreams of fantasy, but by Stead's
ironic structure of juxtaposed points of view. By her
manipulation of narrative stance, Stead shows Teresa's inward journey away from the initial assurance
of her self-defined existence to the inauthenticity of
seeing herself only as she is seen through another's
eyes. Teresa's sense of herself is restored only when
she is helped to regain the responsibility of self-defi-

nition. The change in locus of the moral authority for Teresa's vision is mirrored by narrative changes. The tale is told, successively, as seen by Teresa, Jonathan Crow, James Quick, and Teresa again—each shift of point of view reflecting a corresponding one within Teresa's consciousness. Teresa, and the novel, begin with a radiant, if exaggerated faith in her aspirations and abilities. Strong and self-determining, she has absolute confidence in the primacy of her perceptions and imaginings. Preoccupied not by Beauty but by Honor, she is most concerned not with the way others see her, but with her own desires, needs and ideals. Acting on these determined wants, however, Teresa paradoxically relinquishes the strength of her self-defined identity to definition through the eyes of others. As she narrows the focus of her earlier aspirations for emotional and intellectual fulfillment into a single notion of love for Jonathan Crow, she gradually gives herself over to the authority of his vision, and comes to see herself as he sees her. Since Jonathan's denigrating vision is misogynistic and sadistic, Teresa suffers an intolerably diminished self-image and moves toward a suicidal despair.

She is rescued only by being reseen through the eyes of James Quick's love. After counterpointed scenes in which Jonathan Crow and James Quick do battle for supremacy, Quick wins, and his point of view takes over the story. Both the narrative and its heroine are rescued by the loving generosity of Quick's vision which restores Teresa to herself and the novel, once more, to her perspective. For this, Teresa owes Quick her most profound gratitude: "I can only thank him for giving myself to me," she feels at the end. Quick functions as something of a *deus ex machina* within the novel; nevertheless, Stead's manipulation of shifting narrative perspective to reflect her heroine's changing self-conception is a brilliant technique. Its capacity for both identification and distancing reflects the simultaneous sympathy and irony of her vision.

The problem of assuming the narrative (and moral) authority for definition of character is central to the novel and to Teresa's development. Teresa begins and ends this story by insisting on her right to self-definition. In perceiving herself as subject, not object, Self, not Other, and acting on that perception, she assumes traditionally male prerogatives. While Stead refuses to join the battle of the sexes under the banner of feminism, she understands experience to be shaped by the cultural division of gender roles. Stead has named her central character for the saint George Eliot also admired, but she reconceives the notions of both heroism and femininity that Eliot assumed.[5]

Stead's woman hero defines herself by rejecting social definitions of femininity. Teresa thinks of herself in the imagery of a male hero: she is an Odysseus who will adventure on the sea, not a Penelope waiting steadfastly at home. Her fantasies have been formed by images of epic heroes. The early songs and tales she had heard "made her think that she could escape by sea . . . she had the heart of a sailor. How could she be satisfied on the dull shore?" She sees her present life as a night passage to Cytherea, "to our secret desires . . . a kind of Darwin's voyage of discovery." Her journey to England will be an Odyssey: "Each Australian is a Ulysses," she claims. *For Love Alone* both values and criticizes this classical conception of heroic individualism, as the conviction of independence which enables Teresa to act also reveals its limitations. Stead shows in good faith a woman's creative self-development, while recognizing the inevitable incursions of the social, political, and economic environment against just such development. Nevertheless, the energies needed to explore and extend these limitations require from

Teresa the active self-assertion of a traditionally
male style of heroism rather than a passive feminine
one.

The image of Teresa as a hero is the central metaphor of *For Love Alone*. Through it Stead connects
her story of an individual odyssey to larger concerns
with the patterns of behavior society prescribes for
men and women. Stead's treatment of the intersec-
tion between the personal and political is one of the
distinctive strengths of her style. In all her fiction,
Stead is committed to the probing exploration of individual sensibility, but she understands that to be
deeply connected to larger social forms and forces. In
a perceptive article, "Christina Stead's New Realism,"
Terry Sturm argues that Stead has invented a new
form of realism that can "register the contours of her
characters' experience from within, without manipulation, without 'tailoring reality to fit thereby'. . . .
It does not proceed reductively, like much politically
committed fiction extracting a 'typical' reality from
beneath the surface of the 'merely' personal in her
characters' lives." For her, the individual and the
typical are not opposed: "Her novels are saturated
with . . . ideologies of sex, of family, of economics
and politics and culture. Ideology is part of the texture of her characters' individual lives, inseparable
from their experience and from the way they respond and react to events. . . . Christina Stead
dramatizes ideas at points where they are not quite
conscious in the minds of her characters, where they
clash in confusing and often destructive ways with
inarticulate aspirations and needs."[6] Never ideological because she is never abstract in her presentation
of concepts, Stead gives the political concrete and intimate form, while she distances the personal by political perspective. Her analysis of sexual politics, for
example, gives generalizing force to her highly individual portrait of Teresa.

Stead describes social structure as it is felt and articulated within individual consciousness. Her understanding of the family as at once a crucible of individual and social sensibility, so well deployed in *The Man Who Loved Children*, again informs *For Love Alone*, where patriarchy takes the immediate form of the relationship of father and daughter. Teresa's resistance to accepted feminine social roles is first resistance to her father. The novel opens with a sensuously powerful portrait of Andrew Hawkins: "Naked, except for a white towel rolled into a loincloth, he stood in the doorway, laughing and shouting, a tall man with powerful chest and thick hair of pale burning gold and a skin still pale under many summers' tan. He seemed to thrust back the walls with his muscular arms. . . ." The seductive narcissist we have met before, as Sam Pollit in *The Man Who Loved Children*, Andrew teases, denigrates, and cajoles to make his daughters provide him with the admiration on which he feeds. Like Louisa Pollit (whose motto was Nietzsche's "Throw not away the hero in thy soul"), Teresa defines her independence by refusing her father's incestuously toned manipulations and seductions which would shape her to continued compliance to serve his needs; with his prescriptions for femininity she rejects his vision of her identity.

One of the grounds on which the family battles are waged is the definition of proper behavior for a woman. Andrew, like Sam, would have it both ways. He insists that his daughter be womanly, while simultaneously denigrating women. When Andrew grabs Teresa in a quarrel, and she shakes free with an angry "Don't touch me," he warns her, "Men don't like an unbending woman." "I am unbending," says Teresa. When Andrew inveighs against coaxing, lying, wheedling, and flirting, Teresa asks indignantly, "have you ever seen me coax or kiss?" "Have I ever begged for a single thing?" No, Andrew admits, she has not; but she must know how to lure men. Expert at catching the nuances of tone and maneuvers in family dramas, Stead renders this quarrel with the expertise and conviction of the scenes of family interplay in her previous novel. Andrew calls on his authority to support his contradictory assertions; there are many things Teresa does not know, so she must simply take his word for what's right and wrong. With grandiose claims, Teresa insists, "There is simply nothing of which I am not aware." "I am informed, on the moral side. You're ignoble. You can't understand me. Henceforth, everything between us is a misunderstanding. You have accepted compromise, you revel in it. Not me. I will never compromise."

Though the narrative recognizes Teresa as headlong, explosive, hysterical, proud, she is also dramatized as an emotionally powerful figure, "able to stir them all." The function of her grandiose claims in trying to establish her certitude of integrity against persistent attack is as evident as is their adolescent exaggeration.

When Andrew taunts Teresa, she flies back at him, "you offend my honor! I would kill anyone who offends my honor." Lance, the older of her brothers, sneers with Andrew at the idea: "A woman's honor means something else from what you imagine." "A woman can have honor," declares the younger Leo, a loving boy who admires his sister. When Andrew continues to provoke her, Teresa claims, "Honor is more sacred than life," "I told you I would kill you if you insult me. I will do it with my bare hands. . . . I will kill you, Father."

She does not kill him. Unlike the world of *The Man Who Loved Children*, in this novel, such fantasies are kept in the subjective realm of fantasy, not externalized in action. But this controversy about honor, the essential epic virtue, calls into question the very possibility of classic heroism for a woman. Woman's honor, as Andrew and Lance urge, is conventionally defined as chastity, the denial of sexuality, and the passive resistance to being acted on by others. With an independence that is heroic, Teresa insists on a more active conception of moral integrity. As Stead so subtly recognizes in her portrayal of character, people are always defined in part by their social relationships; women in particular are usually governed by strong affiliative needs. The risk of personal censure and threat of social isolation are powerful enforcers of conventional social roles. Yet, from the beginning, Teresa resists not only her father's but the larger society's conception of women's place and function. Portrayed as independent and critically detached, she differentiates herself from the other young women around her. Teresa feels keenly the constraints of her family and suburban Australian society and determines to escape them. She knows that what she wants is not what that world offers her.

Structurally, Stead announces Teresa's separation from her society by reversing a literary convention. From classical comedy through the nineteenth-century novel, marriage is used as a standard dramatic ending to provide closure, the satisfying sense of completion and the integration of the once erring individual into the stable social order. Instead of ending with a wedding, however, *For Love Alone* begins with one, which represents the hypocrisy and limitations of social conventions Teresa is determined to escape. (D. H. Lawrence, who like Stead decries conventional sexual repressions, puts a wedding to similar use in beginning *Women in Love*, a novel this one often recalls.) This wedding is not Teresa's, but her cousin Malfi's. Its wonderfully realized festivities give Stead the opportunity to introduce an extended cast of family characters in comic display. With each of the other women in the family, she shows another undesirable choice of a way to live, each of which Teresa rejects.

Like Teresa, Malfi is a clever, talented girl, but she forswears her chance for development in a marriage which Stead translates into a defeat of all aspirations. A girl must marry, says Aunt Bea, a boisterous and sloppily dressed old widow, a Dickensian characterization, and the figure of fun women are made when they are no longer young and graceful. The pressing but unacknowledged motive for marriage is made obvious, however, by the presence of another of the aunts. A literary descendent of Jo Pollit, Teresa's Aunt Diana, "the only Miss Hawkins," as she proclaims her permanent title, is the mocked sufferer of a serious "condition"; she is an Old Maid. Evoking the specter of fear that lurks behind the wedding celebration, she strikes terror into the girls' hearts (especially Teresa's, who, like Louie Pollit, resembles her maiden aunt). "Each girl had made up her mind to risk anything to avoid being the next 'Miss Hawkins.'" No more free of terror than the others, Teresa is nevertheless singularly shamed by her perception of the inner motivation of this social ritual. In the vivid scene in which Malfi throws her bouquet and the young girls strain to catch the token that will assure their own marriage, Teresa, in a "blink of the eye, . . . had seen the awful eagerness of the others and the smiling, waiting circle of adults, witnesses of their naked need; and so she had drawn back a bit, with a thumping heart, disappointed but grim, at the very moment the bouquet was thrown."

Stead characteristically mines surfaces, unearthing the primitive emotions beneath social interactions. Not social communion or love or lust motivates these marriages, but a dark terror of isolation. The figure of the Old Maid, which has suffered a long history of social opprobrium, represents not independence, but the denial of all desires. With no social outlet for her needs, she has no avenue of human expression. The alternative seems only marginally better; conventional marriage is portrayed as part of a rigid system of socialization that satisfies few girlhood wishes for love or joy. When Teresa wanders through the poor huts of the fishermen at the foot of the cliffs by the sea's side, she sees the women losing their youth to the harsh miseries of poverty. But the fate of suburban girls is scarcely better:

All the girls dimly knew that the hole-in-a-corner marriages and frantic petting parties of the suburbs were not love and therefore they had these ashamed looks; they lost their girlish laughter the day they became engaged, but those who did not get a man were worse off. There was a glass pane in the breast of each girl; there every other girl could see the rat gnawing at her, the fear of being on the shelf. Beside the solitary girl, three hooded madmen walk, desire, fear, ridicule. "I won't suffer," she said aloud. . . . "They won't put it upon me."

Nor is the gnawing rat of fear to be quieted by having a profession. Teresa is a teacher (of a special class of "feebleminded children"), but the bitter, hopeless attitudes of the women she works with reflect pervasive values. Their jobs give them no pleasure, no sense of self-respect, no absorbing interest. "Sitting blowsily in the teachers' room, standing dully in the playground, patronizing, wretched, dull, deaf to hope and with no thought of a way out, they groused helplessly, in their own minds condemned to servitude for life."

Teresa is no more satisfied with her work than are the other teachers. The children (whose disturbed, sporadic energy echoes the theme of allied madness and creativity that threads through the novel; the energies of both run against social norms) are beyond her help. She is discouraged by the hope-

lessness of their situation and by her own powerlessness. She felt "she had been stuck in there too young,
she was incapable of looking after them, she knew
nothing of any kind, not even to teach madmen." Cut
off from the world, Teresa however does not share
the other women's sense of trapped desperation, but
persists in feeling she has the power to control her
fate. To do so, she goes to business school at night, to
train herself for another kind of job.

While Teresa maintains her feeling of independence and creates choices for herself, she does so in
the face of her vivid apprehension of the limited alternatives in the lives of the women around her. She
realizes that, in their need to marry, women are
under a particular time pressure, determined biolog-
ically as well as socially. Not only must they marry to
have an acceptable place in society, but they must do
so within a very short span of years. They cannot,
therefore, take the risks of experimenting, or looking for what they really want, lest they lose what time
they have:

Yes, we're pressed for time. We haven't time to get educated, have a career, for the crop must be produced before
it's autumn. . . . We put out leaves and flowers in such a
brief summer and if it is a bad summer? . . . Girls are
northern summer, three months long; men are tropical
summers. . . . It isn't necessary—Malfi, . . . Kitty—me!
But they won't even rebel, they're afraid to squander their
few years. The long night of spinsterhood will come down.
What's to be done! But one thing is sure, I won't do it, they
won't get me.

Teresa is gnawed by the same terrors that con-
strain the other women from taking any action.
However, she is able to understand her fear in a way
that lets her act differently. The language of this passage shows the edge of perception that makes Teresa
exceptional. Teresa thinks not in the literal detail of

social convention, as the other girls do, but in wider
analogies. She sees women's individual fears as
forming social patterns, which she understands in
metaphors of general biological production and reproduction and of the natural seasons. This expanded
aesthetic vision generates expanded personal power.
Relying on her more comprehensive structures of
understanding, Teresa is able to move outside the
confines of the social world whose limitations she
perceives and risk the isolation whose costs she so
acutely recognizes.

Teresa's first attempt to leave is a trip to Harper's Ferry, a remote pleasure spot through valleys
and woods sixty miles north of Sydney. While this
journey fails, it rehearses in miniature her later trip
from Australia to England which will succeed. This
episode typifies both Teresa's characteristic way of
acting, and Christina Stead's characteristic narration
of her heroine's actions. Restless with her teaching
job, Teresa one day simply leaves, taking a train to
her Aunt's house in the country. From there she
vaguely plans to walk to Harper's Ferry and then back
to the city: having made this walk which betokens
freedom to her, she imagines she will return to find a
room and a job and save the money to go to a European university (as far as her fantasy takes her). None
of her plans are founded on concrete information:
"As to Harper's Ferry, she had asked no more questions about it than about fees at the university. She
had never looked at a map. . . . She had a vision of
a dreary wild crossing, ancient trees; beyond that
nothing, but it was her way."

Her way is always to act on the basis of her
strongly dreamt fantasies, which exposes her to dangers for which she is unprepared and unprotected,
but also enables her to take paths that are out of the
ordinary. Stead draws both Teresa's imagination and
the world around her with a richness that gives cre-

dence to Teresa's special capacities and heightened powers. Stead's complex conception of character permits her extensive and intricate exploration of individual personality without the loss in solipsism that is prone to afflict modern fiction. Since individual character for her is both framed in and interconnected with social situation, her exploration of one is an exploration of the other. Her metaphors consistently integrate the physical world with the psychological. Concrete observations of a wide range of objects and activities place her minute, penetrating psychological analysis within a wider social framework.

Stead textures this novel, like her others, with multiple portrayals of different families, all of which enact what she sees as typically destructive family possessiveness. Potentially incestuous sexual energies ferment beneath the surface of family relations (as is most clear in this book in the scenes with the Hawkins brothers and father) and become allied with the pervasive possessiveness with which families seek to keep their children entangled in their webs. Teresa's aunt and uncle and twenty-nine-year-old unmarried cousin Ellen in the country are like her Aunt Bea and cousin Anne in Sydney. The kinder parents in these families are not harshly and egotistically manipulative as Andrew Hawkins is with his children, but they are nevertheless softly possessive. By spoiling, babying, clinging, they keep their daughters clutched to them in a way that threatens any chance the girls have for independent adulthood; both Teresa's cousins despair of marriage. All of Stead's independent heroines isolate themselves from their families. It is only "a girl without a family" who "can do what she likes." (Never nurturing or supportive, families in Stead's fiction are always entrapping and reductive.)

Stead's dramatization of family dynamics is an analysis as well of the social reproduction of sexual repression. The youthful rituals of courtship of her cousin Ellen's friends seem to Teresa trivial and humiliating, and she rejects them as she does her family, walking off alone through the woods. Those woods, however, reverberate with the cry of a mad man, who lives confined with his mother, denied all sexual and creative outlets—a cry that echoes with repressions and longings from the depths of society and of nature itself. "The cry was too great to be that of hunting, pursuing things. . . . Was it the howl of empty Creation, horrified at being there with itself in its singleness; or is it the cry of the chase I am on? . . . that lonely, dreadful cry," thinks Teresa. Walking alone at dusk, Teresa is pursued by an old man who exposes himself to her; an action and threat she does not understand, but which seems to her unnatural "madness," "a shame and disgrace." The loneliness, denial, physical and psychic threats of Teresa's larger solitary journey are foreshadowed here. On this first venture both her own fantasies and external realities are blurred for Teresa; they will become slowly more clear as she suffers the consequences of her ignorance. For her second journey, she does learn to attend, minutely and painfully, to practical facts and economies. But that voyage, like this one, is motivated by just the darkly romantic imagination that propelled her toward Harper's Ferry, and the image of freedom.

That imagination is at once Teresa's greatest strength and greatest weakness. Her distinctive vision isolates her from the ordinary forms of social intercourse, making her less knowing and more vulnerable than others. It also enables her to start her independent venture and ultimately to forge different forms of action, relation, and creativity. Stead convinces us of Teresa's creative capacities by endowing Teresa with a style of thinking as rich in complexity as her own literary style.

Stead portrays Teresa from the start as set apart
and reveling in her fantasy life. Teresa considers her
real life the secret one she makes for herself in the
privacy of her room, where she is free to live in her
imaginings. She sees beneath the surfaces of things a
turmoil of passions, and she is convinced that she
sees a truer world than others do. Teresa's "long
walks at night through the Bay . . . her voluptuous
swimming and rolling by herself in the deep grass of
the garden and her long waking nights were part of
the life of profound pleasure she had made for herself. . . . She was able to feel active creation going
on around her in the rocks and hills, where the mystery of lust took place; and in herself, where all was
yet only the night of the senses and wild dreams, the
work of passion was going on." "In her bare room
. . . she reasoned with herself about the sensual life
for which she was fitted. She smelled, heard, saw,
guessed faster, longed more than others, it seemed to
her." Teresa "saw insistently, with the countless and
flaming eyes of her flesh, the inner life. . . ."

Both Stead's portrait and Teresa's image of herself highlight this imaginative intensity. Like a pre-
Raphaelite painter, in a typical pose after Teresa's
nightly swim, Stead glorifies Teresa's sensuality and
romanticism: Teresa

stood panting with pleasure near the middle of the room.
Then with a silent, shivering, childish laugh, she closed the
door, quickly and softly. She stripped off the bathing-suit,
which she hung out the window to get completely dry and
felt her flesh, cold as marble in the warm air. She shivered
again with excitement and went to kneel at the uncur-
tained window [looking towards the sea] . . . "Oh, God,
how wonderful, how wonderful!" She muttered half-intel-
ligible exclamations which were little more than cries of
ecstasy as she stood in the window. . . . She leaned over
the sill, her round arms and full breasts resting on the
woodwork. Her flesh was a strange shade in that light, like

the underside of water beasts. Or like—she began to think like what. She did not care if she never went to bed; the night stretched before her. . . . She abandoned herself and began to think, leaning on the window-sill.

One of the novel's effective scenes shows Teresa with other women on the daily ferryboat ride across Sydney Bay to work. While the other girls elaborate with great intricacy their theories of the etiquette of trousseaus and engagements, Teresa sits apart, equally but differently preoccupied, reading "Louÿs's *Aphrodite* and Ovid's *Art of Love*, illustrated." The others never discuss the theme that dominates her imagination: love, which she conceives to be "a turbulent, maddening, but almost silent passion, a sensual understanding without end."

By looking through the lenses of her own deeply felt emotional life, and the intellectual glasses of the reading she has done, Teresa has an altered perception of social forms. With Stead, she pierces the surfaces of social convention to reveal the deep institutionalized ways in which a culture controls human feelings and utilizes emotions for social control. The vast preoccupation with the forms of courtship and marriage that Teresa scorns in other girls regulates and distracts from fears and passions that she and Stead tap at their most primal level.

Like Madame Bovary, Teresa has formed her expectations on literary romanticism, in the books she has avidly devoured: "This was the truth, not the daily simpering on the boat and the putting away in hope chests; but where was one girl who thought so, besides herself. . . . At each thing she read, she thought, yes, it's true, or no, it's false, and she persevered with satisfaction and joy, illuminated because her world existed and was recognized by men. But why not by women? She found nothing in the few works of women she could find that was what they must have felt."

Teresa finds in fiction affirmation for passions

women do not acknowledge. Literature serves to validate and free her feelings; at the same time, through its tutelage she develops a vision of partial truths, often remote from experience. Critic Elizabeth Sabiston[7] finds this pattern common for the female heroes of the bildungsroman. They are often trained by literature rather than experience, giving them both the liberating strengths and the limitations of perceptions at once freer and more naïve than the ordinary.

Stead takes Teresa's intellectual life entirely seriously. She devotes to it the imagery more often deployed in portrayals of sensual awakening, but seldom used with such concentration for a woman's intellectual coming of age. Stead makes vivid the excitement Teresa feels when she finally gets a chance to demonstrate her intellectual capacities. Having gone to a teacher's training school without academic status, Teresa is at first pale and timid in the university night course in which she enrolls. But soon she finds herself exploding with some of the theories she has concocted in her solitary brooding. ("Everyone likes the obscene; that is real life, [artists] more than others, because their violence is more.") Soon she is arguing "with the rash loftiness of the autodidact." She has "a wooden, naïve, but energetic skill, like a vigorous man talking in a foreign language, strangely, upside down and yet so full of ideas that even aesthetes listen to him." She has "discovered to herself and to [these university folk] a prodigious memory, she confuted them out of her own books and rapped them over the knuckles with what they had told her. She had once . . . offered to make a citation 'from English literature' on any subject whatever mentioned to her. . . . She had few ideas, and argued in an unacademic way, but the magnificence they had thrust on her and that she had read, came whirling at them out of her mouth."

Teresa impresses these "educated" people and

her heady success is wildly exciting to her. One day she goes to the class of a Marxist professor, and "this one afternoon, alone, she realized her dream of the classroom stormy with debate." "This was the moment when she was in flower. Fruit might come, but this would never come again." "The girl with no experience admitted no limitations . . . eagle's feathers sprouted."

As always, Stead places the exaggeration of this paradisal imagery at a slightly ironic distance; Teresa will learn her limitations to diminish the exuberance of her regal pride. Nevertheless, the verbal energy Stead accords the flowering of Teresa's mental powers emphasizes the central value of intellect and imagination for her heroine. Jonathan Crow will join Andrew Hawkins to warn Teresa that men do not like "bluestockings"; but Stead shares her heroine's belief in the necessary channels of growth. She supports her on her journey in search of intellectual and imaginative power, which she too envisions as vital to maturity.

Stead gives Teresa both powerful daydreams and outward means of expression for her creative energies. One of Stead's persistent themes is the destructiveness of unrealized creative powers. Without the capacity to find external channels of expression, the inner life preys upon itself and becomes destructive rather than generative. (Most of the characters in Stead's first novel, *Seven Poor Men of Sydney*, are unable to connect inner with outer realities; one ends a suicide, another in a mental institution.) The ways the young Teresa finds to express herself put her in danger of being labeled an eccentric; but she perseveres in them nevertheless. She has an old green dress that "she had embroidered with all kinds of things, pagodas, butterflies, geraniums. She wore it only at home on Sundays, in the mornings, because it was thick and she need wear nothing underneath it;

but . . . the Bay children had seen it, touched it, asked her about it. She did not know herself why she kept this dress and wore it. She did not want to be eccentric, but on the contrary, to be noble, loved, glorious, admired; perfection as far as she could be perfect." Yet, though she fears "they would think her a freak," she wears her dress anyway.

Teresa's urge for creativity is opposed by the fear of being a freak that haunted Louie. But, as was true for the younger girl, her wild vivid fancies find their outlet. She escapes the tensions of family quarrels by covering papers with designs like her embroidery. She "combined all sorts of strange things . . . patriotic things, the fantastic heads of prize merino rams, with their thick, parting, curly, silky wool and their double-curved corrugated horns, spikes of desert wheat, strange forms of xorophytic plants, pelicans, albatrosses, sea-eagles, passion-flowers, the wild things she most admired." Teresa's style is similar to Stead's. Her drawings display the eclectic profusion of precisely observed creatures and the wild taste for the exotic that characterize Stead's prose. Teresa too will ultimately give legitimacy and focus to this fruitful imagination by writing.

Before she finds her place as a writer (and Stead diminishes rather than emphasizes this aspect of her heroine's maturity in the novel), Teresa's imagination will propel her into the vast and empty spaces of unexplored territory where her strongly felt perceptions serve both to free and to trap her. She sees the principles of constraint underlying social conventions, yet she falls prey to an instrument of just such repression in Jonathan Crow, whom she sees not as he is, but as her fantasy distorts him. Thinking she is escaping from the ideological control of her father, the family, and the society whose rules they inculcate, Teresa imagines she creates a unique and free shape for her life. Jonathan, however, shares Andrew Hawkins's egotism and misogyny; Teresa unwittingly repeats at his hands many of the demeaned patterns of behavior she thought she had resisted in her father's teachings.

Stead cannot ultimately explain Teresa's attraction to Crow any better than Teresa can, but she does dramatize it with conviction. With Crow, Teresa is working out not only problems particular to her character or to his, but also the difficulties inherent in a society where relationships between the sexes are structured by domination and subordination. Stead uses Teresa's relationships with Crow and Quick to explore the interdynamics of sexual politics and the existential heroism of inventing new forms of relation. She does this through a steady examination of Teresa's experience; neither of the men are created as fully or roundly as is Stead's heroine. Teresa, in fact, keeps reacknowledging how much her own consciousness delimits her perceptions even when she thinks she has moved beyond its confines. Yet Stead does portray Teresa's growing recognition of sensibilities other than her own; a growing objectivity in her perceptions of the world outside herself.

With Teresa and Jonathan Crow, Stead dramatizes the effect of sexual repression—not as an abstract idea but felt as it damages each of them, differently, but profoundly. Jonathan suffers the costs of material and spiritual poverty, visited on Teresa through his sadistic attitude toward women. Jonathan, like Andrew Hawkins, endures a split between high-minded verbal idealism, which Teresa takes literally and so believes him "pure" and "chaste" and a misogyny which sends him for sexual relations only to maids and waitresses, women he considers degraded. Idealistic herself, Teresa is unable to distinguish Jonathan's ideas from reality, and more and more takes on and into herself the denigrations of his ideas about women. Her former idealized heroic self-image is eaten away by guilt into something near despair.

Typed by his name, Jonathan Crow is a carrion bird who feeds on the destruction of other life. Although he has a sad history of poverty and Oedipal entanglement, sociological and psychological explanations for his character are put in Jonathan's mouth as whining, self-serving rationalizations and never elicit our sympathy. Thin, "poorly dressed, always in black," Crow is penurious and mean-spirited. In him, Teresa's heroic self-control is reduced to a self-pitying "martyrdom of penury." Lacking the fantasy that illuminates all of Teresa's actions, Crow's inner world is sterile. A caricature of "the soul-twisting pedagogue," he substitutes barren ideas for desires and feelings. "He had trained himself from earliest childhood to stoicism and had no daydreams; nor did he dream at night of what he could not have. What he could not buy, it was unmanly to desire. In the course of years he had reduced himself to a miserliness of mental life." The importance to Stead of the self-creating energies of fantasy and inner emotional life are reemphasized here by the destructiveness of their absence in Crow.

Repressed himself, Jonathan preys on repressed sexuality in others. His particular victims are the innocent, intellectual young women who come to hear his university lectures on love. "A bookworm with scarcely any knowledge of women but unfortunates," he fears women, but passively encourages them. While "he dreaded more than anything a tangle with a woman, the threat of paternity," "women liked him too much and he yielded to them. He yearned for their advances."

Like Jonathan's other followers (his own love cult, a "group of admirers of himself, sedulously collected"), Teresa uses Jonathan to focus her own romantic fantasies of love and learning. "His university talk was wonderful to her"; she conceives it in images of pastoral romanticism: "The university seemed to her a gleaming meadow, in which beautiful youths and girls strolled, untangling intellectual and moral threads, but joyfully, poignantly, and weaving them together, into a moving, living tapestry, something into which love, the mind, the soul, and living beauties like living butterflies and early summer flower-knots were blended." Teresa believes that if she can emulate Jonathan, and like him work her way out of poverty and get to a European university, then "she too could spend glorious days, full-blown hours teasing out the ideal and the real." (Ironically, Teresa does tease out the difference between the ideal and the real, but not in the academic way she expects.)

When Jonathan confides in her, and puts himself in her hands, she is flattered by the "teach me" of his "empty, delighted soul." His self-demeaning statement ("I have no will of my own, I only want to be saved and I don't care who does it. Let it be you.") appeals to her heroic self-conception. She thinks, "She could show him the world of Orpheus and David . . . Orpheus and his lute made the trees and the mountain tops that freeze dance to him when he did sing, the mountains skipped like lambs for David. . . . Why should [Jonathan] be miserable when the world was his? He had only to look at it as she did. The world was hers and she had no doubt for the future."

Jonathan's style of manipulation is passive-aggressive. Operating always at "no cost to himself," he maneuvers others into positions of active responsibility. "The restive, tumultuous breed of women always did the work of passion for him." Lured by her own idealism, Teresa delivers herself up as Jonathan's victim. She makes the agonizing decision to write to Jonathan to initiate a love relationship with

him into a symbolic test of courage, and frames it in
the language of an heroic ordeal, whose failure is
humiliation and isolation, whose success is transcendence. Feeling that a man would have the courage to
act and declare his love, she must too. "She was
ashamed of her timidity and aimlessness. . . . If I
haven't the courage for this, I'll fail everywhere. It
was a symbol; this or a life without men, a body without children. If she won him, she would succeed, and
in some mysterious way conquer her life and time."

The decision to be the active partner in a love affair becomes an act of revolution, leaving Teresa in
the isolation of a moral inventor. She "believed that
no woman had ever done this bitter, shameful, brave
thing before. . . . She was in the howling wilder-
ness. It was like a crime, she felt, in her terror, and
she was a lost woman . . . she went about with all
the feelings of a young anarchist preparing to over-
throw authority in secret."

Stead's political metaphor here is not incidental.
The active self-assertion of the hero's role contra-
venes the receptive passivity socially prescribed for
women. Teresa is not only assuming the responsibility for shaping her fate and learning to accommodate
herself to reality as any young hero must, but, in
denying the accepted division of activity and passivity to transcend gender roles, she is taking on the
challenge of an existential hero, to invent a new reality. The strength of her ability to act, however, is un-
dermined by the framework in which her actions are
judged. As the relinquishing of narrative point of
view to Crow reflects, Teresa dooms herself when she
delivers to Jonathan the moral authority of definition. Once she accepts his conception of their relationship and his assessment of her behavior, she is
trapped by his sadism into impossible binds. Jonathan maintains control, blaming Teresa for all the
overtures for which he makes her responsible. The

more actively Teresa takes the initiative, the more firmly she is enmeshed in his web. Without the genuine power of defining vision, Teresa is Jonathan's helpless victim.

Jonathan plays with Teresa like a puppet, exposing her feelings without sympathy, using her revelations to humiliate her. Their physical relationship is particularly distressing. Whether they are walking by the sea in Australia, or sitting in Jonathan's room in London, the charged atmosphere between them builds with expectations of sexual love, which Jonathan always thwarts. Teresa puts her hand on his, and Jonathan, "as if she were dirty or vulgar . . . coolly withdrew his hand, placed it on his knee and then began brushing a small speck off his clothes." His lack of response leaves Teresa "afraid and ashamed." She feels dirty and inappropriately aggressive, failing to see that he had encouraged her and that his negative response helps create her feelings of shame.

Their first, misconceived walk in the Australian hills forecasts the pattern of all their subsequent interactions. When they fail to become sexually involved, Jonathan blames Teresa for what has so awkwardly gone wrong; Teresa blames herself:

Teresa, going home, was the prey of the voices. One said: "If you had made a move, you would have done better"; the other said: "Men despise women who make the moves." By the time she reached the Quay, Jonathan thought: "I should have done better, but she was coy to bring me on and I won't be the first victim of my own atavism, led by the nose in that degrading mimicry of the chase simulated by woman to enhance her own value in men's eyes." Teresa, by the time she had gone to bed, had altered her ideas to, "It's my fault. If I'd been bolder, both would have been happy by this time." She thought: "none but the brave deserve the fair."

Teresa defenselessly accepts Jonathan's conceptions which are buttressed by social platitudes about

femininity, unaware that they are colored by hostility. Later, when she finds that Jonathan had been
writing love letters to five different girls in Australia, leading them all on, it is not Jonathan who seems
culpable, but the girls. Jonathan believes that he was
simply carrying on an experiment, and finds the
girls' responses disgusting. He is revolted by "their
degrading avidity." They seem to him like five garbage cans, "some half-full, others disgorging their
fragments of spoiled food." Listening to him, Teresa
"felt the fragments of food, the tumbled contents of
the bins, pelting at her, covering her with decay and
smut, but all the time he pretended it was reality, the
truth about men and women, that he was telling
her." That garbage pollutes Teresa's feelings about
herself, as the dirt and mess of Henny's world permeated her vision and shaped her rhetoric and contributed to the grotesque vision that colored *The
Man Who Loved Children.*

In spite of her unusual initial assurance, Teresa
is now acting out her conflicts in a typically feminine
way. Unlike the more self-protective response of
male heroes, who more typically project the rage of
frustrated desires or self-disgust onto an external antagonist with whom they can do battle, Teresa instead
internalizes it at the cost of her own self-esteem.
Stead here dissects with precise clarity a self-blaming
mechanism of feminine psychology. The theme of
guilt repeatedly poisons Teresa's reflections about
Jonathan and her behavior with him. It is painful to
watch the way Teresa goes back to Jonathan again
and again. After her most trenchant perceptions of
his destructiveness, after he has treated her most
cruelly, instead of being angry, Teresa feels the need
to comfort him in his misery. This dynamic is repeated after the most brutal exposures of hatred between them, and resolves even the culminating scene
of their continually frustrated relationship. Just be-

fore Teresa and James Quick discover their love for
each other, Teresa and Jonathan make an excursion
to the country, where a severe storm traps them for
the night in the shelter of a decaying sawmill. In style
and vision, Chapter 33, "The Deserted Sawmill," is
reminiscent of the scenes of sheer male-female antagonism in D. H. Lawrence's *Women in Love*. In
Stead, as in Lawrence, the physical setting images the
human turmoil: a fierce storm batters the broken
mill. Water rushes turbulently beneath the black
gaping holes in its floor, and the man and the woman
confront each other in a moment of pure hatred. As
they stare at each other across a distance, "the same
thought flashed between them. 'He (or she) could go
without regret, why doesn't that thing of misery do
it.'" Yet, though Teresa sees Jonathan's vicious hatred,
though he abandons her during the night, still, when
a few days later he asks her to come see him as usual,
"she did not think for a moment of refusing him. She
thought: 'He needs me, I cannot refuse just because I
am sick of it.'" And she goes back to him once again.

Without being able to explain why Teresa remains attached to Jonathan, Stead shows clearly the
effects of that attachment. Teresa's self-image is
transformed. By the end of her affair with him, she is
a debilitated, despised and self-despising creature,
that lowest thing of all, a rejected woman, who wants
to live only to die. Teresa, who once defined herself by her own standards, has accepted definition
through Jonathan's eyes. By accepting his denigrations of her as true, she has seriously damaged her
own life-impulse. She has tried to please him by attempting to meet his impossibly conflicting demands,
and she blames herself for her inevitable failure. She
thinks of "the rigamarole of her buffoon Odyssey
torn out of privations of which Jonathan knew
nothing; . . . ashamed of all she had done, because
every hour of it was only a stronger proof that she

was a detestable thing, an ugly, rejected woman, distorted and lost. She was lost." Teresa has twisted the
full force of her will away from life into a melodramatic affirmation of death. Now ironically like
Jonathan, she is preoccupied with her "coming martyrdom" and is finishing a book to leave when she
dies. "The Testament of Women" or "The Seven
Houses of Love" (which parodies St. Teresa's *Interior
Castle*, a treatise on the seven mansions of the soul)
will tell "the ages . . . through which abandoned,
unloved women passed before life was torn out of
their clenched, ringless, work-worn fists." "To die
terribly by will" is her final stage. The distance between Teresa's image of herself as the heroic Odysseus who left Australia sure of her honor and power,
defying the conventions which bound other women,
and this "detestable thing" who broods on suicide, is
stunning. This is the nadir of Teresa's hero voyage.

Ironically, Teresa has made herself the very
image she rejected of the female hero as martyred
saint. Teresa seeks, with fierce determination, an
adult life that will integrate rather than deny her
sexual and assertive impulses. However, to do so, she
inadvertently treads the path of masochism and martyrdom. The most violent action Teresa ever takes is
against herself. Teresa sets for herself the most extreme ordeals of physical hardship and social isolation; she inflicts on herself the very repressions she is
determined to evade.

Before she can go to England, Teresa devises a
plan of minutely detailed self-denial to enable her to
save the money she needs for her passage. In the consistent metaphor of the novel, she frames her task as
a heroic ordeal. She felt that "she was behaving as
behaves a gallant and brave man who passes through
the ordeals of hope deferred, patience, and painful
longing, to win a wife. She might win him, it was up
to her." She takes a job as a secretary in a hat factory

and for three years denies herself all pleasures and
most necessities to save the money she needs. Once
she made her resolve, "during the next one thousand
ninety-six days, she spent no money on herself, either
to go to a movie or to buy a stick of chocolate or to
buy a newspaper."

Stead details Teresa's ordeal with the most con-
vincing precision. Teresa adopts an economics of
hoarding and denial in which no amount of energy is
too much to spend to save a few cents. Though "already she felt the resistance of the body," she walked
the "two miles back and forth from work every day."

The tram ride only cost two pence, so that it might seem
folly to wear oneself out in this way, but she was afraid to
give in on any count and in some ways the endless walking,
walking, meant England. . . . She considered the wear
and tear of the body and beauty as nothing. With beauty
and health she could not get one wave nearer England, but
even though her bones poked through and she was carried
aboard, she was welcome, if she paid her fare, she could sail
the sea like any free soul, from Ulysses, to the latest
skipper of a sixteen-footer rounding the world. She thought
of death, indeed, but only as an obstacle that might prevent her sailing and must be circumvented.

Everything else is subordinated to Teresa's fierce
purpose. Like Louisa Pollit who demonstrated her
stoicism by holding her hand in a flame, she considers her body nothing more than a vehicle of her will.
Though, as others observe, there is something mad
about this, Teresa is willing to make any sacrifice to
be able to be a Ulysses who can "sail the seas like any
free soul." She asks nothing of anyone else, but is resolved to win her freedom without assistance.

Teresa ignores her minimal physical needs. "For
four winters, whatever the cold, she had worn . . .
no coat, and she often arrived home wet through, but
pretended that she felt nothing and could never take
cold. She had a deep cough which shook her whole

frame and did not leave her even in the summer . . . [and] a perpetual hunger." "She had only one dress at the time, which she washed and ironed every two days and darned in places, especially under the arms above the waist where her arms, swinging as she walked, rubbed holes. In sitting, she had to arrange the dress so that the mending did not show, and when the darns doubled, she took an old newspaper from home, always the same newspaper, which she carried under her arm."

Teresa feels she must remain isolated to continue her struggle for independence. She holds herself apart from her family, confiding nothing to them, and refuses to join the workers' union at her office. She even rejects the romantic advances of a kind and ardent young man with whom she works. A slighter version of the James Quick figure, Erskine is fond of Teresa and demonstrative, and like Quick, uses images for Teresa that reinforce her romantic self-conception. (She is so pale and beautifully distracted, "like a woman out of Shakespeare. . . . Yes, out of Schubert too, Death and the Maiden in one person." But Teresa refuses him: "I have a great destiny. . . . Glory and catastrophe are not the fate of the common man. . . . If I stay here, I will be nobody. . . . I'd fall in love with someone—you might make me, . . . then I'd get married and stay here. I can't do it." Both the focused ambitions of Teresa's romantic self-idealization and her lack of confidence keep her apart from the pleasures her immediate life offers her. She refuses Erskine both because she expects a special destiny and because "she had so whole-heartedly accepted Jonathan's cool treatment and thought it just that she did not believe any man could love her."

Teresa lives more and more in a state of extremity. Her psychological polarities are acted out physically, and she achieves painful ecstasies like St.

Teresa's by enduring extreme physical deprivations. She is so perpetually hungry that indulging the forbidden sin of buying a sweet drink overwhelms her with "a wave of pleasure and gluttony." She is so fatigued that "a loud sound made her secretly tremble and start. She steeled herself against all tremor . . . the starting at a noise and the suppression cost too much energy." "She developed the acuity of a savage, in sound and in smell." Teresa loses her sense of propriety and one day even finds herself begging for food. "Having a distant goal," she feels so far removed from others that "she had no real shame . . . and she did not even look in the faces of the people" she passed.

Teresa's feelings are heightened to the point of ecstasy or agony. She has removed herself almost entirely from the world around her and withdrawn into herself. Her stoic isolation is not unakin to madness. In spite of her intensified sensuality, her love for Jonathan is transformed into an ascetic dream, in which all thoughts of sexuality are repressed. Teresa feels that "all familiar joys were forbidden to her."

She had come to think of her wild dreams as impure and kept them apart from Jonathan, who was to her holy, pure, admirable. . . . She told herself that if she ever allowed one impure thought to creep into her mind now, she would never have Jonathan: it would be her punishment, and a just one. 'Love has nothing to do with all that.' Her former fancies fell away, withered, things hideous and unspeakable began to take their place, since the room could not be left empty.

The renunciations of Teresa's ordeal are seen in the novel as necessary to enable her to act, yet they simultaneously become a denial rather than an assertion of her own needs and desires. Having started as a vigorous, active, healthy young woman, by the time she leaves for London, Teresa looks much like an anorexic child. Looking in the mirror (never her habit before), she thinks, "It was very curious and touching, even to her, to see certain delicate and rounded forms like the limbs of a pretty, sick child. As a child she had been large, robust, brown and firm, now she was like a child with tuberculosis." The physical effects of her deprivations reflect the diminishment of her emotional energies and her fantasy life. Ironically, by playing what she conceives of as a strong, heroic role as a woman of independent initiative, Teresa, with Jonathan's help, has made herself into a new kind of female victim; she internalizes both Jonathan's revulsion and her own to make herself as sick and weak as the most frail, fainting Victorian heroine.

Teresa has reached the limits of her independent strength. Her rescue now comes only through the grace of an outside agency. James Quick, her first employer in London, becomes her kindly savior and restores her to herself through his love for her. Quick, like Crow, is a character of simplifed outlines, as idealized as Crow is denigrated. Nevertheless, his effect on Teresa's consciousness is clearly drawn. Through her relation with him, Teresa moves beyond her intense involvement in her own fantasies and feelings to a relationship with another person whose separate life begins to assume some reality for her. Quick restores to her her faith in herself in a more realistic form; his view of her is not only more generous than Crow's, but also less exaggerated and kinder than her own initial self-conception. Teresa's concerns with the expression and fulfillment of her creative energies return to prominence and she emerges as a lover and writer, not in fantasy but in practice.

An American, thirty-seven years old, James Quick had come to England to manage the business at which Teresa becomes a secretary. He has a wife of ten years in America, but their marriage was now

loveless and dispirited, though neither quite had the
courage to dissolve it. Like Teresa, Quick is alone in
London, with few friends, and lives abstemiously,
"neither drinking, eating nor loving much."

Stead describes Quick as an ebullient man, and
her description mirrors that exuberance:

James Quick was middle-sized, white-skinned, black-eyed,
with a silent, lively look and speaking lips and, in fact, a
soft and truculent loquacity. He was a subtle black and
white man, a prepotent, agile, clean, sweet-smelling sloven,
a heady man, a sitting man, a man who loved to live by
candlelight, pushed out of doors by an unspeakable greed
of men, a little more—and a fisher of souls, but not this, he
was, not dangerous, not ambitious, not proud, but with
capacity, of old English stock, mature and steeped in a language, cured and treasured up. . . . His looks were those
of a grand-uncle, a family lawyer, but his nature was a rebellion against the protector, a business man, and the
grand-uncle. . . . He would have looked best, portly and
ready, in a black coat with white ruffles slightly soiled, and
from time to time, after being excessively aware, bel-
ligerent, angry, denunciatory, he suddenly assumed these
invisibly, was courtly, lady-loving. . . . He loved women
as equals; that is, as men love friends, knowing and humbly
loving all.

The narrator is inclined to hero worship James
Quick, though this gay, headlong overabundance
does not idealize him into featurelessness.

Stead judges her characters primarily by the fullness of their inner lives; Quick's fantasies are as rich
and warm as Crow's were withered and distorted. He
brings to Teresa an imagination to match her own,
and indeed, Teresa fills his imaginings as she never
did Crow's. The week after she has come to work for
him, Quick finds himself feeling fresh and buoyant
and wonders why. "But he went on thinking pleasur-
ably and soon he found the glare of his pleasure was
concentrated on the office . . . and on the young

woman that he and [his partner] had engaged one morning last week. . . . He thought of her face particularly; it haunted him both in its paleness, without colour or powder, and the shining of the blue or green eyes. He kept seeing them. . . . He went on thinking of the woman's face, her manner nervous, anxious, hungry, her timidity in her independence. . . ." "He thought, it was Old English, the face, antique, something that he had seen in old print shops."

The passages in which Quick thinks about Teresa are flooded with images of heat and light. When his many thoughts about her one night lead Quick to realize that he must love her, he smiles at the idea. "Scarcely, however, had James Quick thought, 'Why, I must be in love with this woman,' than the improbability of it struck him and he clouded over again." He considers her simplicity, inexperience, and thinks of all the reasons he ought not to love her. "But in thinking this, an irresistible smile kept rising to his lips, a radiance brightened in his breast, as if a sun about the size of a twenty-dollar piece was rising over his heart and he could not rebuff this pleasant idea any more than a person coming out of the wintry night can resist getting warm."

Reversing Petrarchan convention, Stead portrays her knight-errant as a sun-god, garbed in metaphors of warmth, animation and freshness. Quick's name itself is emblematic of the life he restores in Teresa. "You light everything up when you explain it," she says to him in wonder. "The world has changed for me since I knew you." "I was dead to the world, and you've restored me to life."

Through Quick, Stead reintroduces the heroic imagery for Teresa that had been lost through Jonathan's influence. Imagining her as a "Burne-Jones girl in a grape colored robe, and something more pre-Raphaelite, Dante, death," Quick revives Stead's romantic images for Teresa from her days in Australia. Intrigued by her seriousness, tender about her naïveté, Quick also thinks of her in images that celebrate her strength of character: "She argued with him about everything, she always thought he was wrong. He, who knew so much, and she, who knew so little—it made no difference—she seemed to think she and the rest of the English came postgraduate from God. He chuckled. 'The philosophical Teresa.' He had had plenty of secretaries who teased, kidded or flattered him. She never once agreed with him. 'Yes,' he said, 'that's it, that's what she is, a ship's captain, or . . . a rebel lieutenant, perhaps the reincarnation of Mr. Christian of the *Bounty*.' He laughed aloud."

Quick's rescue of Teresa is effected as his point of view takes over the novel. Stead somewhat mechanically arranges a scene in which Crow and Quick meet to discuss one of Crow's essays. Quick immediately sees the self-deceptions and power manipulations inherent in Crow's thinking. Jonathan's egotism makes him the perfect gull, and Quick easily maneuvers him into revealing his twisted and degrading feelings about Teresa. "No wonder Miss Hawkins looks like Karenina after the railway accident," thinks Quick, who has been puzzled by his secretary's haggardness and distraught manner. "Crushed by a one-horse pedant." "I'll talk it out of her as he's talked it into her," he vows.

He does what he promises: the narrative adopts his perspective of Crow, and eventually Teresa does too. Through his love, Teresa is freed of her prolonged attachment to Jonathan. "It was just the illusion of a love-hungry girl," Quick tells her. "Paralyzed with surprise in her mind and heart," Teresa says slowly, "I believe I never loved him at all." Teresa "had often wished she could have the mind of another person for a while and this evening she felt

as if it had been given. [It] had spun her away from
Jonathan and she was free of him." Teresa is released
to the freedom of a new vision.

Yet Quick's power is overwhelming as well as
healing, and Teresa reacts against it. Control, and its
loss, becomes a major problem between them. Quick
floods her with new and elevated images of herself,
with new desires and hopes; but while his are as exciting and ambitious and fulfilling as Crow's were
diminishing and debilitating, they are still Quick's
visions and not hers, and Teresa, used to thinking for
herself, is unable to give herself wholly to the proffered tutelage of Quick.

Quick assaults her in a storm of words, telling
her his plans for her glory:

He would bring her books, music, take her to concerts,
theatres, if she wished, send her to the university . . . make
a brilliant woman of her . . . a woman of wit and lustre . . .
who would shine anywhere. . . . He would take her to
Paris . . . he would make her over entirely. . . .

Then he mounted the snake-faced, vulture-winged
Pegasus of passion and sang the physical joys they would
have. . . . Marriage was not what she thought it . . . but
an academy of love, with one tutor, as Abelard and Heloise,
and all this she could have, love, joy and all in the world
that women were supposed to desire, as well as those things
that the women really wanted, in their hearts, dominion,
learning.

Although Quick's dreams for her are elevations
of her own aspirations, Teresa's sense of control is vi-
olated when Quick spins worlds with his words. She
tells him, "With you, I feel like the devil's appren-
tice: I set the pot boiling and I can't stop it—it runs
all over the floor, all over the village, all over the
world and the tides keep rising."

The sun imagery of their courtship clouds into
storm imagery. The first consummation of Teresa's
and Quick's sexual relationship is not ecstatic as

Teresa had anticipated, but bittersweet, filled with the pain and ambiguity as well as love that foreshadow their future conflicts. Later, when Quick greets her on her return from a train trip, his kisses overpower her: "She was confused by this hurricane. . . . She was paralysed and without emotion. She did not know where she stood any more than if a high tide had rushed in and swamped the road where she used to walk. . . . She suffered already from the intensity of her husband's passion, she sensed that in it was doubt, fear, and much suffering. . . . But now she was overwhelmed by his storm . . . a sort of anger arose against Quick that he was pushing her to the wall in this way."

Their love encompasses both attraction and resistance: "She felt both completely united to the man and yet aware of the awful empire she was giving him over her, and it was always at this moment that she pushed him away brusquely." "She had given herself too much in saying she loved him, and now she feared him." As Teresa resists the absolutism of the clichés of "falling in love," being "swept off your feet," Stead resists metaphors of loss of self in love, in favor of images of struggle and resistance.

Stead offers, characteristically, both social and individual explanations for the difficulties Teresa encounters in the love she has so long sought. Women, she says, "love, but they are taught that their love is ridiculous, old-fashioned, unseemly, and inopportune." "The oblique remarks and casual slurs of relatives, the naked domestic drama of hate of parent and child, lead them to the belief that love does not exist, that it is a flare-up between the sexes, a fever, or a nugget which must be capitalized as soon as found." Teresa has lived these economics of love in her relation to Jonathan Crow: "all her life she had expected to give passion and never thought of its being given to her. She had wished for the night of the senses but not anticipated a devotion of every day and night. Quick laughed at her, calling her his "Hard-luck Annie," but he had no idea of how his "constantly proffered love, sympathy, and help troubled her; she was used to thinking for herself. . . . She respected him for his loyalty, which she understood because she too was loyal, but . . . she was embarrassed by this devotion of the man whose idea of heaven was the rapture of married love."

Quick's love makes an important transformation in Teresa. "What surprised her was that there was not only James Quick but another breed of men who loved women who loved. She saw at the same time that her horrible disease, her love, which she had covered up for years, was admired by this kind of man; instead of being loathed, insulted and sent to her death, she was adored. She changed at once." While Quick's affirmation is liberating for Teresa, she finds to her surprise that the marriage which gives her so much does not satisfy her. She "had felt in her heart for some time, emptied of the old need and ambition, an unemployment and dryness which startled her. It was her secret. . . . She thought *this* might be marriage, and if so, marriage itself was arid, for this end of all striving and even lusting in love was wrong and not the part of any mature, joyful human being." "For herself, she knew that the satisfaction of this great desire only made her more restless and energetic than before." "Too formed by adversity and too . . . ambitious by nature to take pleasure in her marital union alone," Teresa "was conscious of two desires, to accomplish her Testament, which had now become the 'Triumph of Love,' and to get to understand and love men." "She wanted to penetrate and influence men, to use them, even without aim, merely for variable and seductive power. . . . Her hunger had made her insatiable . . . she wanted to try men."

The exuberance of Teresa's newly discovered

powers is as real as is their exaggeration. Stead allows her to feel their pleasures before she is confronted with their necessary limitations. Stead, at this point, might have elaborated further Teresa's development as a writer which becomes, for Stead herself, a realistic outlet for her imaginative energies. The exercise of these newly affirmed creative powers in love is more problematic. In *Women in Love*, D. H. Lawrence creates for his married lovers a union that reaches depths of mystical satisfaction. Stead, who seeks to plumb a similar wellspring of feeling, does not have Teresa reach such heights of happiness within marriage. The images of transcendence, security, and joy are evoked not by Teresa and Quick's union, but by the elation of a transient love affair. Stead characterizes her heroine's primary love relationship by a complicated rhythm of give and take, approach and avoidance, fears and satisfactions. It is only in a brief encounter with Harry Girton, a young friend of Quick's who is about to go off to fight in the Spanish Civil War, that Teresa expands into the fully realized joy of self-fulfillment.

Teresa finds herself increasingly attracted to Girton. He touches off Teresa's sensual fantasies, for which Stead uses the paradisal, oceanic imagery of a fused, undifferentiated primal sensuality, explicitly evoking images of childhood delight: Teresa dreams and daydreams of him:

She now knew a bounding ecstatic gaiety she had not felt since her early girlhood. . . . The golden young man called up in her mind . . . an endless succession of light images, golden days, golden globes within which she lived in the murk of London. There were flashes of light, a day which was always dawning, and her feet lightly touched on the shores of a smooth sea, and such feelings of childhood, these visions which come to a child lying on its back under the sun in the grass . . . through him she began to live the sunburnt, wind-blown, nonchalant days of singing in the grass which had never been; she felt her flesh running into his and clinging to him, as if they had never been sundered and as if this and all life would go on in this glory for ever, as if no years would ever pass over their heads and as if, at the same time, children were springing endlessly from his or her loins. There was honey in his thighs and new-pressed unfermented wine in all of him; and, mad with love, she sucked them both into her eyes, only then understanding love of man.

Stead's description of the consummation of Teresa and Girton's affair continues with language that is not so much physical sexual description as it is the imagery of this fantasy of paradise and transcendence. "Their bodies evaporated. 'We are made of smoke,' said Teresa, panting. 'Like those genies in bottles in the Arabian Nights,' . . . we got out." "She was in a strange state of ecstasy, she seemed to float upright like a pillar of smoke." "She was astonished at her feeling of wanting nothing." These transcendent moments of self-realization give Teresa a feeling of mystic oneness with herself: "She was withdrawn into an inner room of herself and here she found the oracle of her life . . . now perfectly visible." "Lifted high, the mind was, now, by a great surge. . . . She continued in a fit of absence, the black river before her, the world, it seemed, silent around."

If Stead concedes her prose to romantic ecstasy, she thereafter retrieves it to a more realistic plane. Teresa's elation comes with her release from the severe deprivations and misery she has endured. Her ecstatic moments are placed as peaks in an ongoing dialectical emotional process which qualifies such heights as soon as they are experienced. They herald, she realizes, not continuing delight but the beginning of a long ongoing struggle, which, however, can now be engaged on more realistic terms, with more hope of realistic positive fulfillments. "For the long

and bitter time, the time of her imprisonment, she
had steeled herself too much against misfortune; she
had never dared to hope or to be glad, in fear of failure; and it was only now that she was able slowly to
relinquish her fierce grip on life, to relish the aban-
don of the senses." Sensual gratification brings her a
new vision:

Suddenly a strange thought came to her, that she had
reached the gates of the world of Girton and Quick and
that it was towards them she was only now journeying. . . .
She suddenly understood that there was something beyond
misery, and that at present she had merely fought through
that bristling, black and sterile plain of misery and that
beyond was the real world, red, gold, green, white, in
which the youth of the world would be passed. . . . This
was beyond the "Seventh House"—and when she understood this, that there was something on the citied plain for
all of them . . . she knew why she continued restless and
why the men, having so much in the hollow of their hands,
keep on striving. At this moment sprang up in her, for
them, an inarticulate emotion of excitement quite beyond
anything she had ever felt. All on this fabulous . . . journey seemed divine, easy and clear, as if she had a passport
to paradise.

   This journey will come to seem less easy and
clear. Her excitement will be qualified by an acknowledgment of inevitable conflicts between individual fulfillment and mutuality, between selfishness and selflessness as well as between assertion and
loss of self in love. The conflict between her love affair, and what Stead comes to refer to as her marriage
(though Quick is not in fact divorced from his American wife) is resolved for Teresa by her loyalty to
Quick, but not without a sense of loss. Trying to sort
her passion for Girton from her love and concern
for Quick, rediscovering her loyalty to Quick, like
another sun dawning, resolves her feelings and permits her renunciation of Girton: "In between these

terrible fits of passion, she realized a new and
wonderful feeling, her duty to James Quick. It was
like the hope of a child; when she fixed her eyes on it,
everything else vanished and her heart became un-
selfish." But this resolution is not simple; nor does it
promise ever to be. Such conflicts will occur again.
"In this rough and tumble of need, egotism and
love," Teresa wonders, "where was the right thing
to do?"

The ending of *For Love Alone* reasserts not
Teresa's newfound harmony with Quick, but the cir-
cularity of painful repetitions of ignorance and mis-
perception. As Teresa and Quick go out for a walk
one night, Teresa sees a gaunt, ghoulish figure standing under the blue light of a lamp. After a moment's
repelled reflection she suddenly realizes that she is
looking at Jonathan Crow. A casual observation of
Quick's about Crow's color blindness (a fact unknown to Teresa) startles her into realizing just how
little she ever knew Jonathan. The last assertion of
the novel is Teresa's bitter sigh: "It's dreadful to
think that it will go on being repeated for ever, he—
and me! What's there to stop it?"   *2/4344*

When *For Love Alone* first appeared in 1944,
critical responses to it were sharply polarized, and
largely by moral rather than aesthetic judgments.
Critics tended to ignore Stead's careful qualifications
and respond to what was seen as the romantic egotism of the fiction. The ending was seen as a glorifica-
tion of female egotism which critics either praised or
reviled. Colin Roderick appreciated watching "the
gradual unfolding of [Teresa's] personality" and
meant it as a compliment when he said that Stead
"glories in the power of the feminine ego."[8] But that
is what most distressed the reviewers who did not
like the novel. Diana Trilling criticizes Teresa for
seeking personal power rather than love.[9] In *The
New Republic*, Marjorie Farber finds the glorifica-

tion of a woman's power an egotistical romantic fantasy.[10] A chorus of voices warns that Teresa, exultant at the end, is riding for a fall.

One suspects that the reactions against feminine egotism are more intense than they would be with a similarly compelling male character.[11] Though this novel is a romantic assertion of Stead's heroine's independence and individual strength, it is not without complexity. Lionel Trilling has said that we demand in our heroes "such energy as contrives that the centre shall hold, that the circumference of self keep unbroken."[12] William James defines identity as a sense of what is "most deeply and intensely active and alive" in oneself.[13] Teresa achieves just this energy and dignified autonomy. This novel affirms the integral process of growth and radiates the communicated energy of authentic self-discovery.

Teresa and Stead arrive at a conception of love in keeping with this sense of identity. Enjoying the freedom Quick's love gives her, Teresa thinks, "How miserable I would have been if I had had to go on for years, wondering whether I should love another man! But now I know, this is the only love, but not the first and not the last. I will know how to make myself a life apart. If James robbed me, I would dislike him for my empty heart, but as I know how to cultivate my heart and mind in secret, now, I can only love him for giving myself to me."

Reinforcing Teresa's values by returning the novel to her narrative perspective, Stead too celebrates love not as self-sacrifice or surrender into merged identity but as self-affirmation. The novel ends with a reconceptualization of the social institution it starts by rejecting. Marriage is recast, not as a passively accepted convention, but as a mutually chosen relationship of loyalty, defined by the two partners' creative reinvention of commitment on the basis of their own needs and desires. Like Teresa's

creation of her own trajectory, this act of social invention is heroic. Teresa realizes her ambitions for
an independent life, rich in work and love, by stringent self-denial and determined solitary action outside all institutions of community or support. The
novel exalts her remarkable independence and final
access to personal power. But Stead conceives the
movement of Teresa's growth and of her relationship
with Quick as neither a linear development nor the
pessimistic circular repetition of the novel's last
image. Progress is rather spiralled moving forward
even as it repeats old patterns, in a continuing dia-
lectic of struggle.

This novel celebrates, as do none of her others,
Stead's ideal of stoic female heroism. In her subsequent fiction these solitary accomplishments recede
to become yet another embodiment of what Stead
sees as all-pervasive, manipulative human egotism.
Her later protagonists diminish in size, become more
ironically conceived, more critically apprehended.
The positive presence in the later novels recedes
from the protagonists to reside in a wise narrative
voice.

In *For Love Alone*, however, Stead creates a
haunting and powerful portrait of a woman of genius, of intellectual, emotional, and physical vitality
who does learn to love and work. With grim intensity, Teresa struggles to find a creative outlet for her
deeply introspective sensibility. She does, and her
relation with Quick, like the more conventional resolution of marriage, serves to bring her back into
social connection after her dark voyage through her
own inner world. Stead treats Teresa's struggle with
dignity and respect, in a tone of high moral seriousness. Stead's attention to social structure as it is felt
and articulated within individual consciousness gives
a representativeness to her heroine. Teresa herself
grows beyond her initial sense of heroic specialness

toward one of shared community. Stead's language creates a continuous interpenetration of people and places, landscape and feeling, private events and public. While Teresa's individuality is highly valued and distinctly portrayed, the dimensions of her portrait are extended to place her struggle within the common social fabric.

For Love Alone anatomizes the costs of a particular social form of ordering human experience—its renunciations, pains, and conflicts. Stead invents a heroine able to push back the limits of experience, to widen the boundaries of constraint within social connection. Teresa's accomplishment is not in the perfection of what she creates, but in the power of the act of recreation. Teresa is celebrated for her capacity for individual acts of imagination and will that enable her to extend the limitations of the social system whose product she is, and whose repressions she shares, to make room for a broader vision of human need and possibility. That Stead has created this capacity in a woman hero is itself a distinctive expansion of traditional limitations. With considerable narrative skill and emotional force, Stead has succeeded in creating what is rare in literature—a portrait of a woman as an existential hero.

4

No More Heroes:
The Development of a Voice
and a Vision

Stead's two autobiographical novels are her best. In them her own story provides a focus that her other fiction often lacks. The Domestic Gothic technique of *The Man Who Loved Children* achieves a synthesis of fantasy and observation that yields her strongest and most original prose style. Over more than forty years, Stead has written eleven novels and two volumes of short stories. Looking at the arc of development of all the fiction, we can trace the continuities and changes that lead to her best work in *The Man Who Loved Children* and *For Love Alone*. In the novels that follow them, the tensions they had resolved reemerge and another struggle between the inner and outer world, expression and repression, sympathy and judgment is waged before new experiments once more generate an equilibrium in the controlled moral and aesthetic vision of her late work.

Some things remain constant. For Christina Stead, the animating concern of the novel is always an interest in people. "The object of the novel is characterization," she asserts.[1] Her own "private passion" is "the study of personality."[2] Stead is interested not in a specific class of people, but in the passions that animate all sorts of diverse personalities.

"Everyone, to a greater or lesser extent," she writes, "is a fountain of passion, which is turned by circumstances of birth or upbringing into conventional channels—as, ambition, love, money-grubbing, politics, but which could be as well applied to other objectives and with less waste of energy."[3] Stead is consistently egalitarian in finding the obsessive character types that interest her in every social class and occupation, age, sex, and nationality. The obscure and unattractive especially fascinate her.

"Everyone has a wit superior to his everyday wit, when discussing his personal problems, and the most depressed housewife, for example, can talk like Medea about her troubles," Stead says.[4] She has always been especially acute about these extraordinary passions in ordinary people; it is the tragic heightening of passion in the inner life of everyday that generates and sustains the excesses of her fiction: that is what her novels are about. Her novels do not, therefore, provide us with a series of plots with clear outlines to discuss. We can, however, trace motifs and images, persistent character types and concerns that define the inner world which is to such a great extent the source and form of her fiction.

All of Stead's work is characterized by excess. It comes from the unrestrained play of her brilliant verbal imagination and powers of observation, but also from her continual devotion to the truths of the inner life, which are by nature extreme. Stead never makes an absolute boundary between inner and outer: the intensities of the secret emotional world are always as much reality to her as daily events and observable actions. Her prose, her characterizations and plots are shaped and misshaped by fidelity to this inner realm.

Criticism of Christina Stead circles around the issue of excess. Even her greatest admirers admit to her luxuriant overabundance, her "natural excess

and lack of discrimination."[5] She is at once called
old-fashioned, undisciplined, and painful; inventive,
humorous, original, and absorbing. While the chaotic richness of her narrative, with its abundant
digressions and repetitions, its menageries of characters and lengthy conversations rendered with the
accuracy of a tape recorder, is praised for its "mi-
metic zeal"[6] that imitates "the messy, disorganized
ways of life,"[7] Stead is also criticized for shunning
the economies of storytelling and the structure of
suspense in plot. And she does. Her fiction demands
"consecutive acts of attention,"[8] though it rewards
them. What she is best at catching is not order, but
chaos. Her style is characterized by a persistent particularity. She operates by "accretion of detail."[9]
What Mary McCarthy calls Stead's "enormous energy
potential" derives from her capacity for specificity.
Stead's form is diffuse; her most profound organiz-
ing principles are psychological. Her narratives are
structured by compiling dramatic scenes to develop
climaxes of emotional crisis.[10]

From the start, critics observed that "the unde-
clared war between the ordinary and the weird,
richly imagined"[11] wages perpetually in her work.
Reviewer Frederick Gardner perceives the tension of
"the outlandish dreamer vs. the social historian giving us the essence of this man, that couple, that
movement, that nation, that epoch—and her best
prose takes its energy from the conflict."[12] Fantasy
always mingles with realism in her work: Stead's
early tales are overtly gothic; throughout, her grotesque imagery is reminiscent of Dickens. *The Salzburg Tales* evoke a "mood that rejects the probable,
the plain, the quotidian."[13] Equally, in the late *Puzzleheaded Girl*, "plots transpire in an atmosphere
of demi-realism that is frequently disorienting and
sometimes incredible."[14] Mary McGrory complains of
"excesses of style and situation" in the satiric *Letty*

Fox. "All is distorted, turgid and overblown in her world, with sex rampant and passion unbridled," she writes.[15] Other critics, however, have appreciated the expressive virtue of what some consider gothic melodrama. Christopher Ricks observes that Stead is fascinated by the extreme rhetoric of our private conversations with ourselves.[16] Crucial to an understanding of Stead is an appreciation of her technique of embedding fantasy in a realistic context to unearth exaggerated feelings and grandiose rhetoric of the inner life. Stead's style is defined by the distinctive union of these two dimensions of reality.

While her interest in people (and the depths of their personalities) stays at the center of Stead's fiction, her way of perceiving and representing them changes. The development of her style is marked by a changing equilibrium between the grotesque images of the inner world of feeling, and images of the outer world, addressed through satiric realism. Early on, Stead's stylistic vision is polarized. Fantasies of the feeling world are abundant; she achieves distance from their turbulence through satiric detachment. There is little conjunction of the two realms. Both her prose style and her characters grow to develop a functional balance between fantasy and satire, expression and control, feeling and intellect; her work will always swing between these poles. The accomplishment of the Domestic Gothic style is the counterpoise it achieves that expresses the range of feeling of inner fantasy while keeping the perspective lent by intellectual understanding and social observation. This parallels a course of development for her characters and a development in her techniques of characterization. Characters learn to move through and beyond the world of their own fantasies to externalize their desires in action and interaction with other people. And Stead perfects a narrative technique for creating a complex fictional world that can focus on one character's inner life while allowing a number of different individuals, each with a fully developed internal world, to coexist in the same dramatic universe.

It is just this freedom that characters perpetually deny to one another. Stead sees people persistently trying to violate the separate realities of others, whom they wish to make puppets in their own dramas. In her early understanding of such egotistical tyrants, Stead tends to divide the world into oppressors and oppressed, strong and weak, tyrants and victims. This habit of thinking in polar oppositions is itself characteristic of the inner dynamics of a young mind. As her work matures, these polarities move in a dialectical process toward synthesis. Tyrants and victims come to be the same individuals; as she examines the manipulative techniques of the weak, she sees the tyrannies of egotism enacted by those who were themselves its victims. The heroes she had once seen escaping into their own inner worlds, or running away in stoic independence, come to seem an inevitable part of the interconnected human fabric in which independence is only another mask of egotism, a disguised form of taking without giving in return.

In her characters, Stead shows that neither loss within the inner world of feeling nor suppression of feeling by satiric detachment and independence from emotional bonds is an escape from egotism. As she develops her technique, instead of using irony for satiric detachment that mocks and denies feeling, as she does at first, she uses it to hold multiple points of view in a counterpoise that allows in her fiction's world an acknowledgment of the simultaneous reality of equally rich, vital, and valid separate sensibilities, and so gives distance from the egotistical self-absorption of each. It is this ironic equilibrium of multiple points of view that lets her late work present a vision of the transcendence of egotism that so shapes and devours the world of her early fiction. Similarly, Stead develops a flexible constraint in her prose style, in which fantasy is neither denied nor given free reign, but placed by intelligence to animate her prose without consuming it.

The Salzburg Tales (1934)

Stead's first published work reveals the deep resonances of intelligence, wit, and imagination, the incisive observation of character, the sheer linguistic fertility that mark the originality of a genius. In *The Salzburg Tales*, whose literary form lends itself to revelation of the polarizations of the inner fantasy world, we can trace the themes and issues that shape all of Stead's fiction in its progress towards integrity of voice and vision.

The Salzburg Tales is a quickly written collection of stories dazzling with a young writer's erudition and luxuriant prose. It erupts with fantasies, and also glib, clever satires. Choosing for her first work both a conventional literary form, and one embedded in the collective fantasy life of oral literature, Stead constructs a set of framed tales, like those of Chaucer or Boccaccio. In the frame fiction, visitors at the Salzburg music festival pass their time entertaining each other with the tales of the collection, a concatenation of enormously varied literary genres, including saints' legends, pastoral parodies, Yiddish jokes, romances, classical legends, ghost stories, satires, melodramatic tragedies, and sheer fantasies. These stories, set anywhere from classical and medieval times to the personal present, to the timelessness of imaginary realms, rove widely through time and space. They take place in city, country, desert, in heaven and hell. As do her novels, the tales focus on

children, adolescent girls, middle-aged men and
women, old women, sick and well, aging men, married
couples and single lovers, families and wanderers.
Their personages come from all classes and profes-
sions: musicians and teachers, businessmen and
students, doctors and philosophers, lawyers and ste-
nographers, policemen and architects, ministers and
peasants, bankers and writers.[17]

In the exuberant prose of this volume, full of
verbal tours de force, literary allusions, and wild
wordplay, the polarities of Stead's style are immediately apparent; her voice of romantic and psychologically probing fantasy wars with her coolly controlled
satiric realism. Her prolific imagination teeters on
the brink of excess, often falling over, as it will always, frequently shunning the traditional economies
of storytelling. If her form is not constrained, she
does exercise stringent intellectual control on feeling. Unusually honest about the blackest desires of
the human heart, Stead controls her examination of
deeply emotional sources of behavior by exerting the
constraints of an ironic intelligence.

The satires of these tales serve also to clear the
underbrush of received opinion, to free Stead to
come to an original moral vision. In the *Tales*, she
takes on a number of the world's major philosophies.
Ecumenical in her mockery of religions, she treats
Catholicism, Judaism, Buddhism, and atheism with
equal irreverence; she satirically dispatches human-
ism, primitivism and Utopianism, Communist faith
and bourgeois honesty. While Stead shares with
Christianity a belief in inherent evil, the organized
church seems to her just another destructive family
run by hypocritical priests. Its "brilliant visions of
hell are made out of the thousand pinpricks, back-
aches and disappointments of the wretched millions
of the earth."

Stead always refuses the moralism of abstract rhetorical systems. None of the distinct and palpable miseries of human life, none of its physical or psychological texture is ever obscured for her by ameliorative doctrine or theory; individuals never become mere types or counters in an abstract theological or social scheme. Her profound attention to the particularity and complexity of the inner regions of the primitive imagination prohibits such a vision.

The Salzburg Tales plumb what one character calls the "excessive passions, obscure griefs, unspeakable longings and perplexed desires" of the "primeval psychic world," to unearth some of her own deepest underlying feelings and fears, which will reappear in differing forms throughout her fiction. The many gothic tales in this collection act out overly in plot the fantasies that Stead's later work incorporates into imagery: violent fantasies of forbidden sexuality, uncontrolled aggression and grotesque punishment. Sexuality tends to find expression as incest, love affairs lead to disfigurement and death, murder and mutilation are the consequences of most passions.

Stead has always had this access to fantasy's extremities and insists on the importance of fantasy to quotidian existence; she refuses to draw an absolute line between the two. Devoted to fairy tales as a child, she says she shares the theory of the "Franco-American writer, Julien Green, that everyone is affected if not formed for life by a folk-tale, a legend of childhood. I was enthralled by the legend of Roland and Oliver. I don't know how many times I read the legend of Roncevalles; and in my inner life there was always a Roland seeking an Oliver."[18] She also likes to tell the story of her grandfather's migration to Australia as motivated by a Dickens novel, and of her own dream of leaving Australia as shaped by reading George Henry Lewes's biography of Goethe. "That was the very first dream I had. And then it all built up. But it really began on this little fantasy."[19] Fantasies all bear fruit, she claims, though often not the expected ones.

This habit of mind, which refrains from creating rigid boundaries, is an important one for Stead, and it is manifest in all the ways she talks about literature and about life. "The essence of style in literature, for me," she writes, "is experiment, invention, 'creative error' . . . and change; and of its content, the presentation of 'man alive.'"[20] "I don't set out to do different things," she insists, "but when you've got a subject in mind, the style alters itself. It really does . . . it comes naturally."[21] While there may seem to be a certain disingenuousness in this disclaimer by such an original stylist of conscious attention to style, Stead is consistent in her refusal to separate style from content, life from art. Her characters are all based on real people she knew, she freely admits. "Oh, yes, you can't invent people, or they're puppets. [Novels based on real people] are the best, because the characters carry it along. . . . You recognize the human energy, the vigor in it. But as for writing about puppets, well, . . . puppets are nice. I have a puppet; I like puppets. But you shouldn't write about them."[22]

When she writes about the short story, the sense of human experience is more explicitly collective, but it is still human experience, rather than aesthetic form that focuses her discussion: In a *Kenyon Review* symposium on the short story in 1968, Stead explains the impulse to write, and the impulse to read, in terms of human needs: We go to the story in "the hope of recognizing and having explained our own experience." "The story has a magic necessary to our happiness." It speaks to our "desire for the great legend, the powerful story rooted in all things which will explain life to us." The "ocean of story" is made up of "the million drops of water that are the looking-glass of all our lives." "What is unique about the short story is that we all can tell one, live one, even write one down; that story is steeped in our view and emotion. . . . Give writers a chance, start magazines, open columns (and by writers, I mean everyone, not professionals, I mean anyone with a poignant urge to tell something that happened to him once) and there will be no end to stories and what stories carry that make them vital—genuine experience and a personal viewpoint. It isn't necessary that these stories should be artistic or follow formulas or be like Chekhov or the last metropolitan fad, or anything. . . . The essential for us is integrity and what is genuine. . . . That is what is best about the short story: it is real life for everyone; and everyone can tell one."[23]

The tensile strength of Stead's style derives from this habit of thought, one I have elsewhere called "fluid boundaries" and suggested as a style derived from the particular development of the female personality. The refusal to conceptualize experience in rigidly defined categories allows for openness and strength of vision, and a genuine capacity for growth and change.

In the early *Salzburg Tales*, the blurring of boundaries allows Stead access to the fantasy world and its thought processes. The *Tales* not only articulate specific fantasies in grotesque imagery and plot, but share in the oversimplifying perceptual categories of the inner world. Before a certain stage of moral development, in youth, one's habits of thought tend toward absolute polarizations. There are clear goods and bads, heroes and villains; choices seem absolute, compromise impossible. Such a world is simplified, drained of moral complexity. The romance form, of which tales are a subgenre, takes as its literary realm this stark world of black and white. In Stead's *Salzburg Tales*, characters and their choices are concep-

tualized in terms of extreme polarities. Even fantasy
and quotidian reality are set in absolute opposition:
A Philosopher in the *Tales* declares: "I only tell fairytales for I would rather be seen in their sober vest-
ments than in the prismatic unlikelihood of reality."[24] Stead's growing vision will find a way to unite
the truths of fairy tales with those of every day. But
within these early stories, there seems to be no possibility of such a synthesis. Fantasy and irony are opposed rather than united: one must feel or protec-
tively think, but cannot do both simultaneously. One
loses oneself to one's emotions and is destroyed by
fire, or keeps oneself distant from all feeling and is
destroyed by ice. This articulation of choice as the
conflict of unreconcilable extremes itself prevents
resolution.

In *The Salzburg Tales*, characters are destroyed
both by dwelling too much within their fantasies and
by being too remote from that world of emotion. One
of the personages describes the people he knows who
have been ruined by seeing too deeply:

I know a poet who takes drugs and has ruined his imagination, which is haunted by pools of blood, entrances to
morgues with icicles hanging on the keystone, pale-faced
ladies, horses in winding sheets and bulls whose hides are
covered with craters like the moon's; and his sleep at night
is interrupted by shrieks, heavy sighs and long mutterings.
I know a man who went mad and who now has to listen till
the end of his days to the garrulous follies or the shrieks of
madmen who have imagined more than they can bear. I
know a close-knit family where the grave dissensions of the
husband and wife . . . have ruined the children's health
and their chance of making a marriage, and where the
youngest screams at the nightmares he sees in his sleep.

The alternative, being cut off from even one's
painful wishes and feelings, is more destructive.
Another poignant character in the *Tales* suffers as
much from lack of access to his fantasy life as others

do from an excess of imagination. The architect in the tale "Silk Shirt," an orderly man with a "too succinct heart," cannot tap his dreams and is therefore without passion or purpose in his life: "I am full of inexpressible melancholy: I feel as if my heart will break, and it seems to me that the dark is full of forms which I cannot see, but which if I should, would lessen my trouble. But I cannot reach them any more than the fancies I have in my work, which always end by eluding me. It seems to me that I am among dreams which I have dreamed on all my past nights and forgotten. It seems that I have gone through life with a cataract in my eye, or silk veil hung between me and the brilliant clarity of daylight forms: when my heart breaks, the veil will be rent—too late."

Stead's imagination is closer to the poet's than to the architect's. *The Salzburg Tales* are full of just such morbid images and ruined children as the first speaker describes. The root of this vision is in the family, the persistent and crucial subject of Stead's fiction. One need not be a Freudian detective to see that the family life she describes and embodies in *The Man Who Loved Children* appears throughout her fiction as theme and image, substance and aesthetic form. The language generated in its crucible is the language of her prose.

The greatest vitality for Stead is found within the matrix of the family, which is both product and source of her conception of human nature. She is fascinated by the intricacies of family life and able to render them brilliantly. Yet her vision of the family is complex and ironic. For Stead, each individual is an insatiable egotist, craving infinite love, but cold and unloving himself. Each struggles to get as much as he can from others, while remaining free of their demands: what everyone wants to take, no one has to give. Under the guise of friendship or love, Stead's

characters use one another exclusively for the gratification of their own narcissistic needs. Stead's characters perpetually want too much and get too little.
They have fantastic longings, but at the same time
they live in an unusually ungiving world. Not only
because they want so much, but because so much is
wanting, they are inevitably disappointed. The primal
reality for Stead is an initial lack of love and gratification; that deprivation creates a vision that ensures
continued deprivation: when her characters find
what they seek, they perceive it not as satisfying, but
threatening. Not until toward the end of her fiction
does she develop an alternative vision of wants and
satisfactions.

Stead's novels are full of destructive families or
wanderers. No abiding social institutions connect her
characters in continuing intimacy. Home is never safe
or sustaining; family members devour each other
like greedy cannibals. Freed from family domination,
people form either remote, unsatisfactory associations in which they scarcely touch and regularly desert one another, or doomed passionate affairs whose
intensity destroys not just the love but the lovers as
well. For none but a few of Stead's late, minor characters is there ever love or friendship woven from
small everyday interaction into a stable, lasting fabric.

Her characters long for love and loyalty, but in
the dark world of Stead's early fiction, loyalty is
equated with possessiveness, and what poses as affection is repulsive. What would be coziness to Jane
Austen is suffocation to Stead. An intense emphasis
on family loyalty cloaks the fear that each is really a
freak who would be abandoned to isolation if other
family members were free to choose whether to go or
to stay, rather than being held by iron bonds. When
family loyalty is epitomized by the unchanging devotion of dogs (as in *The People with the Dogs*), or the
"blind, instinctive, unquestioning perpetual love" a

father in *House of All Nations* demands from his
daughter in return for bringing her up, loyalty is no
better than bondage. Yet Stead's early work is haunted
by the fear of disloyalty. In *The Salzburg Tales* one
family has a deformed child, whom they hide away in
the attic as something less than human; ultimately
they sell his drowned body to a circus's freak show.
Stead's characters fear that with the release of the
seemingly inimical powers of their fantasies they may
become freaks or madmen or murderers. Such root
insecurity makes them long especially acutely for
fidelity. But permanence and change are equally
frightening; the forces of stability are those of ossification. Families provide a continuity of relationships,
but in return, they fix "everyone with a single grimace
and symbol as in a tapestry. . . . A character cannot
change—it would be inconvenient."[25] In the obverse
of Freud's family romance in which a child thinks his
parents offensively low-born, the family in her 1973
story "Fairy Child" insist their normal, healthy son is
a demon changeling. Unwilling to question their idealized notions of themselves, they want to commit him
to an institution for the retarded, interpreting his
simplest acts of self-assertion as perverse and mean
demands.[26]

Family relationships are constructed to feed
parental narcissism, shaped to relations of domination and submission, enforced by humiliation and
manipulation. As, in *The Man Who Loved Children*,
the angers and egotisms of the Pollits leave little
room for tenderness or warmth and the children
never get the nurturing or love they need, so throughout Stead's fiction, children starve for affection, and
its symbol, food. A mother in *The Salzburg Tales*
prates incessantly about her genius for making fish
sauce which is so good for her son, but, as he relates,
she "can never succeed in killing a fish [so] we have
no fish at all, and no fish sauce. . . . But she worries,

my mother, for fish is good for the brain, and she thinks I should eat fish perpetually." In another of the *Tales*, "The Guest of the Redshields," a poet is fed on talk of food. His strange hosts offer him so many detailed choices about exactly what he would like to eat, without ever producing food, that he finally cries in despair, "I cannot cope with the verbal resources of your universal larder. Let me only not starve!" In *House of All Nation's* brilliantly satiric scene, "The Stuffed Carp," an ostentatious couple offer a dinner so elaborately rich and exotic that it sickens rather than satisfies. Fish (the subject of her ichthyologist father's study) appear throughout Stead's fiction as images of false wealth or empty words, food that does not nurture.

From her early tales to one of her most recent, "Milk Run" (*The New Yorker*, 1972) Stead connects the motif of food to want of satisfaction. In this gentler, more nostalgic reworking of her family themes, a little boy who spills the milk he is sent to fetch, suffers not only from its loss, but from a more basic lack of affection from his parents. They take no notice of his stories of the bully who plagues him on his milk run; when he spills his milk, he is too tired to go back to refill his pail, but fears even more going home, where "they might beat him—worse, shout and deplore." The child does, however, out of his misery find a token of luck. Looking down at the spilt milk, he finds a gold coin, a symbol of a possible richness of personality salvageable from a distressing and destructive childhood. In spite of this modulated hope, however, the most poignant feelings of this story are of the solitariness and humiliation of childhood, and the inadequacy of family life to support or protect or nurture. Faced with hypocritical geniuses of empty rhetoric like Sam Pollit, characters in Stead's world cannot trust anyone or anything outside themselves to gratify their most elemental needs.

They become Dickensian solitaries, unprotected in a hostile world.

Children in Stead's families are hurt by their parents, the more so the longer they stay attached to them. Daughters are often crippled by their fathers in a tragic way, sons held close by their mothers in an equally debilitating but more comically rendered fashion. Beginning with "The Marionettist" and "Overcote" in *The Salzburg Tales*, where girls are psychologically or even physically crippled, fathers try to keep their daughters tied to them, and often succeed in preventing the girls from creating emotional lives and families of their own. Letty Fox foreshadows the shallow waifs of *The Puzzleheaded Girl*, all of whom suffer prolonged attachments to their charming fathers which keep them immaturely dependent and purposeless. The father-daughter relationship of Sam and Louie Pollit persists throughout Stead's fiction.

Although mothers feel the same possessiveness towards their sons, women leading traditional lives seem to Stead constrained, diminished, and somewhat impotent, and most of the domineering mothers she portrays are ineffectual comic figures. (Her model of mother-child intimacy is probably the distances and resentments of the stepmother-stepdaughter bond of Henny and Louie in *The Man Who Loved Children*.) In *The Salzburg Tales*, the Roman mother who tries to seduce her hermit son from his sainthood, and the small old woman who tries futilely to compete with the sexual power of her son's fiancée, are comic figures, and a little poignant. The virulence in *The Little Hotel* of Madame Blaise's possessiveness of her son, or of the constraint on his ability for adult love exercised by Robert Wilkins's mother, is treated by Stead with considerable satiric distance, while fathers' manipulations of their daughters are Stead's prototype of tragic tyranny.

Father-daughter (and brother-sister) love in Stead

always verges on incest, and incestuous erotic fantasies are a variant of the narcissism that so pervasively
rules relationships in Stead's world. Parents' possessive attractions to their children are another expression of their wish to assimilate another personality
into their own, to dominate another existence to suit
their own needs. (Michael admits this of his love for
his sister in *Seven Poor Men of Sydney*, while Sam
Pollit keeps both the sexuality and the egotism of his
desires from his awareness.) One of the three original
Salzburg Tales Stead rewrote from memory of lost
earlier versions,[27] "Triskelion" is overtly about an incestuous triangle and is permeated with imagery of
sexual self-disgust. This tale takes its title from an
ancient three-legged symbol which Freud takes as an
image of male genitalia.[28] Each time this apparition
of "three legs sprouting from a hub, bound together
at the ankles to form a wheel" appears "trundling
along at an unnatural rate towards the Entrance," it
forebodes disaster. The tale is a murder mystery, resolved by the discovery that a girl who has had a long-
standing sexual relationship with her father has
murdered him for being unfaithful to her. The girl
and her mother are rivals for the affections of a second man; ultimately the daughter, having borne a retarded son, commits suicide. The tone and landscape
of the story are equally bleak, filled with imagery at
once sexual and grotesque.

Stead's treatment of adult romantic love in *The
Salzburg Tales* is not entirely different from her
version of incestuous love—and the two are not unre-
lated. Her lovers are drenched in the romantic mythology that craves impossible obstacles to maintain
intensity. The yearning for an inaccessible object,
the traditional paradox of courtly love, derives from
the primarily forbidden wish, the incest fantasy. The
theme of romantic love rouses in Stead especially extreme reactions. She sets herself at an ironic distance

from the lovers of the *Tales* who destroy each other with their ingrown passions, having various narrators of the tales declare: "Nothing is more disagreeable to me than to see a friend or an intimate become obsessed as if they had a tic, and cherish what is quite indifferent to another." Or "Horrors and death's heads . . . let themselves into civilized households under the cloak of romantic love: it is a kind of disorder, an anarchy to which weak ones are prone."[29] This extreme and protective cynicism is in a constant interplay in Stead's work with vulnerable emotional revelation. Caught by her attraction to what she fears, she keeps a satiric distance from subjects she is nevertheless drawn to treat. In this early work, the deludedly passionate gives way to the tonelessly detached. Unable to gratify fantasy wishes, characters repress their desires; satire can ossify the abundant flow of her prose.

In *The Salzburg Tales*, lovers live in a tormented, tragic world. Rapt in their *egoisme à deux*, longing for utter loyalty and perfect passion, they devour each other. Typically, the love of Willem and Helena in "To the Mountain" is mad and death-obsessed. Absorbed in their ardent symbiosis, Willem "looked at Helena with a peremptory possessive passion, as if she were a drug that he ate and inhaled, necessary to the cherished derangement of his senses." They both cherish a premonition of a "tragic destiny" and invest all their emotional and material resources in shaping their grotesque death. Helena dies of a disfiguring skin disease; Willem cuts out her heart and leaps with it into the seething crater of Vesuvius, under whose shadow they have always lived.

In "The Gold Bride," another lover, like a Browning monologuist, loves his wife with such a possessive passion that he prefers a golden statue of her to the living woman, so that he can be assured of keeping her. This intense romantic possessiveness,

not unlike the crippling family loyalty she decries, is
an object of Stead's satiric criticism. But it is not the
only component of romantic love that arouses her ire
and anxiety.

Sexuality itself, rooted in incestuous eroticism,
is frightening as an uncontrollable passion. But it is
also feared simply as a form of self-assertion. Women
in the *Tales*, as in many of our cultural myths and literary classics, are punished not only for breaking
moral codes, but also merely for being talented, and
acting on their gifts. Helena, in "To the Mountain,"
before her love affair was an attractive, gifted organ-
ist, "a brilliant young woman, ample, tall, . . . no-
ticeable for the youthful pomp, insolence and gaiety
of her bearing." The story that most clearly articulates this cultural motif is "The Prodigy." In it, a
young girl who is an exceptional violinist follows her
steadfast musical ambitions, at the cost of great suffering. She must forswear her family and demean
herself by posing as a diseased prostitute in order to
continue her studies with her music master. In the
end, she is raped, then murdered. The narrator of
her tale finds her violent death the natural conse-
quence of her ambitions: "What is wilder, more reck-
less and weaker than a rebellious woman?" he
queries. "History, reason and intuition all tell her
she must fail in this world of men."[30]

In this story, Stead ironically frames a narration
of the profound cultural constriction on female development that inhibits women's active self-assertion. Such constraints are internalized in a pervasive
feminine self-hatred. The portrayal in *The Salzburg
Tales* of female sexuality supports a theory that critic
Ellen Moers began to develop in *Literary Women*[31]
of a female grotesque style, rooted in self-disgust.
Moers suggests that barren, rocky plains and hills are
as frequently women's images for their sexual parts
as the ocean metaphor Freud designates as feminine.

Both images appear frequently in Stead, and both
tend to be grotesque. In "Triskelion," the landscape
is female and sinister, unspeakably bleak and threatening: "The curlews cried by the lake, at dawn and
dusk, and nothing was more appropriate to the
dreary wastes of sand-rooted underbrush, the overgrown shrubbery full of tarantulas, the dreary wastes
of turbulent ocean, always peaked and foamy, and
the bleak and ravaged headlands." The dreary, ravaged, poisonous, entrapping landscape of sexuality is
terrifying. The mother in the tale cries, "How I hate
this everlasting gush and hiss of the sea, and those
swishing trees. . . . I hate nature: it is full of cries
and tears like a female madhouse."[32]

In *The Man Who Loved Children*, Stead showed
brilliantly the linguistic and psychological chain of
inheritance of internalized feminine denigration. In
these first tales, all specifically female functions re-
lating to sex, pregnancy, and birth evoke grotesque
imagery from Stead.[33] A pregnant woman in "The
Mirror" dreams she is underground drowning, watching from beneath "the surface of the germinating
earth horribly suggestive roots and cotyledons . . .
waving violently and tossing their sensitive blinded
tips as if in the grip of primitive ruthless passions."
She sees her mottled flesh decay and rot, "the weeds'
roots sucking up all that is fluid in me," as she imagines her death, sliding "deep into unconsciousness,
like a body floating quietly to the bottom of a river."
In another tale, "Day of Wrath," a woman's adulter-
ous love affair is concluded by having her young
daughter Viola drowned in a bizarre ferryboat accident. Viola is found, after a week, "standing in the
green gloom" of the sea, "prisoned by her poor weak
foot, decaying, but with her arms still floating up; a
water maiden tangled in a lily-root, and not able to
reach the surface."

The struggle to come up from under the surface,

to emerge from the life-in-death drowning within the self, entangled in inner images of monstrosity, is an emblem of a particularly female struggle which all Stead's heroines wage with their own innerness. The imagery and bloody violence of plot of *The Salzburg Tales* embodies the fear that realizing sexual or aggressive energies or desires is potentially disastrous. Stead's later work incorporates these fantasies into imagery instead of acting them out as events in plot, but the theme so blatantly exposed in the *Tales* is a crucial one for women writers. Ambivalence about self-assertion is a central issue of feminine psychology. When women are afraid to act independently, the blocking of the impulse for self-expression causes frustration, which induces anger. But that anger particularly is prohibited by cultural images of benevolently nurturing femininity, and so turns inward, along with initial aggressive urges, against the self, and further denigrates women's self-image. Adrienne Rich has noted the number of women writers "marked by the depressive mood, their sense that to act was to court destruction."[34] This constriction too becomes part of the inner image of monstrosity.

Stead finds two resolutions to this circular dilemma. As her heroines develop through the course of her fiction, they learn both to recognize and to resist these violent inner feelings. The conceptualization of oneself as either monster or hero is eventually shown to be oversimplified and unrealistic. These images are tested against reality as Stead's heroines move outwards to engage with another world of love and work with other people. They learn to stop thinking in terms of angel-demon, good-bad polarities, and grow toward more realistic conceptual processes and modes of behavior.

Similarly, Stead transforms this feminine dilemma through her prose. The dichotomy of richly grotesque, uncontrolled fantasy and unenriched sat-

ire in *The Salzburg Tales* grows with the novels into
the brilliant style I have described as the Domestic
Gothic, in which Stead is able to express simultaneously the melodramatic passions of the inner life and
well-articulated perceptions of the social and material world. Drawing on an uncertainty about self-
boundaries that derives from feminine conflicts about
aggression, Stead creates a form in which confusions
about self and world are put to good aesthetic use.
Women often develop the pattern of self-definition
psychologists have described as one of "weak ego
boundaries" in which the self is defined in terms of
others to such a degree that the clear distinction between self and other is not so clear. We have seen this
habit of mind at work in Henny Pollit in *The Man
Who Loved Children*. Stead's grotesque style capital-
izes on this tolerance for boundarilessness and develops its expressive virtue. Her Domestic Gothic
mines the frustrations of constraint and inhibition to
find expression for the feelings generated by being so
confined. It taps the fantasies of the constricted
inner world, overcomes the ban on aggression and
thus releases energies for creative use. This capacity
not only to tolerate but to utilize boundarilessness
and chaos that can be so threatening to identity and
self-esteem enables Stead to order the very unyield-
ingness of human experience to order. This style is
her most original and brilliant.[35]

Stead's skill at dramatization develops along the
same lines as does her prose style. Problems of characterization and plot arise from similar issues of the
relation between inner and outer realms. In her early
novels, Stead's characters tend to be too locked
within the inner world of their own fantasies, and as
a novelist, Stead relies too heavily on the narrator's
or characters' conversations to make characters come
alive. As her work matures, instead of relying on discursive statements, she embodies character more

dramatically. As the same time, her characters learn
to move beyond confinement within the world of
their internal language to act and interact in an external domain.

The novels in between *The Salzburg Tales* and
The Man Who Loved Children swing between the polarizations of fantasy and social satire. Stead's first
and second novels, *Seven Poor Men of Sydney* and
The Beauties and Furies are both about protagonists
too lost within their inner worlds to realize their own
desires; and both novels suffer an excess of introspective, analytic talk, a deficiency of dramatic characterization. With her third novel, *House of All Nations*,
Stead moves almost entirely to the realm of brilliant
social satire, temporarily putting aside her more personal materials.

Seven Poor Men of Sydney (1935)

Set in Sydney, Australia, during the Depression, *Seven
Poor Men of Sydney* is Stead's first novel, published
in 1935. The poor men of the title are three friends
who work as printers: Joseph Baguenault, a young,
conventional lad who, by virtue of his dullness becomes the novel's only real survivor; the garrulous
Tom Withers; Baruch Mendelssohn; an intelligent
expatriate American Marxist (an early version of the
James Quick figure, also modelled on William Blake);
and Gregory Chamberlain, the press owner. Their
circle encompasses the cynical Tom Winter and Kol
Blount, "a paralysed youth" given to philosophical
disquisitions, as are nearly all these characters, who
have long theoretical arguments about politics, religion, art, life. The most interesting poor man is the
seventh, Michael Baguenault, Joseph's cousin, an intensely introspective youth never able to create a
place for himself in the world. He suffers the most
acutely and dramatically.

The imaginative landscape of this book is bleak; grotesque poetic scenery mirrors the characters' miseries. Stead is profoundly aware of the ways deprivation suppresses the vitality in people. All of these men are thwarted by poverty or paralysis, spiritual or physical. They are diminished by economic and emotional constraints which prohibit the realization of any of their longings. The political philosophy offered by these characters to help articulate their condition is Marxist; however, while Stead insists on the importance of material conditions to the spiritual life, her perceptions are never limited to material first causes.

The only personality in the novel that approaches full development is Michael. But his own development is limited by the very problem with which both Stead's characters and Stead as a novelist struggle in all her early work. Michael is an introverted, melancholy sensibility, perceptive but inturned with the self-centeredness of adolescence. His inability to find expression culminates in his suicide. While Stead will learn with later novels how to better embody this sensibility in character, her prose from the start takes its lushness from access to the rich inner world of fantasy and feeling. This novel starts with a description of Fisherman's Bay, Sydney, and one family there. The decaying physical profusion Stead's prose evokes parallels the psychological complexity and decay it foretells:

There was a family there named Baguenault, which had settled in the bay directly after its arrival from Ireland thirty years before, and had its roots growing down into the soil and rocky substratum so that nothing seemed to be able to uproot it any more, so quiet, so circumspect in the narrow life of the humble, it lived; but disaster fell on it, and its inner life, unexpressed, incoherent, unplanned, like most lives, then became visible as a close and tangled web to the neighbors and to itself, to whom it had for so

long remained unknown. Who can tell what minor passions running in the undergrowth of poor lives will burst
out when a storm breaks. . . . Michael Baguenault pad-
dled through his childhood round the beaches, helped the
fishermen haul their nets. . . . He ran with other little
boys in frayed trousers to the beach to collect driftwood
and coke for the kitchen, and would return late for breakfast with blue hands; . . . The beach provided not only
fuel, but also dead fish, swollen fruit, loaves, pumpkins,
shoes and socks, broken straw-boaters—all varieties of
food and clothing cast up from ships and sewers. Once,
when a five-thousand tonner was wrecked near the Gap, a
hundred tons of butter floated mildly in to the beach. . . .
There were crabs in the rock-pools, little oysters spread all
round the bay, and the waters were rich in fish. . . . There
was even a great house there, in the last stages of decay,
weathered by wind and sea, and standing in a neglected
garden with old trees. . . . The fences were down, and the
house was inhabited fraternally by human, barnyard, and
vermin tribes. The goats, ducks, geese, dogs and horses left
wandering about the streets of the neighborhood oftener
wound up in the backyard than in the pond. . . . In the
corners of the house bats flew, swallows dropped mud and
dung from every beam, and from all the cracks of the great
whitewashed stones at the back ran cockroaches, beetles
and rats . . . large spiders hung in the outhouses, and
fearsome-looking but innocent crickets and slaters dwelt
under the bits of wood and sheets of corrugated iron fallen
off the roof into the grass. The house attracted Michael
and the other children with the same charm as a stagnant
gutter.

Rooting her characters firmly in their richly
conceived environment, Stead always plants them as
well in the context of their families. We see a good
deal of Michael's mother, and especially of his sister
Catherine, the novel's other main character, though
she is not included in the title. Michael and Catherine
are the first incarnation of the incestuously bound
brother and sister who reappear throughout Stead's
fiction. Their relation is an ultimate expression of

Michael's destructive egotism. Michael tells Catherine: "I have come to love my sister as myself, for you are myself . . . in you is the very reflection of my own thoughts, my mind and my desires. A man cannot love himself, but all men do, and so there is no satisfaction in the world, for we must clasp another body, informed by another spirit to ourselves." While the possessive narcissism Stead finds in all families will be more subtly and intricately developed in her later novels, the immersion in self-love it represents is clearly shown here. Michael takes all the world within his own sensibility, then cannot escape from those solipsistic confines.

A more active spirit than Michael, Catherine too suffers as a rebel who can find no place for herself in society. The astute Baruch sees in Catherine "the middle-class woman trying to free herself, and still impeded by romantic notions and ferocious, because ambushed sensuality." All of Catherine's considerable artistic and political energies are defeated; her struggle against conventions wears her out. "A woman should be a woman," Catherine's mother complains. "What's the good of her being a rebel? Where did it get her?" Catherine broods, "I've fought all my life for male objectives in men's terms. I am neither man nor woman, rich nor poor, elegant nor worker, philistine nor artist. That's why I fight so hard and suffer so much and get nowhere." Catherine leads a gypsy life and survives by retreat into a mental asylum.

Michael, however, is unable to survive at all. He is troubled by some of the feelings that plagued Louisa Pollit; described by his sister as "emotional and sensual . . . his mind lost in antique Celtic fogs," he feels thwarted everywhere. He complains bitterly that he is unable to tell jokes and

that makes me simply despair. It means there is something else, a sort of animal success which I haven't and can't get.

Another thing, when any one twits me or insults me, I can't stand it; I want to cry or kill them, or commit suicide. Even if I answer back it does no good. I go on thinking over the insult for weeks and crying inwardly. It kills me, this wounding and this hatred it stirs up in me. But other people are not like that. They give back as good as they get, and everyone is happy. . . . But to me, it's like murder. And all the time I feel foggy.

The mingling of Michael's human personality with the sea in the romantic passage that describes his suicide is a grotesque expression, blending inner and outer worlds, of the total loss of identity in death:

He wrapped his coat around him as he wished to wrap the deep sea round him and its sleep fathoms down. He wished to sleep, to have the water sing as now for ever in his ears, and the inextinguishable anguish in his mind to be hushed. So he stood fixed, with fixed and troubled look cleaving the sea, in whose heart he has always found more repose than in any human heart, which understood his miseries through its own rages and revolts, his inconstancies through its tides, his longings through the bottoms grown with various plants and barnacles from foreign ports, and the turbines plowing its waves.

The wind sways him like the rooted plants and grasses, whistles through his hair as through the pine trees opposite: he is already no longer a man but part of the night. The pine trees crowd him to the ledge, the light wheels, down underneath is the howling parliament of waters deciding on his fate. The gusts on rock and ledge as spirits hold his heart in their shadowy hands and squeeze the blood out of it; darkness only runs through his veins now. He takes a step nearer the edge, and at the same moment this idea splits him from head to foot: "what if I should fall upon a rock?" He falls into the sea, the wave a moment later cracks his skull against the submerged pediment of the cliff, and his brains flow out among the hungry sea-anemones and mussels. It is done; all through the early morning the strings of the giant mast cry out a melody; in triumph over the spirit lost.

Stead's romantically lyrical prose exhibits the
unifying poetic sensibility that develops into one of
the great strengths of her style. Here, however, it remains colored by the adolescent sense of specialness
that sees in black and white dichotomies which doom
the man of finer perceptions. Michael is drawn in
strict opposition to his cousin Joseph who, Catherine
says, "has no understanding whatever of the muscles
and nerves of the world" and because of his "tranquil
stupidity," survives. She contrasts him (unfavorably)
to her more compelling brother who "eats his own
flesh." Stead, however, softens her judgments of
Joseph's limitations by providing multiple perceptions of him through the eyes of different characters.
Baruch Mendelssohn more tolerantly believes in the
possibility of development of even "the quietest and
simplest man." He is fond of Joseph and defends
him. Stead will later develop this technique as a
vehicle for the finely ironic perspective of her mature style. Here, in spite of Baruch's kind tolerance,
the sympathies of the novel lie with the doomed
Michaels of the world.

From the start, Stead unites social realism with a
gift for lyric prose, but this novel, like its characters,
remains trapped within itself. This is the book that
Teresa in *For Love Alone* works on in the darkest
days of her depression when she first comes to London, and in which her employer sees signs of potential genius. In "The Seven Houses of Love," or "The
Sorrows of Women," Teresa works out her suicidal
impulses and despair. Australian critic Dorothy Green
is no doubt right when she claims that all of the
characters of *Seven Poor Men of Sydney* are aspects
of Stead's own personality;[36] that does not distinguish this from most other novels, except that here
the conflicting voices of inner dialogue remain
largely disembodied in long passages of philosophical discourse. Stead cannot yet create fully sustained

characters or dramatic events. Nevertheless, this novel
has, as William Blake observed, "mountain peaks."[37]
Taking fresh liberties with the novel form, it is the
first expression of a highly original sensibility and a
large talent, and filled with brilliant flashes. In its
descriptive passages, its richness of throw-away lines
("She stared at him as if he had shown her that she
was only a bag of bones imagining itself to be a
human.") and particularly in its account of Michael
and Catherine, it foreshadows the major strengths
and themes of Stead's future development.

Most of Stead's early work treats sensibilities
like Michael's—intense, rich in fantasy, inturning.
He is the forerunner of later Stead heroines who try
to accommodate their inner world to outer reality.
Elvira Western, heroine of the next novel, *The
Beauties and Furies*, fights this battle in terms of
sexual relationship, trying, like Madame Bovary, and
with the same success, to find expression for her sensual fantasies. Not until Teresa in *For Love Alone*
will this struggle be victorious.

The Beauties and Furies (1936)

In the thirties, Stead wrote quickly and regularly.
The Beauties and Furies was published in 1936. This
novel like her last is full of talk, about Marx, Engels,
and Hegel; capitalism and freedom; but mostly about
love. In the line of descent from Madame Bovary to
the liberated heroine of 1970s popular fiction, Elvira
Western leaves her kind, staid older husband Paul,
an English doctor, to join her young lover, Oliver
Fenton, in Paris. Set in Parisian cafés, streets, and
bedrooms, the plot is motivated largely by the
manipulations of Annibale Marpurgo, an Italian
lace-buyer Elvira meets on the train to Paris, who in-
terferes with her life from then on. Something of a

set piece of Jacobean villainy, Marpurgo constructs a romantic subplot. Out of the reach of the manipulations of his invalid wife, Marpurgo shares with Oliver an attraction to the self-confident young Parisian Coromandel, an antiquary's daughter. Marpurgo arranges encounters that discredit Oliver with both Coro and Elvira, and send him back to England. The actual structure and devices of plot, however, are weak and of minor importance. Elvira's character is the story's central interest and the real source of the disintegration of her affair with Oliver.

Elvira is trying to escape from the debilitating limitations of a conventional life (a significant theme for Stead, but one neither she nor her heroine have yet found the best way to handle). Searching for fulfillment, she finds she is unable to sustain her new freedom. Her ambitions are vague and her fantasies literary. Unable to commit herself to either husband or lover, she vacillates between them. Nor does she have occupation other than trying to make this choice. When she finds she is pregnant, she has the same trouble trying to decide whether or not to have an abortion—and both decisions consume endless pages of prose. In the end, she does return to her husband and England, leaving without a note one night when Oliver is out in the country with Coromandel.

Uttering one of the novel's many aphorisms, Oliver proclaims that "All middle-class novels are about the trials of three, all upper-class novels about mass fornication, all revolutionary novels about a bad man turned good by a tractor." The emotional intricacies of this novel do work themselves out in triangles. When Paul and her brother Adam come to Paris to try to retrieve her, Elvira realizes she would be most happy keeping both Paul and Oliver tied to her: "I wish we could live like this . . . all three. . . . Her eyes, growing roots of seduction, sucked in their

breaths, her prolific ego, masked in pathos, had
them in its tendrils." Elvira's brother and Paul's
sister Sara, who comes to keep house for him when
Elvira is gone, are flickering reminders of the powerful threes of family ties so often present in Stead's
fiction.

Stead also uses the multiple relations of her
characters for the purpose of characterization.
Marpurgo is a "psychological detective" whose ele-
ment is "making an easy survey of human frailty,"
but all these characters are prone to psychological
dissection, and Stead characterizes each of them by
the articulations of the others. Oliver sees that
Marpurgo "is an ascetic, he despises women and yet
he is lonely, he tries to net them with eloquence, and
then he lets them fly free again." Marpurgo, who
speaks "with the voice of eternal enquiry of a person
speaking to himself" calls Oliver "an oscillating
hedonist," "a pure physical function," without integrity of feeling or belief, whose Marxism is merely a
modern fad. He warns Oliver: Elvira "is weaving you
into her cocoon." Oliver accuses Marpurgo of being
"demoniac," "bandying our fates, giving advice, . . .
No one has any privacy with you around. You're a
vulture picking the eyes out of romance, baring a
man's brains before he's dead." While many of these
accusations seem just, the characterizations remain
more analytic than dramatized.

The chief of these psychologizers is Elvira. She
thinks and feels extensively, but neither thoughts
nor feelings ring quite true. Elvira is a woman of free
ideas and constricted emotions. She has a passion for
self-analysis and for examination of others: "I don't
listen to conversations," she says, "so much as understand the psychological weaving that is going on
underneath. I see everything dissected." Her radical
analyses, in long passages of conversations with Oliver
and others, of sexual politics could have been written

in the 1960s instead of the 1930s. She articulates theories of the constraints of marriage and the freedom of women, of desire, abortion, the need for freer sexuality. "I feel so bitter," laments Elvira, "when I think that, even though I give up my old life of wifehood, there is no freedom for me, a middle-class woman without a profession. They should give me a street-walker's card. . . . The real thought of the middle-class woman . . . is the problem of economic freedom and sexual freedom: they can't be obtained at the same time. We are not free." She counters Oliver's socialist assertions: "It's all a formula. You could exploit a woman in a house making her wait on you and cook for you, turning her into an idiot with ideas about mouseholes and curtain-rods, while you wrote essays on labour-unions. It's just the same, I see no difference."

The lack of freedom Elvira laments is, however, determined from within as well as from without. For all the conviction of her analyses of the plight of the middle-class woman, confined to dull suburbs, without economic independence, without creative work, nevertheless what we see of the function of her ruminations in her own behavior frames her intellectual perceptions with a different emotional truth. Her obsession with self-analysis becomes an end in itself. For all her introspection, Elvira lacks a clear sense of the reality of other people. She makes Oliver listen to long accounts of her doubts and reservations about him, unconcerned with the effects of these revelations. When Paul comes to Paris she passes a day with him "in irresolution. Elvira spent hours with Paul reviewing the whole of their past life. She was mournful, and yet this cataloguing adjustment of claim and blame, self-revelation, unearthing of symbols and unrecognized prophecies, the eternal game of hide-and-seek she played with all men, satisfied her ruminating mind." Unaware of her own emotional complicity in the constraints she feels, Elvira thinks endlessly, but is unable to act. We come to see her ultimately as self-absorbed, weak, indecisive.

While Stead, like Kate Chopin in *The Awakening*, has created approvingly a sensual heroine who is frank about her sexual desires and pleasures, she condemns her on other grounds. In a long scene, Elvira bathes languidly, walks naked around the room, posing in front of her mirror, rouging and powdering her body, kissing her shoulder. She thinks "of her body, knowing by experience that that made her an enchantress. She smiled deeply to herself with the full realisation of her female powers"—and egotistical power strongly colors her sensuality: She had "ensnared" Oliver "with her practised married wiles, frankness, tender brutality of speech, the little armory of pet names and expressions she had slowly woven with Paul, the caresses and savant libertinism. To her he was a child: he could never escape her if she wanted him." "She would have liked, though, to sleep all night alone wrapped in her . . . coat with Oliver in another bed, but near. . . . She wanted so to keep him enslaved, not to gratify him." Elvira protests that she had not really wanted to marry her husband: "I wanted him to love me, but . . . I wanted to be myself, not a wife, with children. I wanted to do something creative . . . perhaps writing." While Stead is sympathetic with this ambition, the situation is more complex than Elvira's rhetoric allows. An astute critic of social constraints, Elvira herself is ultimately unable to love. In the letter that enticed her to join him in Paris, Oliver had written, "Oh, do wake up, come to life before it is too late: before the thorns interlock and crib you forever." His suppressed metaphor bears consistent weight. Styled "a beauty who never reigned," Elvira is a Sleeping Beauty, passive, drowned in melancholy self-absorption, dependent on the initiatives of others, sensual primarily in fantasy. Incapable of the stoic self-denial a Stead heroine needs, she lacks the energy, courage, and integrity to sustain the independent life she imagines for herself. By the end of the novel she decides, "I was not passionate . . . I never had a great passion, only an immense but quite lifeless passion for my own troubles; melancholy I am." When Elvira and Coromandel meet, curiously, most of the conversation is Elvira's self-analysis. She tells Coro that she has come to realize that she had always been "pitifully eager to talk on that pathetic subject of her lonely heart." Coro finally thinks her "an inferior will and girlish character in a nature instinctively subtle, sombre and critical," and this is Stead's final judgment too.

While Stead passes harsh sentence on Elvira, she also makes her a large and sometimes compelling character. Herself a careful examiner of feeling and thinking, she crafts a sensual language of passionate thought. We have watched as Elvira "wound herself, slow, cold, beautifully diamonded, as a snake, round the problem." Elvira thinks of Paul and "her heart closed round the dark image as a glove on a hand."

Stead's brilliance of phrasing matches the intelligence of her analyses, even though the dramatization and plotting of this novel are weak. Elvira Western is of interest as an early version of the character Stead will treat most sympathetically and successfully as Teresa Hawkins in *For Love Alone*. With the transformation of Michael Baguenault into Elvira, the shift from a male to a female protagonist moves Stead towards a more direct confrontation with this type. For all of its weaknesses, *The Beauties and Furies* is a step forward in Stead's development, and not without appeal on its own behalf.

House of All Nations (1938)

Stead's next novel, *House of All Nations* (1938) is a mammoth and damning critique of the decadent world of international banking in Paris between the two World Wars. Largely abandoning the inner arena and autobiographical sources of her earlier fiction, Stead focuses on the activities she observed working as a secretary at a bank in Paris. The social satire that, from her first tales, coexisted with her explorations of fantasy, here takes dominance; her flights of imagination are edged with wit and irony in this savage tour de force of social criticism.

Most of Stead's novels have rambling plots, but this one, laid out in over one hundred scenes, is panoramic, scanning the lives of a huge cast of characters. Jules Bertillon, with his brother William, heads a bank which he runs exclusively for his private profit. Jacques Carrière, an old and vicious antagonist, and Aristide Raccamond, who works as the bank's "customer's man" (spurred by his ambitious wife Marianne) contrive to enmesh Jules in a scheme that drains his money, then expose his fraud. Also noteworthy among the 126 characters Stead asks us to pay attention to are Henri Léon, a grain merchant whose appetite for sex is as voracious and undiscriminating as his greed for money, and the bank's economist, Michel Alphendéry. Brilliant and eloquent, Alphendéry is another of Stead's humane Marxists, who resemble William Blake. He provides the novel's center of moral vision.

In *The Beauties and Furies*, Oliver had proclaimed that "all upper-class novels are about mass fornication." *House of All Nations* takes its title from the name of a whorehouse, but the passion from which it derives its obsessive vitality is "money-grubbing," on a grand scale. As she herself observes, all of men's obsessive passions—for money, sex, ambition, or love—in Stead's hands equally reveal the potential of the human spirit for egotism, self-delusion, and vitality. The worst of these characters amass money and lovers with a mechanical lack of spirit that makes their lives barren. Their passion is for accum-

ulation, not use or pleasure. Jules Bertillon is as
morally corrupt as the others, but his abundant
charm and creativity make him fascinating to Stead.
"Endlessly, primevally fertile," Jules is a builder of
illusions, the chief of which is the bank itself, fabri-
cated on confidence tricks, run by wheeling and dealing. "It's easy to make money," Jules declares. "You
put up the sign BANK and someone walks in and
hands you his money. The facade is everything." Alphendéry tells Jules that as a result of the "corrupt
fairy tales" and "carefully whetted greed" of capitalism, he has chained his inventiveness to a sterile enterprise; his fantasies will become grotesque, he will
be bereft in the end, Alphendéry warns, because he
has no social function. "You want to build and what
have you built?" he cautions Jules. "You have long
ago lost the sense of money that a poor man has,
when a hundred-franc note means relief from pain, a
thousand-franc note means marriage. That is money.
What you have are counters. You might as well have
matches. . . . You see, because you are fine and fertile, that is not enough. You think if you increase it
suddenly with a great swoop of villainy, steal from
everyone that confided in you, make a great scandal,
see your money grow overnight from a bean to a
beanstalk, that you will catch the hen that lays the
golden eggs. But if you do it, Jules, I warn you, you'll
be just as unhappy as before. You've built a hothouse
here to force your fantasies in. . . . They'll grow
twisted, leaves will turn into flowers . . . the world
will be monstrous and topsy-turvy . . . because you
are without a function."

In another flight of metaphysical wit, Stead
shows gold, like love, to be invested with just those
emotional desires it cannot satisfy: "The word
'gold' . . . has undertones of sensual revel and
superstitious awe and overtones of command and
superhuman strength. . . . This joyful sensuality

comes not only from its brightness . . . nor . . . the
worshipful value of a very small bar of it . . . but
also from a lifelong association of the world 'gold'
with the idea of ultimate wealth, perennial ease, absolute security. It is an absolute and in its presence
the anxious heart breathes sweetly and the blood
laughs and the toiling brain sheds its dew of agony.
. . . It has in it everything that man desires in a wife,
that cannot, precisely, be purchased with gold." But
amassing money, for most of these men, is an animating passion, and end in itself.

In this world of corruption and mythomania, illusion and delusion, Jules is an attractive charmer.
Almost godlike, he stamps "images of himself on wax
hearts, his own fraud, currency"; his bank is a tem-
ple, a "palace of illusion, temptation and beauty." A
fraud whose obsessive imaginative powers are compelling even to his victims, Jules prefigures Sam Pollit, the man who loved children, a compelling character type for Stead. When Jules's schemes collapse,
and he disappears with all the bank's money, de-
frauding his friends, colleagues and clients, some of
them nevertheless hope that he will return and re-
furbish the myth. Ready to believe again, "his old
friends, and even the most pertinacious of his credi-
tors, hoped that he went and made immediately a
shining new fortune with which he would come home
presently to flash in their eyes. For he had by now
benefited by the immorality as well as by the mythomania of the financial world and had begun to be
relacquered in the minds of the rich. For others,
though, it is true, he still remained a rankle and a
hurt, the charmer who deceived."

While scene after scene of this novel reveal the
obscenity of conspicuous consumption of money, sex,
food, goods, and these greedy men and women are
sharply satirized, Stead maintains both the fascina-
tion and the ironic distance with which she treats

other kinds of deceivers. Although her political critique is socialist in its premises, she finds these capitalist businessmen subject to the same human flaws,
and compelling for the same reasons, as people of
other occupations. Her largest characters are those of
vital imagination; her meanest, those without fantasy
or verbal power. Jules Bertillon and Michael Alphendéry, in their affection for one another, display
the same somewhat cynical tolerance. Alphendéry is
idealistic, kind, eloquent. He has "a way of weaving
thought and word continually, his chief pleasure,"
and a "supple, perpetual, illuminated eloquence
which was his to command." A man with "the courage
to be kind and unassuming" he insists that life is not
worth living when men "live and work for themselves
alone." Jules thinks his ideas lunatic, but is fond of
him nevertheless. "I don't mind communists," he
says. "I think they're nuts, that's all. But decent nuts.
Because they're not serious." And Alphendéry, though
he is serious, does work, loyally, for the bank, motivated by inertia, the need for money, and his affection for the Bertillons. Stead's perception of human
complexity is too subtle to be purely ideological.

Stead uses for this book the materials she
gathered when she and Blake worked in a Paris bank
in the thirties. She credits her employers as one of
her sources: "Those boys told me everything. People
always tell a writer everything, especially in business,
because they think the poor romantic soul won't
really understand that sort of thing, you know. They
do tell you everything."[38]

And "everything" has gotten into this novel.
Stead's detailed knowledge of financial dealings is
extraordinary in its extent and accuracy. Her acute
observations extend the traditional range of the English novel to complex economic analyses not often
within its province. Yet "one should not suppose that
Miss Stead has turned her back on fantasy," cautions

a reviewer in 1938. "If her knowledge of private banking, of bucketeering and grain options, of foreign-exchange speculation and account gathering, of stock manipulation and politic-financial intrigue is little short of miraculous, she scatters the bright fragments of her information across the skies of her novel in the disorder of stardust."[39]

Stead's accustomed themes are all here—the war between men and women, parents and children, the rich and the not rich; exploitation by those in financial or emotional power, the substitution of manipulation for love. A book as extensive as the next is intensive, this novel gives itself to satiric portrayal of the public world. Its scope and distance represent developments in Stead's narrative technique that free her to turn next, more directly than she ever has before, to the autobiographical materials from which she constructs her masterpiece, *The Man Who Loved Children*, in 1940 and *For Love Alone* in 1944.

If *The Man Who Loved Children* dissects, places, and so transcends the narcissism of the family, *For Love Alone* both exalts the stoic heroism Stead deems necessary to escape its stranglehold, and at the same time, begins to achieve some perspective on this new version of egotistical self-absorption. Stead's protagonists undergo a metamorphosis parallel to the one which transforms her prose style. In *For Love Alone*, Teresa mines her fantasies to act on them and thus learns to temper the extremities of her imaginative life to more realistic behavior. Like Louisa Pollit, Teresa counters the denigrations and denials of family life by assuming a pose of stoicism. In her later work, however, Stead looks back in chagrin on her heroine's stoicism and recasts it as a further drowning into self, rather than a means of transcendence. The constriction of relationship and disciplining of emotion by which Stead's women achieve independence endangers their capacity for interdependence.

The women of Stead's later fiction are characterized more by the means by which they inflict suffering than by what they themselves suffer. The developmental task of tempering exaggerated self-images to reality does present difficulties of heroic proportion for Stead's female characters. Everyday life offers them not mature fulfillment, but inhibition and subtle denigration. Conventional social patterns limit women's means of economic self-sufficiency and emotional gratification. For rejecting traditional feminine alternatives, Teresa pays the price of isolation. What seems self-reliance in her independence, in less imaginative characters comes to seem another mask of egotism; Stead's later wanderers are more irresponsible and childish than they are heroic.

Before Stead wins the recognition that shapes her mature vision, her work shows a process of fragmentation and rejection. In *Letty Fox*, the novel that follows *For Love Alone*, Stead splits her heroine in two, letting Letty embody all the active virtues, and isolating and rejecting introspective artistic dreaminess in Letty's sister Jacky. This criticism constitutes a recoil from Teresa Hawkins's kind of heroism, which unites fantasy with practical action. Attempting to deny the "morbid poetic melancholy temperament"[40] she repeatedly tries and fails to deny in herself, Stead condemns one of the greatest strengths of her own sensibility; Letty prefigures the most negative transformation of Stead's woman hero. Stead starts to write in a more exclusively satiric mode that upsets her productive equilibrium of fantasy and satire and ossifies her fiction. After *A Little Tea, A Little Chat*, and *The People with the Dogs*, her voice was silenced. When she started to write again, her conception of her heroines had significantly altered.

Letty Fox: Her Luck (1946)

The somber introspection of *For Love Alone* and the
critics' response to it evoked a reaction in Stead's
writing. *Letty Fox: Her Luck* is the first of three
satiric novels, set in New York City, which progressively examine increasingly purposeless characters.
In 1947, Stead writes, "In [*For Love Alone*] I tried to
present a girl of no social background who just believed in love, but whom society forced into the same
sordid mess that entrapped Letty Fox. American critics couldn't understand this girl, so I decided to give
them something they could understand—a young,
pretty New York girl, talented, with a good social
background, who nevertheless finds promiscuity necessary in her search for security."[41] In her comments
in our 1973 interview, the novel bears more of the
burden of dissatisfaction than the critics: "There was
a certain amount of labor in writing *For Love Alone*.
After I'd written that book which is gloomy and
serious, I thought, . . . instead of being bogged down
in all this stuff, . . . well, I'm going to write about
quite a different kind of girl, who's wide awake, or
apparently so. (Of course, nobody's wide awake in
sex.)"[42]

   Stead does give us a heroine different in style
and character from Teresa Hawkins. Liberated city
girl of the 1940s, child of divorced parents, still emotionally attached to her father, Letty grows up, lives
on her own in New York, works in office jobs, runs
through various love affairs, and finally marries,
more for financial and emotional security than for
love. Stead gives Letty that "blast of energy and self-
confidence" that her predecessors lacked; but it is at
the expense of their thoughtfulness and richness of
fantasy life. Letty tells her own story (Stead's first use
of the first person narrative, and not a particularly
skillful one). Its tone is vivid, witty, bright, and ultimately superficial. This novel is more a picturesque

satire on what is cast as American materialistic values
than it is a novel of development. Letty is at once a
mouthpiece for Stead's commentary and herself an
object of the satire.

At the center of the novel is a critical examination of marriage, its preludes and alternatives.
Letty's mother, Mathilde, had despaired when "she
had acquired all the advertised products, love, a
husband, a home, children, but she had not the advertised results—she recognized nothing in the landscape." She warns Letty, "All married women were
pariahs from life itself." As Letty watches her friends
grow up, the lively, smart schoolgirls disappear and
are replaced by "middle-aged women, dull, smug,
neurotic." They sit in the park in dowdy house-
dresses and curlers "playing watch-dog to baby carri-
ages . . . looking vapid, as if they'd never been to
school and never read a book. . . . Although sorry I
had no husband and baby, I could no longer rub
shoulders with these thwarted and miraculously
stunted youngsters," says Letty. She fears that if she
marries she would "just silt down into primeval mud
like the rest of the girls." "It's like being a sardine
in a school of sardines. You can't tell one from
another. . . . I do not intend to be canned in cot-
tonseed oil. I do not intend to be eaten, if I can help
it," Letty determines.

Her own family is a living attack on the myth of
marriage. The first of the novel's two books provides
a family history, but the rogues' gallery of Letty's
extended family houses a display of caricaturized
portraits. Her father, Solander, a charming conversa-
tionalist, has left the family to live with his lively
mistress Persia. She is called by all "Die Konkubine,"
and in a covert way, accepted as part of the ongoing
life of this fractured family configuration. Letty's
mother, who gave up an unlaunched acting career for
marriage, is listless, passive and full of her own sor-

rows, able only to moan and mourn. Letty and
Jacky's youngest sister, baby Andrea, is a "post-
humous child" of the marriage, the product of one of
Mathilde's final and unsuccessful "feminine" strategems to hold her husband. Besides several uncles,
their wives and girl friends and other family friends,
there are two grandmothers, each a characteristic
Stead sketch of one type of old woman. Grandmother Morgan has taken over her ailing husband's
business and runs a country inn. Now that all her
seven children are grown, she is "just beginning to
feel her energies" in both economic and romantic en-
terprises. She joins Henny Pollit's mother, Old Ellen,
as one of Stead's feisty, cynical old women who, past
childbearing, are free to be as frank, iconoclastic and
exuberant as they wish—"members of a joyous,
ribald camarilla, hardy women, more like men."
Wholly unsentimental, she dispenses pragmatic advice on marriage: She has no sympathy with women's
illusions of love; marriage is a business matter, laws
were made so women could trap men into providing
economic support for themselves and their children.
Wives, on their parts, should tolerate their husbands'
affairs, keep the house running and be smart dressers
to keep the men coming home. Quite her opposite,
Grandmother Fox is nervous, timid, weak, queru-
lous. An aged child, she mutters to herself and
subjects her children to long tiresome monologues,
trying to manipulate them into caring for her. Like
Mathilde, she is passive and dependent. "She had
always been a queer little thing, sharp, angry, disappointed." With its layers of generations, this is a
family of vitality and continuity, if not conventional
form. While the institution of the family does not
match its image, it does endure and thrive.

   The novel moves between New York and Paris,
where mother and daughters go in pursuit of
Solander and Persia. Letty grows up, goes to work,

and runs through a string of lovers, another set of
satiric sketches. Most of them are older, married and
rather seedy. A rather unsuccessful practitioner of
Grandmother Morgan's philosophy, Letty ends up
giving men money, rather than getting it from them.
She believes their promises of forthcoming divorce
and marriage, and moves from one to the next with
unblemished faith. Eventually she decides that "I
was one of those marrying women who married even
her casual lovers." Worn down, she tires of living
"spiritually and mentally, from pillar to post (pillow
to post!) and from hand to mouth." "I wanted now to
become part of society myself and have a husband in
the regular way." In the end, Letty marries an old
friend, Bill Van Weeks, "whose pastime in life was
splitting with his parents" until his millionaire
father dies and disinherits him. "Tired of struggling
so hard," Letty "wished never to wish for another
man." Married, "at last I feel I have something to live
for . . . I did not need money. I did not need
society. I was never alone and never despaired. What
else can one hope for?"

Letty has run down, rather than developed. Her
family history, though recounted at length, has no
explanatory force in the shaping of her later life. In
this novel, Stead has externalized and divided com-
plexities of character in a way that leads more to
satire than to understanding or development. Just as
the two grandmothers represent extremes of dependence and independence, Letty and Jacky are polarizations of traits united in Stead's preceding heroines.
Teresa was both imaginative and pragmatic. Here,
Jacky is thoughtful where Letty is active; artistic and
romantic where Letty is practical. Jacky has the
literary tastes of Louisa Pollit and Teresa Hawkins:
she regularly falls in love with the "immortals": Shelley, Spinoza, Bertrand Russell. She is a good artist
and keeps a private book of personal sketches; she

takes all things seriously. Letty says, "Jacky never was humorous, she lacked this quality. She intended to move into history with all sails set." Letty considers her sister one of those "persons of obscure unpopular talents [who like] to dream their lives away, masochists who like to swim upstream." Never wasting her energies on introspection or private expression, Letty likes politics, writes for the school paper, where "I learned," she says, "without tears, how to prostitute my talent, putting in little things to please the faculty advisor and editor." "Sophisticated," confident and slick, she is successful, especially socially, in the literary business. She knows "where the dog lies buried," goes to parties with the right men, and so gets on very fast.

Letty is a product of the values and institutions Stead's satire debunks. She has gone to progressive schools, been raised with the post-Freudian permissiveness that Stead always mocks. When Letty visits a psychoanalyst, she laughs at his diagnosis of her Oedipal attachment to her father. "I am tired of a place where instead of getting out the old family album, they now get out the old Oedipus complex that made them what they are today. It's the same, but not in such good taste."

This novel, however, offers no alternative conception of character formation. Letty is one of the many girls in Stead's novels still attached to their fathers. She is a precursor of the shallow American waifs of the novellas of *The Puzzleheaded Girl*, who wander listlessly around Europe, forcing others, especially older men, to take care of them. Letty is more likable than they, more energetic and openspirited, less successful a manipulator, but she shares their lack of moral coherence. For all her frankness and energy, Letty never engages the narrative's sympathies as Teresa does. Her witticisms and analyses are clever and sometimes brilliant, but her lively patter skims the surfaces of emotional and moral issues. The history of her childhood, family, work, lovers, marriage never materializes with the conviction of a lived life. Both she and her story, finally, lack inner coherence.

The brilliant equilibrium of fantasy and realism Stead achieved in *The Man Who Loved Children* here falls to the side of satiric realism; emotion goes underground. The next of Stead's New York novels will find her mode of satire ossifying to rob her style of the animation of the inner world. *Letty Fox*, however, still has sparkle and spunk. A reviewer in the *Times Literary Supplement* finds its principal quality "an immense vitality and an enjoyment of life as a painful comedy."[43] *Letty Fox: Her Luck* is an intelligent book, full of insights, aphorisms, and caricatures, but not illuminated from within as are *The Man Who Loved Children* and *For Love Alone*.

A Little Tea, A Little Chat (1948)

Stead's irony at its coldest and most bitter freezes *A Little Tea, A Little Chat* (1948) into dark sterility. Set in New York, but peopled by new incarnations of the worst of the characters from *House of All Nations*, this novel follows a spiritless, philandering, middle-aged man, Robert Grant, through his dissolute moneymaking schemes and loveless love affairs. For him, "the talk of love had become a daily hunger . . . he was starving, never satisfied." The detachment of his emotionally constricted life, however, insures his starvation. His mistress, Barbara Kent, is as cynical and selfish as he. Without the redemption of the imaginative fertility and rhetorical powers that animated the larger philanderers and con men of the earlier novel, the life in and of the novel is so degraded that it loses all color and grace. Grant dies, appropriately enough, of heart failure. Critics condemned the book, complaining that exposing pettiness and vice seems hardly worth the effort when none of the characters is attractive enough to elicit our concern. This novel is a rewrite, ten years later and in a minor key, of *House of All Nations*, without any of the greater novel's charm or scope. It forecasts the beginning of a period of dormancy of Stead's creative powers.

The People with the Dogs (1952)

The People with the Dogs dissects a very different segment of New York society. Its colors are softer, less acid-etched than those of *Letty Fox*, or *A Little Tea, A Little Chat* but it too portrays the destructive egotism and power manipulations within human affections. Centered, more or less, on the thirty-three-year-old Edward Massine, a likable but purposeless landlord who devotes little energy to anything or anyone, the novel is primarily a critique of the zany extended family to which Edward belongs. Rather diffuse and rambling, like Edward, the novel is peopled by the profusion of characters he meets in rooming houses and on the streets. The many New Yorkers whose life stories we hear are mostly tattered idealists: actors, musicians, German puppet-makers, Russian emigrés, old anarchists.

Listless though affable, Edward Massine lives for the family instead of himself. He has become "a sort of eunuch . . . in the affections," unable to commit himself to a woman or a career until he extricates himself from his large and loving family. The Massines believe in loving all mankind; their dream is to provide a roof for everyone, which they come near to doing at Whitehouse, their large country estate where they all retreat for the summer. The

entourage of family and friends encompasses not
only Edward's Aunt Oneida and her husband Lou,
but also Victor Alexander, an old suitor of Oneida's
who has built his own little house there. Their principles are of inclusion, not exclusion; but their very
generosity masks emotional constriction. A friend
cynically tells Edward: "You only understand the
communal life, that's why you don't want to marry,
isn't it? . . . You need abundant multiple life
around you. . . . Fruitfulness with grapes and rab-
bits dropping over the edges of an oak table on a
woven cloth—and many dogs and dishes and many
children and many days? Isn't that you fundamen-
tally? . . . You're married to many." To Stead this
communal ideology generates an unsatisfactory sur-
rogate for love; its superabundance is repellent.

The main proponent of this lush life is Edward's
Aunt Oneida. This effusive woman cares "only for affections," and insists, "'to live in a community is the
way to live. . . . We must live for others, mustn't
we. . . . Oh, we musn't live for ourselves. . . . I've
never lived for only one person,' cried Oneida franti-
cally, 'I couldn't! Oh, I must live for all my darlings.
To live for one person only is death, the end.'" She
becomes hysterical at the thought of Edward's marrying, and insists that he does not want that kind of
bourgeois life of possessive jealousy. She coquet-
tishly seeks to keep Edward enmeshed, in order to
maintain the fabric in which the family thrives. "We
need you," Oneida insists, "'if you left us the whole
old life would dissolve. Where would I be?' 'Only
with me,' said Lou," her husband.

But that is not Oneida's idea of love. The "sweet
close honeying ones who were her intimate life, her
perpetual joys" are her dogs. The lives, sicknesses,
and deaths of dogs, each of whom has its own personality, are as much a part of this novel as the human
lives. "I think a love of dogs makes you understand

human beings," claims Oneida. "You learn to take
care of everybody. . . . If children take your food it's
because they know they have an equal right with you
and they take more than their share, they're monsters, they know they must grow up and live longer
than you. . . . Children are Frankenstein's monsters!
They grow up and leave you; but dogs never leave
you." Dogs epitomize to Oneida the unchanging, im-
prisoning loyalty that defines family love for her and
by which she is herself damaged. In her profuse affections, Oneida remains "sheltered from crude and
bestial life, from passions," from the savagery
Edward says is in all of us, and therefore from any
deep capacity for loving.

This collective family love is debilitating also to
Edward, who has been unable to make any adult
commitments. When Margot, the woman he has been
with for twelve years, tries directly to wrest Edward
from the family's surrounding fortress, and insists
that he make up his mind, he is unable to decide to
marry her, and she marries someone else. Sunk in
ennui and depression after her loss (and that of his
dog Musty) Edward goes uptown to Harlem to stay
for a while in the rooming house of his old friends,
Philip and Nell Christy. Philip, a cynical, often
drunk optician in his fifties, lives with his old sister
Nell who devotedly cares for him, and his dog Lady
to whom he is devoted. From time to time, Nell
wonders if she has wasted her life, loving this brother
who is almost like a husband to her. When Philip,
trying to save Lady, is killed by a trolley, Nell too
wants to die. As Edward helps nurse her, the two recognize a kinship in their purposeless lives: both live
sheltered from reality in the sticky cocoon of family
love. After a long period of meditative solitude with
the Christys, Edward begins to change. He starts to
write, falls in love wth Lydia, a divorced actress, and
finally marries her. (He recognizes that he is at-

tracted to her because she looks so much like himself
"and [that] seemed to mean that they were meant for
each other; but he did not say anything to Lydia
about it. It is the sort of compliment that only works
in love and then is dubious," Stead comments wryly.)

Edward's resolution, and the novel's, are not
without ambiguities. Edward and Lydia attend a
party on the Massine estate. Though he has resolved
to go away with Lydia, and escape the octopus tendrils of the family vine, he feels sad and torn: "I can't
bear to see the Massine Republic change," he says
with tears in his eyes. In the last scene, Edward has
announced to his Massine tribe his marriage to Lydia
and they await a toast. We see the family standing
about, "not especially arranged, but in a natural order. . . . There was no silence or constraint, no im-
patience and no flurry. In this moment, as in all
others, their long habit and innocent, unquestioning
and strong, binding family love, the rule of their
family, made all things natural and sociable with
them." But the last line of the novel is the ambivalent toast: "Brothers and sisters: We love each other
and today is St. Valentine's Day."

We have seen what this love of brothers and sisters for each other is like. *The People with the Dogs*
treats more softly the incestuous pairs of *Seven Poor
Men of Sydney* or *Dark Places of the Heart*, but the
pervasive family narcissism here too inhibits just
what the incest taboo functions to promote—the
movement outside the family unit to form affectionate bonds with larger networks of people. Stead is
more gentle with Edward than she is with any of her
female protagonists. The Massine family is lively and
charming too. Informed by the utopian ideals suggested by Oneida's name,[44] they are not the crass
American materialists of the two preceding novels.
In all her fiction, Stead portrays characters from the
political Left, and her own premises are grounded in

socialism. However, though Marxist critic José Yglesias believes Stead's criticism is directed at the bourgeois nuclear family,[45] here, an open, extended
communal family proves equally threatening to individual integrity. In a fragment from a still unfinished novel about expatriate American radicals in
the thirties, Stephen and Emily Howard quarrel
about communism and family love: Emily is ecstatic
about "closewoven" family life. "'The family is the
heart of man; how can you tear it open?' Stephen
listened smiling, grinning. . . . 'Any family life is
poison.' . . . 'Stephen, listen to what I say! Family
love is the only true selfless love, it's natural communism. That is the origin of our feeling for communism: to each according to his needs, from each
according to his capacity; and everything is arranged
naturally, without codes and without policing.'"[46]
Stead's beliefs seem closer to Stephen's than to
Emily's.

This portrait has more genuine comedy in it
than Stead's other American satires. Still, to Stead all
affections remain suspect. While the Massines feel
nostalgia for a way of life that is passing, Stead is
never nostalgic about anything that comes from that
cradle of nostalgic sentiment—the family. Stead had
left the U.S. in 1947 and was traveling with William
Blake all over Europe. Whether because of this itin-
eracy, as she claims,[47] or because of something in-
trinsic to the development of her fiction, *The People
with the Dogs* was to be her last novel for a decade
and a half.

The Little Hotel (1975)

Stead says she has a trunk full of writing unpub-
lished during her long period of silence. Some of the
fragments from that time have been coming to light

in recent decades. Published as a novel in 1975, *The
Little Hotel* is a reworking of two short stories first
published in 1952 and 1968.[48] It therefore combines
themes and tones from Stead's earlier and later
periods. The novel reiterates and extends a central
motif of the early fiction: the only escape from the
destructive narcissism of families is satiric detachment of attitude and literal flight to wander free but
solitary, far away from any home. The tone of the
work, however, modulates into the tone of Stead's
late fiction: a calm and detached acceptance of the
lot of man- and womankind.

Families in Stead are always destructive. The
characters who escape their tentacles to leave home
become wanderers, seldom forming new families of
their own. *The Little Hotel* shelters a small, wild collection of such people. Its narrator is the garrulous
young Swiss woman who keeps the hotel, though, due
to a defect in construction, the narrative point of
view often switches to that of Mrs. Trollope, one of
her guests. The two give us their rambling observations of the hotel's various occupants, all rootless
exiles of the postwar 1940s who speculate in international currency; "rich people . . . grudging every
penny, going shabby," as one character observes.
There is the mad Mayor of B. (mad men and women
appear with regularity in Stead's novels); a poison-
ously quarreling couple, Dr. and Madame Blaise[49]; a
rich eccentric princess who coddles her singing dog;
Mrs. Powell, a genteel racist and anti-Communist;
and the affectionate, melancholy Mrs. Trollope, who
has been living for twenty years with a financial
speculator, Robert Wilkins. They call themselves
"cousins"; Wilkins controls all her money and refuses
to marry her. Humiliated by the arrangement,
tenderhearted Lilia Trollope is unhappy living from
hotel to hotel, with no real home. "I can't go on all
my life trying to love people at the *table d'hôte*," she

cries. Yet that is just what most of Stead's characters
do. From *The Salzburg Tales* to *The Little Hotel*,
chance concatenations of strangers are drawn together by some arbitrary event or place, where they
provide each other whatever human relationships
are possible.

The European expatriates at this inexpensive
hotel in ever-neutral Switzerland are all endemically
homeless. Their association is determined not by
bonds of blood or love or friendship, only by proxim-
ity and circumstance. "Are they my old friends?" asks
Mrs. Trollope. "Are they the kind of people I would
pick out for myself?" But for Stead, social institutions seldom connect people in continuing intimacy.
"Life seems very small to me this way," complains
Mrs. Trollope. These people do lead constricted
lives, "painedly narrow, like a wince," as critic Christopher Ricks comments.[50] Their isolation takes
different forms; many are crazy eccentrics. Dr. and
Madame Blaise have a long-standing marriage of bitter fighting. (When she dies, it seems likely he has
poisoned her.) Another of the hotel's inhabitants,
Miss Chillard, is a manipulative invalid, one of
Stead's transformations of her independent heroine.
The sick, whining old woman who uses her sickness
to wheedle care from others is a character who reap-
pears throughout Stead's late fiction.[51] "A tanned
bony virgin martyr," Miss Chillard attracts Mrs.
Trollope's sympathy. Mrs. Trollope concludes that
she is "a brave malingerer-errant who was not afraid
of homelessness but of home, and who knew enough
about people to cast herself on the mercy of hotel-
keepers or casual acquaintances; and could not bear
those at home who knew her sadness." "Who would
lead such a life?" wonders Mrs. Trollope. "And I am
leading it. . . . " "Supposing she ended up like that,
with her little aches and pains, in a narrow poor hotel room, despised and harassed?"

The fear of that isolated old age and despised spinsterhood helps keep Mrs. Trollope attached to Robert Wilkins. Their story is told at a slower pace, in more detail and in a more thoughtful tone than any of the other anecdotal lives of the novel. Most of the other characters are revealed in swift, deft scenes which skewer their victims with precise economy. One such scene is an elaborate dinner Wilkins gives for the Blaises and some other guests. (The pretentious dinner of excessive food and talk and little nourishment is another staple of Stead's fiction.)[52]

Lilia Trollope is a bit of an exotic; of mixed blood, her mother was Dutch-Javanese, and she had lived sheltered for many years "in the unreal world of empire outposts." She left her husband and children when she fell in love with Robert Wilkins, twenty years earlier. Now they are a pair who walk together "with the unmistakable trotting and nodding of the long-married." Their long relationship, founded in love, has endured with fondness which, since Robert's refusal to marry her after her late divorce, has turned distant, though still punctuated by the old affections and dependencies. Robert now reads the paper in her face at meals and Lilia feels deeply shamed by his refusal to acknowledge her. Robert has been kept from marrying Lilia by a promise to his mother that he would not marry while she lived. Wilkins's mother and three sisters, "maiden ladies in their fifties and sixties" display just the family-centered narcissism that cripples the children of Stead families. "They do what suits them and that is what God thinks right," says Mrs. Trollope. "They would not give you a cup of water if you were dying in the gutter [and were not a Wilkins]. Secretly . . . they would like to see us all die before them. . . . No one counts but the Wilkinses. . . . It does not even matter if there are no more Wilkinses, they are so precious."

Typical Stead obsessions keep these characters from each other. Mrs. Trollope feels she has to choose "between a wandering old age and that homeland in which she was a stranger." But "if she married Robert? She would be worse off perhaps. He was married to his family; she would always come second." Madame Blaise expresses the Wilkins's vision of family love, with more virulence. She insists that her son is the only person she has ever loved and "I'd like to see him die, rather than see him tied to another woman." Their emotional rootlessness disguises itself as an obsession with money; they move from country to country following changes in currency rates. In his review of the novel, John Updike observes with precision the intertwined dependencies of financial and emotional needs: "Throughout, money or its lack is crucial, and it is the women, rich and poor, who are exploited. . . . Miss Stead, an outspoken left-writer, enriches her perceptions of emotional dependence with a tactile sense of money as a pervasive, unpleasant glue that holds her heroines fast, in their little hotels of circumstance."[53]

Within this constrained space is much distance. Before she does finally leave Mr. Wilkins, Mrs. Trollope complains to him: "At times you seem to me a complete stranger. I am living with a stranger." His reply: "We all are." The various accommodations these people make with loneliness, though sometimes spirited, are all unsatisfactory; yet this "doty profusion of characters"[54] presents us with comic tales of endurance as well as suffering.

A pastiche of imperfectly integrated vignettes and fragments, this novel is also a composite of tones. Madame Bonnard, the original narrator, knows so many stories of her guests and servants, because she is an accepting listener who "understand[s] people without criticizing them." She is unperturbed by whatever eccentricity she reports. Mrs. Trollope's

tone of voice is somewhat different. Reflective, melancholy, analytic, and indecisive, she recalls Elvira
Western of *The Beauties and Furies,* who also could
not decide to leave or to stay with her lover. Mrs.
Trollope, too, is accepting. She comments about Madame Blaise, "I think she is a neurotic, perhaps; but
she is unhappy. People suffer and we call them
names; but all the time they are suffering." She
echoes Caroline, a character in *Dark Places of the
Heart,* as she walks the streets full of human misery;
Caroline's observations serve as a description of the
characters of this novel as well: "In these houses were
strangers occupied in struggling for breath, not much
more. . . . She had seen the riot, scandal that was
the flowering of the force of nature in some, the
strong wildness, that was anger, the perversity, the
nonchalant feeble depravity, the indifference to degradation in others. Though she burned hotter than
ever, and detested vice more than before, she had
also become gentle and indifferent about it: it was
their way and they were human. If people had tuberculosis or cancer they were still entirely human."
Stead does not react as Caroline does with "wretchedness and fatigue." Her overall narrative stance is
neither Madame Bonnard's nor Mrs. Trollope's, but
contains both. This is the matured tone of Stead's
late fiction. She shares their acceptance, their refusal
to label human behavior. At the same time, she
makes unyielding judgments, distanced, thought not
softened, by ironic wit. She appreciates humanity's
suffering—much of it self-inflicted—with insight and
with a continuing enthusiasm for life in all its variegated distortions. Stead's own comment about her
characters' story: "It's no great shakes." "But they
were human beings and it's a human little story."[55]

The root of the tone of acceptance in *The Little Hotel*
and Stead's late fiction is to be found in the new syn-

thesis of vision of *Dark Places of the Heart*. With it she relinquishes the last remnants of a world divided between heroes and villains. Stead has always been acutely sensitive to the omnipresent inequities of power in personal relationships, and has always proclaimed herself on the side of the oppressed. Through *The Man Who Loved Children* and *For Love Alone*, parents and men seemed the strong; children and women the powerless. After her autobiographical fiction, however, her work shows an increasingly complex vision of oppressors and a shift in the designation of the victims. More and more as her work progresses, Stead examines the tyrannical modes of the weak, and the manipulative stratagems of the injured. The dark figure of Nellie Cotter Cook in *Dark Places of the Heart* is a woman and a writer, speaking on behalf of the downtrodden—simultaneously oppressor and oppressed, deprived child and damaging parent. This resynthesis of the polarities of power and powerlessness into a single individual is as severely judgmental as any image created by Stead's early fantasy or anger. The harsh self-criticism it implies, however, becomes a source of self-acceptance, in its leveling of the heroic sense of specialness to the common dimension of shared human nature.

Dark Places of the Heart
(English Title: *Cotter's England*) (1966)

In 1965, *The Man Who Loved Children* was reissued, ending Stead's long silence. The next year she published another major novel, *Dark Places of the Heart*, a scathing character study of another of her deceiving charmers. Nellie Cotter Cook is a left-wing journalist from a working-class family of the industrial north of England, married to George, a labor leader who spends most of his time far away from home. In

her large old house in London, Nellie shelters stray
women; many of them are attracted to her brother
Tom, but Nellie has her own designs on them. Nellie
is the bleakest reincarnation of Stead's favorite type,
the manipulative egotist who persistently preys on
others. In this single sinister figure, Stead recaptures
her entire family configuration. One of her victims
says of Nellie that you carry her with you "as you
carry a bad parent always with you" and Nellie is
the reembodiment of both Pollit parents. Skinny,
scrappy, sickly, spewing black tirades, Nellie looks
and talks like Henny, but she loves like Sam. Disguised in a rhetorical cloud of socialism and sympathy, she strangles her family and friends in webs of
possessiveness.

As the oldest child in her family, Nellie had se-
duced her brother Tom and sister Peggy to dependence on her, "out of her great vanity wanting to be
the only one to show them love; so that no one again
could take them from her." Nellie's greatest wish,
like Madame Blaise's, is that someone would love her
enough to die for her; destroyed by her fierce domination, one woman does commit suicide, her sister
goes mad, and her brother remains a weak and helpless man, forever in her power.

Sitting up late at night, smoking and coughing,
Nellie talks endlessly (and her long monologues are
brilliantly rendered). Devoted to character analysis,
like Stead, Nellie considers herself an empathetic
guide leading her friends in "healthy introspection."
But she is hardly disinterested: "Introspection and
Friendship were words Nellie used for her own pur-
poses: by introspection she meant a shameless curios-
ity and crafty use of her knowledge; by friendship
what only a clique meant; and it was dishonest since
she trapped people that way." Nellie's motivation is
not sympathy but possession. Tom tells her, "You've
got just a little twisted spittling spider thread of

sympathy and you try to dangle a whole human being on it." Nellie is a vampire feeding off those she pretends to protect. Her emotional hungers and craving for possession are all the more horrifying for posing seductively as feminine sympathy.

Most of Nellie's "friends" are her brother's lovers; Nellie wants to keep both Tom and the women for herself. Whenever Tom finds someone new, Nellie has long talks with each of them, alternating flattery and slander to convince them that love is no more than a dangerous illusion: "What is the use of these tawdry loves . . . aren't they always disappointed? Doesn't that prove that it's shameful degrading nonsense?" The burden of this proof is that the listener should trust only Nellie, and love her alone. Like the greedy satyrs of *House of All Nations* or *A Little Tea, A Little Chat*, Nellie and Tom are both insatiable. Tom, soft, gentle, confiding, is appealing to women and bemuses one after another, without making a full commitment to any. These women form a long string: Marion, Camilla, Frida, Caroline, Eliza. After talking all one night to Eliza in one of her accustomed diatribes, Nellie sits back and "black curtains of fatigue dropped all over her mind. She sat in the double dark till morning, with fiery tongues of desire, brain-flame licking the roots of her skull. She had perhaps made another conquest in Eliza but it was not sufficient. The drawback of her easy conquests, she thought to herself, was that they left her dissatisfied: she wanted more."

Nellie traces her craving for psychological analysis to her bleak working-class youth, where "there had been nothing . . . to satisfy their youthful intellectual and moral hungers, so they had taken to drink, vice, unbridled speculation and gnawing at each other. Hunger will prey on garbage, rather than be extinguished in death. But Nellie had not called it garbage, she called it knowledge." While Stead quickly but densely sketches in Nellie's childhood and family, childhood to Stead is never an excuse. Tom and Peggy's accounts of their unloving mother, their exhibitionist father, whom Nellie so resembles, function as self-serving rationalizations. This might have been a study of the destruction wrought on the human spirit by deprivation, but Stead is too relentlessly moral to temper her judgments of behavior with social or psychological determinism.

Nellie herself is without self-criticism. Unreflecting, for all her introspection, she dominates this novel as she does all those who come under her spell. (And that includes the reader: while we see through Nellie in horror, she is fascinating and vital.) It is the nature of Stead's destroying charmers to survive while others die. With Tom, Nellie succeeds in doing what Sam Pollit had wanted to do to Louie: "I made him see he had no one but me, only me for his life long," she boasts. "Naturally, we were close. I didn't think about loving him. It was something deeper, a communion, that comes only once in a life, if it comes at all. He could never have with anyone else what he had with me. We don't have to talk or tell anecdotes. We have a perfect understanding": it's perfection achieved by the absorption of her brother into herself. When Nellie catches a reflection of herself and Tom in a mirror (and this novel of narcissism is full of mirrors), she responds to the single vision: "Not much is it? They're distortions of human beings! Why do we like it, Tom?" Nellie and Tom are the most fully developed and most horrifying of Stead's emotionally incestuous brothers and sisters. As the novel ends, Nellie's husband George has sent for her to join him in Europe, but he dies in a skiing accident just after her arrival. The newspapers refuse to print the grotesque picture they take at his funeral, of Nellie and Tom, hand in hand and smiling.

Stead has once more focused a compelling novel on an essentially repellent character. Nellie is her father's daughter, and heir as well to Sam and Henny Pollit: a character on much the same scale and of much the same nature. Though excessive, like Nellie's tirades and like all of Stead's fiction, *Dark Places of the Heart* fascinates. Its pointed insights and concentrated, forceful prose make this grand dark novel one of Stead's best.

The world of Stead's late fiction is not different from that of her early work, but it is seen from the shifted focus of the figure-ground reversal of an optical illusion. While the same manipulation and greedy human need run this world, its tyrants are likely to be its victims: the sick, the weak, the old, the young, women and children. Characters who had been the heroes of the early work are transformed to satiric caricatures. Simultaneously, the introspective insightfulness that was crucial to the kind of heroism Stead has admired is seen in its darkest aspect, then removed from characters entirely to recede further back into the narrative presence of the fiction. Stead's real hero has always been the artist: the one of complex and changing vision. She has a number of characters who, like herself, are watchful analyzers of human nature, probing dissectors of personality. But from Elvira Western on, Stead has always been aware of a dimension of self-absorption in what seems to be dedicated interest in the inner workings of other people. In Nellie Cotter, Stead portrays a woman who uses penetrating analysis exclusively for her own narcissistic ends. Stead's strongest heroines, Louisa and Teresa, are young women of highly developed inner lives, of complex fantasy and perception, and Stead cherishes these qualities. After showing this personality in its most negative guise in Nellie, however, Stead creates no more heroines defined by this kind of specialness. Stead's ugly duckling does not grow into a swan, but becomes just another duck, to share the flawed nature we all are heir to.

The female protagonists of Stead's late work are

more caricatures than characters. From Miss Chillard, the manipulative invalid of *The Little Hotel*, and her sister character in the short story "An Iced Cake with Cherries,"[56] helpless old women lying in bed find ways to maneuver others into caring for them. The two weaker novellas of *The Puzzleheaded Girl* (1967) ("The Dianas" and "Girl from the Beach") are satiric portraits of listless young American girls, spoiled offspring of permissive parents, who wander around Europe with no more purpose than to turn others into the all-giving, nondemanding parents they have been used to. The final transformations of Stead's woman hero are these shallow, manipulative young girls and sick old women who passively wring from strangers the love they fail to find in families they fail to form. The cynical wisdom of *The Puzzleheaded Girl* is expressed by one of their victims: "We say the handsome use their looks. The ugly use their looks; and the sick use their sickness; and old age uses its age. Don't pity anyone."

Stead remains unforgiving in her judgments. If there are no more sympathetic individuals in Stead's late work, however, there are many like the rest of us—deluded, funny, sad, awful—but human. And there are eyes to see and smile at them. In a pair of minor characters who appear not as protagonists but observers throughout the late fiction, and in the narrative presence they often represent, there is a sensibility that sits back and enjoys this painful but comic human spectacle, without surprise or disdain for anything it has to offer.

The Puzzleheaded Girl (1967)

The spoiled children of *The Puzzleheaded Girl* (a collection of four novellas) are Stead's least appealing egotists. They have the least inner strength, the least imaginative energy of any of her greedy tyrants. Stead no longer sees these young women as victimized, crippled daughters (as they might have been in *The Salzburg Tales*), but portrays them instead from their victim's point of view. Stead approves of neither the origins nor the outcome of their character development. Having brilliantly dissected a childhood that was anything but overindulged in *The Man Who Loved Children*, Stead is curiously harsh with liberal parents who are afraid to stunt their children with any discipline, and overpraise their least accomplishments. Stead mocks both the children and the parents of permissive modern families. Letty Fox has a friend who wants to bring up her son to have "a full life with no repressions." Letty tells her friend that she is preparing her son for a fantasy world: he won't have fifteen bosses all catering to him to bring out his individualism. "You send him to witch doctors too, who make him think there's something divine in his innermost I." But there's not. "You're just training him to be a complete rotter." Similarly, in "The Rightangled Creek" in this volume, Ruth and Laban Davies never cross their son Frankie, never make any attacks on his self-esteem, want never to frustrate or deprive him. (The twelve-year-old Frankie, like his parents, is already a pompous and condescending socialist who despises his poor working-class neighbors.)

Stead's satire embodies the cogent criticism of child-centered upbringing that her husband, William Blake, articulates in his book, *Understanding the Americans*. He writes:

Every one of these parents knows that no adult takes such tender care of the inherent personality of any other. . . . Most persons recall their early days in employment as a painful experience; the world is so much more hostile than one's family, even a difficult family. Yet most people adjust to this, perhaps always with some regret, because, apart from crime or beggary, there is no alternative. The

Americans are practical, economic, yet they train their children, or rather, fail to train them, for a world that does not exist, that of unlimited self expression.[57]

But the virulence of Stead's portrayal of spoiled children is greater than such rational critique alone would justify. To Stead, the progressive theories of these mothers and fathers disguise yet another form of parental egotism: parents inflate their children's need for them, binding the children forever in infantile attachments. A mother in *Letty Fox* who believes in Freud, "to free his libido and her own . . . talked to her son about the Oedipus complex, that is, about incest; and in this strange way, tried to attach the boy to herself." The children who grow out of such families are undisciplined and exploitative. They have none of the strengths Stead admires: self-reliance, stoic discipline, purpose, imaginative fertility. Stead is cold in her dissection of their behavior; she does not do their portraits with the emotional involvement and even compassion she lends to those of her charming tyrants (like the Pollits and Nellie Cotter and Jules Bertillon).

The other two tales of this volume, however, "The Rightangled Creek" and the title story, use the sparer and more controlled style she has developed to transmute the themes and images of her earliest work into a broader and wiser narrative vision. "The Puzzleheaded Girl" retells a version of Stead's autobiographical heroine's family story, but from a different perspective and in a quieter tone. While *The Man Who Loved Children* unites fantasy and realism to tell Stead's own family story so well that by its particularity it becomes universal, in the late work she transcends the angers of personal injury to tell a human story—one with the tragic wistfulness and compassionate acceptance of a tale of the shared human condition. In both these tales appear the

middle-aged couple who are calm, detached, capable
of integrity and of concern for others. (The recurring
William Blake–Baruch Mendolsohn–James Quick–
Michel Alphendéry character seems to bring some of
this generosity of sensibility and tone into Stead's
fiction.) These minor characters voice a growing acceptance of what Stead has all along perceived to be a
truth of both nature and human nature: that people
are both creative and destructive, capable of great
selfishness and cruelty, and also of love and creativity.

This vision finds its most integrated expression
in "The Puzzleheaded Girl." Its heroine, Honor Lawrence, is indeed a jigsaw puzzle of pieces of many of
Stead's women characters. Honor tells repeatedly a
sad family history much like Stead's, but with a strong
coloring of self-pity that never stains the tales of
Stead's autobiographical heroines. Like Teresa Hawkins and Louisa Pollit, Honor has had a particularly
unhappy childhood, constrained by a possessive father and family responsibilities. As she tells Gus, the
good man who pities her (husband of Stead's persona
in the tale),

I have such a long walk to work—my father won't give me
the fare. You see, I have to give him everything. . . . He
doesn't think I ought to have money for myself. He says,
what is it for? And I won't explain. I'm too proud. It's a
long walk. Then I have to go back and cook at night. . . .
My mother died years ago. . . . She wasn't sick. She was
miserable. . . . I have to scrub the floor and wash the
things with water and no soap. . . . I never told anyone all
this before. I suppose it's a bit unusual. But I never knew
there were happy families. I thought that it was all a
lie. . . . [58]

Honor is kin to Lydia and Linda. She uses her
tale of woe to catch sympathetic men; the trusting
Gus thinks her "an ingenuous or a pure soul struggling with the world" and helps her whenever she

comes to him. Another young man insists he loves
her for her suffering: "It's . . . the beauty of your
mind and sorrows that I care for. They're my hope,
my fire, my salvation."

But the author and the women in the story see
something else in Honor. As Gus's first wife detects,
Honor is not a sensuous heroine, as Teresa liked to
think of herself, but "knows nothing at all of the
physical side of love. . . . It's the result of a subcon-
scious taboo. It's a real part of feminine nature. . . .
Such girls exist everywhere." Honor is "chaste." Her
chastity is not honor, but coldness. Asexuality is an
aspect of her general remoteness. Like Teresa, she
always carries with her a book, about art or literature; her intellectual involvement serves to isolate
her from those around her. Self-contained, aloof, she
affects others without herself being affected. Honor
has no part of a sustained relationship, but must always appear and disappear, leaving disaster in her
wake. She answers a young man's profession of affection with a sentiment typical of Stead's earliest cynicism: "Love! I spit, I spit it out . . . It was all lies. It
kills you. . . . There's no love at all." Mari, Gus's
second wife, whom Stead claims is her own voice in
this story, says that Honor "never was in love . . . she
never loved anyone."

Honor is needy, but willing to give nothing in return for what she gets. Selfish and grasping, she lives
off the goodness in others' natures, playing on capacities for pity and kindness that she herself lacks.
Throughout the story, she keeps showing up at the
homes or offices of other people, getting them to
provide her with food, clothes, shelter, or sympathy.
Mari imagines her as "a wraith, a wanderer" perpetually "turning up somewhere . . . asking for help."

Honor represents a different vision of the Teresa
Hawkins character. The stoicism for which Stead
admired her successful women heroes no longer seems

admirable to her. We all need the human connection
such stoicism denies. If we do not give and take directly, we take indirectly. This new insight is accompanied by a change in Stead's narrative voice. In *For
Love Alone*, she identified with her heroine, while
she controlled that empathetic identification by the
ironic multiplicity of narrative points of view. That
novel is marked by a balance of sympathy and perspective. By "The Puzzleheaded Girl," the woman
hero Stead admired in Teresa Hawkins is no longer a
hero, but neither is she quite a villain, for this world
of the late fiction does not divide along those lines.
The waifish puzzleheaded girl becomes an emblematic figure, representative of human nature, and the
tale itself takes on the tone of a parable. Mari calls
Honor "the ragged wayward heart of woman that
doesn't want to be caught and hasn't been caught."
Stead seems no longer to be describing idiosyncratic
foibles, but rather the ultimate isolation of impene-
trable individuality. When Kafka tells such a tale, he
makes us sympathetic to his hero's suffering humanity. Stead rather portrays Honor clearly as a manipulative victim, but one who nevertheless embodies an
untouched separateness that is shared and human.
The tone of this tale is not satiric so much as mysterious and wistful.

　　This motif of separateness is not new in Stead; it
is in play as early as *The Salzburg Tales*. In her first
work, isolation often seems the punishment for the
fantasy of monstrousness, which family loyalty strives
furiously to avoid. Later, it comes to seem an inevitable part of the human condition. Especially between lovers, there is always a distance, though the
mythology of romantic love, with its fantasy of merger
into ecstatic oneness tries to deny it. As early as 1935,
Stead had quoted Proudhon, saying, "It is by possession that man puts himself in communion with nature, while by property he separates himself from it:

in the same way that man and woman are in communion by domestic habitude, while voluptuousness holds them apart."[59]

The natural world confronts man with the same essential otherness as does love, and Stead is firm in asserting the necessity for recognizing its inevitability. Yet the grotesque style in which she makes this assertion utilizes the very fantasies of merger, of violation of boundary which such a recognition of the necessary integrity of otherness contradicts. "The Rightangled Creek: A Sort of Ghost Story" reanimates the gothic mode of *The Salzburg Tales* to show the consequences of failing to grant man or nature their due respect.

"The Rightangled Creek" reasserts the truth that Teresa Hawkins had perceived as she watched the sea from her night window in Sydney: life forces are destructive as well as generative, and one ignores this to one's peril. A young engineer in the tale refuses to respect the power of nature and rolls around in a bed of poison ivy; for his hubris, he dies. Stead insists firmly on the immanence of evil. Those who, like Sam Pollit, refuse to recognize it, destroy others or themselves. The one character in this tale who looks through what a critic has called Christina Stead's "wise old eyes"[60] is not untenanted by ghostly premonitions of nature or ghastly damages to human nature, but accepts them all with equanimity.

As the tale begins, the kind and solid Sam and Clare Parsons rent a summer house in the Pennsylvania countryside, beside a right-angled creek. Having sheltered a succession of tragic families, the house seems haunted by "a great ousting power": even the sensible Parsonses are finally forced to leave. The physical atmosphere of the story is tropical and steamy. Hot, damp, lush, breeding nature always threatens to overwhelm the house's inhabitants. Sam first describes to Clare the house he wants to rent as a nature lover's ideal, "as rich in birds and animals as a Breughel painting." "Clare laughed. 'A Breughel painting! . . . this is where you feel the multitudes, the creeping and running, the anthills and wasp nests, the earth breeding at every pore, there's a sort of horror in fertility and rioting insanity in the hot season. I love it.'" The sinister implications of the Breughel allusion suggest a contradiction within Clare's confident affirmation.

And the other side of what Clare loves is evident in the attitude of another woman, a guest from the city, who complains "'I hate it here. . . . I might tread on a mouse. . . . Why is it artists like to live in primitive conditions, with a john a hundred yards away, so that you can step on a snake going to it; or some bull get you or man rape you; remote from life . . . in a mice-eaten weasel-bitten shack with disgusting little vines that work themselves around your finger while you're reading a book on the back step. . . . There are snakes in the water; watersnakes. Oh, I know I shall get pregnant here; the place is alive,' she shuddered."

The vision of the narrative balances somewhere between those of the two women. In spite of Clare's stated pleasure in this teeming natural world, the house is haunted by the ghosts of disasters; all who have lived there have come to grief. The original occupants of the house were a couple with a daughter who had been jilted in love and borne a baby who died; her sexual and maternal frustrations drove her to insanity. Her protective parents allowed her to nurse her sorrows and frustrations, until her grief turned one day to rage against her mother and father, whom she tried to murder with an axe. Caught by the neighbor, she is now in a madhouse. "She's not like a woman," he explains, "she's like a sick animal or a baby, worse; and she doesn't know who she is."

Unfortunately, however, she is like a woman.

The next family to occupy the house is more seemingly normal, but Laban and Ruth Davies and their
spoiled son Frankie are in fact equally sad specimens.
Laban is a self-pitying drunkard, and Ruth, who "had
been a strong girl, brought up in jolly health, a success in a small town" was now "overworked, uneasy
and cranky: she saw dangers all around them." She
has both her husband and her son to tend; the urge
for mothering thwarted in the mad girl is equally
destructive when fulfilled. As Laban explains about
Ruth, "what she's gone through for us has turned her
from a normal woman into a sort of lunatic, part
prison warder and part village sibyl."

This melodrama is but the hidden life of ordinary men and women. The breeding of the physical
world seeks to oust man; within the human heart, violent passions wreak havoc. This vision of destructiveness is as dark as in Stead's earliest *Tales*, but the
narrative tone and style of its expression has
modulated. Clare, Stead's spokesman in this story,
expresses a delight in the irrational; a quieter grotesque vision that evokes gothic presences more
mysterious than violently threatening. This poised
ambivalence is evinced in Stead's description of
Clare's sensations as she and Sam sleep in this haunted
house: "She heard Sam breathing faintly in sleep.
The living sleeping night was all around, close, form-
less, rich and suffocating as a mother's breast. On the
black breast of night she fell asleep too. The foot-
steps passed her again; she did not hear them; the
bridge gave warning; they slept. The faceless haunter
of the stone house moved slightly through the open
attic door and down the closed stairs; with the
strength of water behind glass, without shape and
ready to pour through, it mixed with the moonlight
at the locked glass door, mixing as blood with water,
smoking, turning. But there was peace in the bedroom; until the skunks came for the liver laid out at

the back door, when, at the musky stench, there was a great rain of mice and Clare awoke, listening, delighted. 'There you are, friends, animals, children,' she thought; and heard many small réal footfalls, squeaks and movements."

Mother nature, like other Stead parents, threatens to be suffocating and unsafe; she is neither reliable nor nurturing—but she *is* fertile, teeming, breeding. Stead finds it necessary neither to deny nor to romanticize the dark side of experience. She continues to focus clearly on what is destructive in nature and human nature; but this delight in the variety of life and richness of language feeds her continuing creativity and is the essence of her genius. Her late work achieves an ironic detachment, a narrative perspective like that of Chaucer's Troilus, observing the human comedy from a great distance, but still able to enjoy even its darkest activity. While her scornful satire continues its hard judgments of human character, there is some more accepting wisdom in the continued devotion of her detailed observations of the most perverse of personalities and the smallest particulars of the natural world. "Whatever moves and has life fascinates her," writes Australian critic Dorothy Green.[61] In this late fiction, Stead's early excesses of style and feeling are more controlled; the compassion and judgment, humor and pain, delight and despair that play through her work have found resolution in a quieter, more accepting voice and vision.

Miss Herbert (*The Suburban Wife*) (1976)

In 1976, Stead published a new novel. Although marketed as a story about a "liberated" woman, *Miss Herbert* (*The Suburban Wife*) presents a heroine who belongs to another class of characters: the long

line of Stead's egotists. Eleanor Herbert's life never
matches her illusions, but she never sees the difference. Like Sam Pollit, Eleanor is sustained by a blind
optimism growing out of self-delusion. But also like
Sam, in spite of the narcissism Stead so ruthlessly exposes, Eleanor is energetic and resourceful, and
even, somehow, likable.

The balanced but unsparing analysis of characters who are far from admirable is Stead's trademark.
Miss Herbert is fairly benign by Stead standards: she
does not cripple others, as do the worst of Stead's tyrants. In fact, other figures in this novel have only a
shadowy existence, due partly to a failure of Stead's
technique, but partly to the limitations of the central
character. The narrative is presented from Eleanor's
perspective: because she sees no one more clearly
than she understands herself, none of the others
materialize very fully. Eleanor is supposed to be a
young, athletic English beauty who takes her experience of men and life before she settles into a dull
marriage in a poor suburb of London, where she
manages a boardinghouse and raises two children
with strict frugality. When her husband leaves her,
she sturdily carries on, trying to pursue her rather
dubious literary ambitions working on the squalid
fringes of the publishing industry.

None of this exists for the reader with sustained
vividness. Eleanor's children are only intermittently
important; the men who appear and disappear in her
life—with the possible exception of her snobbish,
mean-minded husband Henry—are no more than
fleeting caricatures. What is clearest to us is not Miss
Herbert's life, but her delusions about it; not her
marriage and divorce, but the willful blindness
through which she refuses to see them as they are.
Eleanor confuses sensuality with sexuality; she pa-
rades naked in her room or poses in the nude for an
old man, but is afraid of any emotional involvement.

While she has worked as a maid, traveled to Paris, slept with many men, worked hard to earn money, none of her experiences touch her deeply. Her mental language is inadequate to her experience. She feels her life with no more depth of complexity than the clichés in which she thinks and writes. With resilient energy and good cheer, Eleanor Herbert creates fictions that have little to do with the reality of her experience; when one fades, she is left to construct another. Every distorted observation she makes shows that she is what Stead conceives most people to be— an isolated monad, blinded by her self-involvement, rather foolish, rather lonely, but part of a world where no one is much better.

There is an undeniable vitality to the worst of Stead's characters, and especially to the worst of them. In more affable, demonstrative people she sees the same disguised manipulativeness she dissects in her tyrannical egotists. Most of her characters, like Miss Herbert, chase illusions and never know themselves. In an age of devotion to the quest for self-fulfillment, Christina Stead's deepest wisdom is a satiric vigilance over the tyrannies of egotism. She is consistently at her best in only a few works; *Miss Herbert* is not one of them, yet it shows in flashes some of that singular Stead genius.

5

The Optimism of Creation

Stead's best characters are her worst. Critics praise her "grasp of motivation and compulsion."[1] "Stead appeals through the oddness of her characters and the relentless, uniquely resourceful dialogue through which she creates them," writes reviewer Charles T. Samuels.[2] The banker Jules Bertillon in *House of All Nations*, and Nellie Cotter in *Dark Places of the Heart*, like Sam and Henny Pollit are obsessive talkers whose rhetoric is capable of creating a world, and of destroying the entranced subjects who fall victim to it. A disproportionate share of Stead's emotional tyrants are professed and vocal socialists. Reviewer Frederick Gardner guesses that "the recognition to which she leads left-wingers, far from comforting, is appalling. With few exceptions, the American radicals she presents are hypocritical and incestuous, honey-talkers, good livers, enlightened parents of darkly disturbed children."[3] Nellie, the quarreling couple of *I'm Dying Laughing*, the self-pitying Laban Davies of "The Rightangled Creek," and even Jonathan Crow of *For Love Alone*, are like Sam Pollit; their high-flown humanitarian rhetoric always cloaks self-serving egotism.

The prototype of this character is, of course, Sam Pollit—an eloquent, creative, narcissistic, manipulative "charmer who deceives"; his strengths and limitations of character shape all of Stead's work. While she remains fascinated by the type and continually recreates it (and the persistence of her attack is one with the persistence of its attraction for her)—her opposition to it is a crucial aspect of her own style of eloquence. What fascinates Stead more than the substance of these word-magicians' socialist theory is the ironic discrepancy between their altruistic ideas and their domineering, self-aggrandizing behavior. The narrative voice in which Stead so incisively unmasks their sham is more like Henny Pollit's than like Sam's. Unlike the eloquent obsessive charmers she portrays, Stead shuns all rhetorics of abstraction. Never subsuming particular realities into simple generalizations, Stead remains fastened to the concrete truths of immediate individual experience and perception. Hers is a passionate intelligence. Her analyses are intellectually powerful, but she always embodies her larger perceptions in immediate sensual forms. Ideas are created in her fiction as lived experience. Poverty, for example, is never a political concept, but is felt as it determines the daily experience and shapes the inner beings of those men and women who are poor. Stead refuses to oppose the individual and the social, the specific and the universal; neither exists apart from the other.

Her style manifests the essentially political premise of the reciprocal interconnection of personal and social structures of experience. The moral authority of Stead's narrative voice rests not in didactic pronouncements, but in particular observations, concrete dramatization and ironic juxtaposition by which she establishes her larger points without resorting to reductive assertion. In her devotion to detailed particularity, she presents individuals with the full integrity others are perpetually trying to deny them. The complex nature of that individuality is affirmed in the grotesque imagery of her Domestic Gothic style, whose metaphors draw on inner and outer experi-

ence, as if they were of the same realm, uniting inner
fantasies and feelings with outer physical and social
objects. Stead captures, both for individuals and for
social groups, a sense of multilayered interrelation-
ships. Characters, families, events are portrayed as
dynamic, living processes, neither existing nor to be
understood within static conceptual categories. This
generates the "inclusiveness and open-mindedness in
her novels, and [the] exploratory attitude towards
character" that Australian critic Terry Sturm notes.[4]

In this dynamic conception of social life, and of
characters as deeply determined by personal fantasy,
which itself manifests the shapes of cultural structures, Stead unites the insights of Freud and Marx.
But she is less deterministic than either of them.
Neither personal history nor material conditions are
fully defining; she sees the possibility of growth and
creativity beyond what is determined by the interplay
of forces that shape an individual. Nor is Stead a revolutionary. Her belief in change concentrates more on
the inner world than the outer. If they are not separ-
able, still it is change of vision on which she focuses,
rather than change of material conditions. Stead
does not make the tragic egotism she sees at the heart
of human nature seem exclusively the product of a
particular capitalist, patriarchal social system, although she subtly shows how the forms in which it
manifests itself are shaped by that system. Nevertheless, there is no sense in Stead's work that this essential fact of human nature would be eradicated by a
different form of social organization.

Speaking of the Leftist circle of which she and
William Blake were part in New York in the 1940s,
she says, "My entire entourage was active politically,
[but I myself] am not a political person. If I act, it is
in another direction."[5] What we see change or fail to
change in her novels, is characters' capacity to see: to
understand themselves and their world differently.

She defines the essential process of growth as breaking free of the language systems that articulate the
visions of others—parents, lovers, employers, govern-
ments—to create one of one's own, truer to one's
needs and desires. Her quintessential hero, if she has
a hero at all, is the artist. While she dissects with
painful accuracy the forces that militate against it,
change of vision is, sometimes, possible in her fiction,
and is always manifest by the fiction itself. In this resides her faith in the resilience and vitality of the
human spirit.

Objective, ruthless, wholly unsentimental[6] in
her analysis of the human condition, Stead is not
despairing; her zest for observation and delight in
variety animates her fiction. Like a Bosch painting,
her canvas teems with life. Her range of interests is as
wide as her travels—inner and outer. The original sin
at the heart of her universe is the violation of
individual integrity; the miracle of her craft, that she
devotes the respect of detailed perception to the
creation of just those individuals who are most guilty
of that violation. With the respect for individuality
her characters rarely show to each other, Stead
accepts a great variety of human idiosyncracy—and
delights in it. "The creation of something out of
nothing is the most primitive of human passions and
the most optimistic" she writes.[7] This optimism mitigates the force of her dark vision of human nature.
The energetic invention of her endlessly fertile imagination tempers itself with an increasingly calm,
ironic detachment to fulfil the genius of the author
of one of English literature's most original masterpieces, *The Man Who Loved Children.*

Interview with Christina Stead

by
Joan Lidoff

Surbiton, England. June, 1973

Q: What are you doing now?

CS: For five years—I had a book finished and my husband
died and I started to revise it. I slaved at it and it became something else. It was turning into another
book. So I dropped it. I think I was changing, becoming someone else. Well, so I dropped it about three
months ago and I've been much happier since, I must
say. I'm just waiting now. I always have a few projects
going and I'm waiting for one to come out. What I
really want to do is to take one and write it right off, to
clear out all the past. I've done twelve books, more,
twelve published up to now.

There's one that's coming out this year. It's a little
one I wrote when we were in Switzerland. It's not
about us. It's about the people in the hotel, more or
less, mostly the English in Switzerland. It was hard for
them. They were in exile. At the same time England
wasn't in the kind of political state they approved of.
But they were human beings and it's a human little
story. It's no great shakes. A nice little story. I called it
Mrs. Trollope and Madam Blaise, but my English edi-
tors thought that wasn't a good title. We haven't yet
decided on a title, but that's what it's about. [This will
be *The Little Hotel.*] It's about an Englishwoman
called Mrs. Trollope who's living with her lover—who
could marry her, but won't acknowledge her for some

mysterious reason. There's no real reason, except his old mother and some terrible old sisters he has. Madame Blaise is a Swiss woman, who's in terrible difficulty with her husband. It may be all her own fault, but she's in difficulty. And there's a lot of other characters as well. It's nothing festive. Poverty, and that sort of thing.

Q: You've published some short stories from this, haven't you?

CS: Yes, "The Woman in the Bed," and there was one called "The Hotel-Keeper's Story."

Q: What was the novel that you dropped?

CS: That was a big novel, it really was. It was full of passion. But this rewriting and rewriting. After it started to turn into something else, and something else quite dull—it got me in the end. I dropped it. It was all about the passion of—I use passion in almost the religious sense—of two people, two Americans, New Yorkers, in the thirties. They are doing well, but they suffered all the troubles of the thirties. They were politically minded. They went to Hollywood. They came to Europe to avoid the McCarthy trouble. Of course they were deeply involved. And then, they lived around Europe, oh, in a wild and exciting extravagant Hollywood style. But there was nothing to support it. At the same time they wanted to be on the side of the angels, good Communists, good people, and also to be very rich. Well, of course . . . they came to a bad end. They suffered too much. They all lose faith and hope, except for their friends.

I may, will, go back to it again. In fact, I must do. But I want to write something right off. Graceful, with energy, you know. You came at a bad time. I read it to Bill. His eyes had gone. And he liked it. Well, of course his memory was perfect for detail. He remembered all of that. But people don't remember all that, you know. The thirties was a hundred years ago. So I started to go to work and explain it all to people. And it got me down. I don't want to write like that, filling in all kinds of details. These reference books kill me.

Q: What became of that couple?

CS: Well, I don't want to say at the moment. It'll be in the book if I ever do the book. Something bad happened. Two different things. Very bad. They did break up. She did break down. Though who could stand it? It's not their fault.

Q: They were real people?

CS: Oh yes, sure. And that's part of the trouble. I don't suppose now anyone would recognize them. But people would have. Many examples, thousands of course, from America—with their great passion for inquisitions. They're having one now. [Watergate]. They've got an inquisition now.

Q: This novel is *I'm Dying Laughing?*

CS: Yes, that's right. [And the couple was Stead and Blake's close friends, Ruth McKinney and Richard Bransten.]

Q: Were you ever very active politically?

CS: Not really, but my entire entourage was active politically. I'm not a political person, but it's only . . . I don't like to state things politically. But it's wrong of me, because I respect all of that. But if it doesn't come from me, then I don't like it. I know it's wrong. I've learned a lot from all of them. Marvelous people. The greatest patriots. I knew them and respected them. They were my friends. But I myself am not such a person. If I act, it's in another direction.

It may be that when I was a child, which may be the real reason, my father wanted me to be a scientist. He was, you see. And luckily he didn't give me a science name. He gave all the boys science names: Darwin, Huxley, David Starr Jordan. He didn't stick me with a science name. But he wanted me to be a scientist. When I was very young, I used to get dragged to these terrible meetings, weekly or monthly meetings, of scientists, very honorable men and women, of course. But what repelled me, it's shameful of me, but it's true, is the women used to dress very plain: long plain skirts, hair way back, in a bun, and I couldn't

stand it. Not for me! And as for the men, they were jawing all the time and I was too young to care what they
were jawing. As I was the daughter of a *very great orator* I had enough of it already.

Q: So you decided not to be a scientist?

CS: I did quite well in science in school without thinking
      about it. That's what I meant by an underweave. You
      get into it anyway. I got in it to impress my father. I
      didn't mind the classification. I was used to it. I was
      used to calling things by their Latin names very often
      because in Australia there aren't always common
      names for flowers. Not like here. Rose, violet, all those
      things. Wildflowers. But there's nothing like that in
      Australia. It wasn't that. I enjoyed it. But the idea of
      going through my life looking at cells—I couldn't. I
      couldn't.

Q: When did you decide you were a writer?

CS: I never decided I was a writer. I'm not a writer.

Q: You just write?

CS: Yes, that's right. But this thing, professionalism, I
      don't like that. I don't associate with writers. Not that
      I don't like them, but what can you learn from each
      other? I learn from human beings. Or even a cat, a
      hedgehog. But what can you learn from each other?
              They're nice people. I was associated with them in
      New York and at the Paris thing, of course, but that
      was so huge it was anonymous. And in New York it was
      political.

Q: Who were these people?

CS: Oh, everybody, everybody who wasn't a Tory. All well-
      known writers. Americans. I was just an outsider.
      They usen't to answer my questions. They'd just listen
      to me. And I'm not so British as all that. They'd just
      listen. There'd be a silence. Of course I gave up
      speaking.
              Oh, I can tell you—people—Albert Maltz . . . they
      were names in those days. He was one of the Holly-
      wood Ten. Went to jail. Oh it was a terrific thing in

those days. Like being from Naples in an eruption of
Vesuvius. They had lots of them. Lots of crises in the
States in those days. But as for going to pieces recon-
stituting not only the events of those days but the passions involved . . . it was like an eruption . . . it's too
much for me. It's not my nature, not my style. Anyhow, I don't want to go back on that.

Q: You wrote a lot in the States?

CS: Oh yes. I wrote *The Man Who Loved Children* in the
States. It's got a States setting.

Q: Did you live in Washington, D.C.?

CS: Bill was always good to me this way, he was enthusias-
tic. When I decided to transfer the setting to America,
we stayed in Washington and Baltimore, and got all
the details. I simply tranferred where I talk about the
salinity of the Chesapeake [Bay]. Sydney Harbor's a
reach of the sea whereas the Chesapeake is not, [and so
is of a] greater salinity. I didn't mind, because the
physical things I understood perfectly. I was brought
up in a family of biologists. I knew what was what. I
knew what to do.

Q: When you wrote it, did you draw on your childhood?

CS: Oh, of course. Yes, of course. Charming. But it's odd
how many people it appeals to. It makes one wonder
about people's childhoods. . . . Oddly enough, it shows
the magnanimity of men. You'd be surprised at the
number of kind, good splendid men who say, "It worries me so much. Am I like that?" You can see they're
not. The others wouldn't worry of course. I never expected that book—I wrote it to get it off my chest.
Still it just shows you. The modern family. Peculiar
childhood. . . . And yet it is a family life. Yes, it is.
The children aren't marytrs. In spite of the awful
things like the fish throwing. The children aren't
martyrs, are they?
        Last week at dinner I met a teacher from the Uni-
ted States. He said, "When I taught *The Man Who
Loved Children*, two of my women students said to
me, 'I can't read it. Henny is such a bad mother.'" And

you know my father would have said that. He would
have said, "Books shouldn't be about bad subjects."
That's just what my father would say, "Shouldn't write
about a bad woman."

Q: What would your father say about Sam?

CS: Well, he never knew about Sam. The family are very
friendly to me on the subject. It's only very lately I've
come to think how good they are. The family. They
were so friendly about it. But they are.

When I was about fifteen, I thought there was
only one true writer in the world who told the truth
about families, and that was Strindberg. I read many
stories, of course, about good fathers and mothers and
little girls running to their mother's laps, and I
thought it was all lies, all nonsense, like we have commercials now on TV. I thought they were commercials, some kind of story they sold people.

Q: Do you think that families are by nature destructive?

CS: Ah, you're talking about this fellow Laing, who treats
the unbalanced and unhappy, and who thinks this
mental imbalance comes from the family. There's a
certain amount of truth in it, of course. But what
about social relationships? A man in a factory doing
the same job for twenty years, who doesn't want to be,
or who hates his boss.

Yes, certainly family relationships have some effect. But there's one thing that I've learned, and that
is, children grow up anyway. You see some of them,
they've been horribly spoiled, but they grow up anyway, and they're really quite all right. They manage to
survive parental care. Supercare. Probably some are
twisted. But I would say on the whole people are
pretty hard to twist. Because of the social setting. Of
the schools. School has immense influence on children. It's the first valuable break from the family. At
first there may be a crisis in some children's lives because a difference in mores obtains. I think on the
whole it's a very healthy thing for children. A standard by which to judge the family. It's the first way
in which they grow up. And so they're able to stand

family shocks. And of course school shocks too. Then comes the playground. Then the gang. Then they've got four sets of mores. This is when you grow up.

Q: Did you ever have a gang in school?

CS: No, I was a loner. I wasn't sour or blue or anything, but I was a loner. Some good girls were allowed out gardening. It wasn't a gang really, just three or four kids out there at a time, not much. But there were the children at home, there was this gang. So I wasn't one of these morbid, poetic, melancholy creatures. . . .

Q: Are there any writers who were your models?

CS: I don't have any conscious model at all. In fact, I didn't intend . . . I never thought of being a writer. Although all my teachers from the word "Go" figured that I was a writer. But I never thought about it as a profession. My father was a scientist and we all had to get jobs as quickly as possible, because there were too many of us, you know. So he didn't even want me to finish high school, but he wanted me to go on a newspaper. But I had an instinctive repulsion for journalism. I don't envy them their profession. I think it's most exhausting. Here I can sit and if I don't like a thing I can throw it away and do it next week. They can't. They've got to turn it in by seven tonight or four tomorrow morning. Most exhausting profession in the world. I'd hate to be a journalist.

Anyhow, my father proposed it when I was fourteen. I suppose he was having money troubles. I was the oldest. He had six others, so that's the money troubles in question. And he had a friend who was very devoted to him, he suggested that I should become a journalist because I had this facility—I could write. That was perfectly obvious. I refused. I said, "No, I won't. I don't know enough." Even then scared stiff of a journalist. So, all right, he was kind enough to let me go on and finish high school. And then I got a scholarship to do science at the University, and to a business college, and to a teacher's college. Well, the best offer, since I didn't want to become a scientist, was the teacher's college. So I went there. It was financial. I didn't intend to do that. But I had no thought of being defeated or anything. And at home they didn't give two hoots what I did as long as I earned something.

I didn't mind that. It's good for one, that they don't bother about you. Don't build you up into something you're not before you are. That's what I dislike about certain parts of education in America, and it's coming here, and also Australia, of course. That they build little tiny kids up into artists, when what have they done? A few chalk strokes on paper. And they glue it up on the wall. All the guests have got to goggle at it. What becomes of the child? That's not the way you begin life. It's a mistake. What do they turn out in the end? Those kids have been prodded and puffed. It turns out to be nothing. Nothing. It's much better for a child to be treated normally, like a normal person. I knew a writer whose kid wrote some stuff and it had to be printed—properly bound, properly printed, because Daddy too was a writer and the child would feel frustrated or something Freudian. So I bet the child has never written a good line. That's not the way you write. You have to accumulate experience and be a *mensch*, be something. And then if, *Gott sei dank*, or even *Hitler sei dank*, as they used to say, if at the age of fourteen or fifteen the impulse comes, then good, that's natural.

That's really Madison Avenue, that pushing and prodding a child. It's because of parental vanity. Not that it matters, I think. A true artist could probably survive even that. What I think now is against all that. But I do think almost everybody has a bit of artist in him. Whatever it may be, a writer, painter, dancer, whatever it may be. There's nothing wrong with that. Doing it as a class, as a community. I'm talking about pushing the individual because there may be gold in there. That's the real object. Be a big artist, sell hundreds, thousands. Make money. That's really what's behind it. And another fatal idea that belongs to the bourgeoisie, that there's something sacred inside which if you dig out it will make you an original. And again it's a silly idea. There's nothing inside. It must be developed first. Well, there's something in-

side, but what? It's an amoeba, or something like that.
It's got to be developed. But I do think that art is good
for people and everybody can do something. I don't
mean art, I mean the creative impulse. It's an instinct.
A heredity. Birds have it. They build nests.

Q: You taught young children for a few years in Aus-
     tralia. Why didn't you like teaching?

CS: It was quite a nervous strain. It wasn't the children.
     There were a lot of children at home. I didn't mind
     that. But, your time is not your own. You've got to pre-
     pare things. I was brought up to be a modern teacher,
     progressive type. I spent two or three years in a
     teacher's college. Psychological testing and stuff. Four
     years I had of it altogether. Oh, you've got to prepare
     things. And the kids don't know at all anything about
     that. They're just little shrimps. They don't care what
     you prepare. They're just erupting. I didn't have the
     nervous strength. I have plenty of nervous strength
     for books. But all those little shrimps, no. Then I
     couldn't do it. They put me on to what I was really
     more suited for, variant children, feebleminded. Two
     of them were little dears. They were utterly sweet.
     They were deaf and dumb through syphilitic parents.
     What could we do with them? There were all kinds.
     Very interesting personalities. Because they weren't
     overlaid with all the nonsense, the playground non-
     sense, that the other little shrimps were, jumping up
     and down all the time. Well, mediocrity, to tell the
     truth, except for two or three. They weren't mediocre,
     they were exceptional. Unusual. How they responded
     to their situation, which they understood, however
     feeble they were. They were accepted as eccentric,
     feebleminded, and that sort of thing, but they knew it.
         One poor boy—He was fourteen years old, and he
     was fairly well groomed. And he used to work so hard,
     like the clerk in Russian literature. He'd say, "I know
     I'm no good at it, but . . ." and he meant it. He wasn't
     bribing. There was a very feebleminded girl. They call
     it something else, but it's the same thing. Very, very
     low. Her parents dressed her beautifully. She came to

school beautifully dressed. And she was very gentle and sweet looking. She was like something from a German opera, one of those demoiselles. You wouldn't have known she was feebleminded unless you spoke to her. She'd sit there quietly and do absolutely nothing. Absolutely pure and sweet, except no brain at all. Her father used to come for her. He came to see me in the teacher's room and asked me if there was any hope for her. He was crying. It was terrible. Still is terrible. I had to say there wasn't. Because there wasn't. They just had to look after this poor child to see that she didn't get into any accident. Because she was a pretty, attractive girl. That sort of thing. I found it in the end hard to take. Because you won't get anywhere. Later on in biochemistry they will find some answer to those things. But there was no answer then.

Then there was that wild boy. Mad. He really was. I used to like him rather. I tried the tricks on him that you're taught. The plant. I brought a plant to the classroom. "You look after it for me on the weekend, Fritz." He did. He brought it back. Then they told me he'd kept it over the weekend in the washroom. Because he didn't dare take it home. He had two crazy parents. That sort of thing. But it didn't stop him from his outbursts. Because he couldn't help it. It was something biological. I knew that too. I knew quite well that all this nonsense about plants wouldn't help him.

Then there was another boy. He was very feeble-minded. Had no sense at all, but he could draw. He'd suddenly dash out of his seat and seize the chalk. For an instant, forty seconds, he'd draw a picture on the blackboard. And it was very good. It was a flash, then it would die. Rather like the creative talent, you see. It's just a spark, of real creation. It's all he had. And his brain would die, altogether. Interesting. He was a perfect blob, except he had that wonderful thing. Well, I don't know how good the pictures were, but for him, they were wonderful.

No, I just walked out. I wasn't suited to teaching. Other people do. They devote their lives to these chil-

dren and very noble of them. But I couldn't. Didn't
want to.

Q: When did you decide that you were going to leave
      Australia?

CS: A friend of mine, well, two friends of mine, were going
      to University. We have there traveling scholarships,
      which are grants to study abroad at an English univer-
      sity, and two of them competed for the traveling
      scholarship. One was a colleague of mine at Teacher's
      College. She had various misfortunes. She had no
      money, but she was better than he was. But she hadn't
      been able to matriculate, to pass the entrance exams.
      She had come up from Teacher's College, and because
      of this detail, though she was better than he was, she
      didn't get it. So then I said to myself, "I'm giving my-
      self a traveling scholarship." (Just a phrase. I wasn't in
      the running, of course. I wasn't at the University.) I
      was very keen, from the time I read Lewes, the hus-
      band of George Eliot. He wrote a very fascinating biog-
      raphy of Goethe. It's very romantic. Two volumes. A
      huge thing. Very fascinating. And I was very keen on
      going, like Goethe, to one of those German universi-
      ties. I had the impression that they were howling with
      philosophical arguments, a whole life. But since I
      knew French I thought I'd go to the Sorbonne. I had
      no idea how I was going to get there. Stupid ideas you
      have, make you do something. So I stayed. I got a job
      in industry. First I worked for a well-known architect,
      who was really very kind to me, considering my ineffi-
      ciency. I was terrible. But I had done all the work at
      the night school. They were rather nice to me. Then I
      got a job in a big hat firm, where they had an office,
      and a secretary's office. That was me. And showrooms.
      They made the hats upstairs—wool and felt hoods and
      straw hats; the hoods were imported from England. It
      was sent here, they dyed it there. They were really
      making something. They knew all about it.

Q: And it took you five years to save the money?

CS: I had to pay to live at home. My family couldn't get
      along. Although it was a big family. I was the eldest.

The other poor souls hadn't got up to it. Not that I gave so much. I was saving it for my trip abroad. But I did have to buy clothing, and a season ticket for the boat. We always lived round the harbor at that time. I took the ferry to Circular Pier at Central Wharf. And I used to walk, a long walk, up to the hat factory.

Q: What became of your brothers and sisters?

CS: They're all there, in Australia. My eldest brother, who's five years younger than I am, . . . My sister, much younger than I am . . . Next brother . . . engineers. The younger sister went in for typing, shorthand. She didn't like it. Wanted to be a hairdresser, but of course it was infra dig to my father. Father wouldn't hear of it. She had a real gift for it. She could make dresses. All sorts of things. Well, she married. Had children. Plays golf. Has a car. She's a very nice woman, but . . . I hadn't seen her for forty years.

Q: When did you go back?

CS: Ah, the year after Bill died—measure time that way. I don't mean it that way. But the year he died, I felt nervous. And the next year, they wrote and offered me a fellowship in the Creative Arts at Canberra, the National University. They were very good to me there. Very good.

Q: Do you consider yourself Australian?

CS: Oh yes, I am Australian. Of course I'm Australian.

Q: It's been so long.

CS: Yes, but it's extraordinary how it works. It's like someone going back to Texas after being away forty years. You know that smell of the hot earth. That color. Because there's a slight comparison. And the attitude of the people—bold. They're very talented people but they love the outdoors. They don't like complexity. It's unnecessary for them. That's fine. It's like it was in ancient Greece. No compliment to either party.

Q: Were you anxious to leave it when you did?

CS: It wasn't that. It was an intellectual idea. I wasn't anx-
        ious to leave. It's a beautiful place. It's like South
        Africa or something, except for the race problem. Hot
        and dry. A lot of desert. Very hot.

        Then inside we have sort of potpourri. Down the
        East Coast, places of import. Some go to the other
        side, but then, a vast Sahara, clear across the conti-
        nent. It's a Sahara. It's immense. All sand. They're a
        lot of mineral deposits around the edge . . . all the
        fortune hunters. All the digging. It is in fact a Sahara.
        It's very exciting if you come from a country like that.
        You like it. You look back on it . . .

Q: Do you miss Australia?

CS: Haven't missed it. I like anywhere I am. I don't like
        England quite as much as I might, because, of course,
        as soon as I came here I met an American. I didn't be-
        come American, but we kept American company. So
        that I never became English. It's only now that I'm
        alone that I'm meeting really English people.

Q: Bill wrote too, didn't he?

CS: I should say so! He was a tremendous writer! He began
        in Wall Street, as I told you. *Magazine of Wall Street.*
        Not the *Wall Street Journal*, but another one, *The
        Magazine of Wall Street.* He was a financial expert.
        Did all kinds of financial journals. Then he came to
        Europe, in '28 he came to Europe. Became associate
        manager . . . wheat . . . That's where I met him. A
        very big commodities firm in London had so much
        money it was starting a private bank. And one of the
        managers of the firm was our friend, Alf. And he in-
        vited the others to come and do the bank side. And
        they needed a secretary and I became it. Remained a
        life partnership.

Q: How did you get the job?

CS: I had just arrived in England. I had to get a job. You
        should have seen me! But I had got here. And I had to
        find a job. I went to an agency. There was a woman I
        didn't like at all. I couldn't stand her looks. She said,
        "I have a job for you. They'll like you." I was mad, not

taking it. I went all over town, to all kinds of other agencies. When I heard the salaries they were getting, not much. So I thought, "Well, I'll try there." I could easily have missed it. And then, as soon as they saw me . . . I must have looked like a dead duck. But I think the clincher was—Bill told me years afterwards—that I looked so shy and at the same time serious. I was carrying a book of Bertrand Russell. And I think that got him. So he engaged me. And, in fact, for life. And I thought he looked nice too. Very nice. I thought he looked marvelous. So pure. What girls think! But I wasn't wrong, really.

Q: There was a long time when it seemed you stopped writing—fourteen years.

CS: No. You see, Bill wanted to travel, so we traveled all around the place, all over Europe: Holland, Italy, Switzerland, France, even Spain. I wrote *The House of All Nations* in Spain. And we lived in different places. In a hotel room. Generally we ate in, or we'd go out to eat or Bill would bring me something. I always had this typewriter, been with me all my adult life, and I wrote everything on it. It's actually my home. But it wasn't really very productive. Bill did his best for me. He'd go out and do the shopping. I think I let him down. He liked living abroad. He liked living this way. He didn't want a home. Neither did I. We always said—I said, "You're my home." He said, "You're my home." And we really felt that. We didn't want a house and garden and refrigerator. We really didn't. And I still don't really. But we were always in a different country, and typing in the hotel bedroom. I got used to it. We always had a nice lot of windows. I think that . . . On the other hand if I'd always lived in one setting and my books turned out the same . . . Well, who knows? I'm not complaining. It was his life. And if he wanted to live that way, I wanted to live that way. Any way he wanted to live. Until the time came when I said, "I'm losing my English. I want to go back to England." And he said, "Well, you've done what I've wanted to do, so now I'll do this."

He really wanted to go to Australia. A bit difficult, because he was a foreigner, and you needed all
sorts of money, and you had to give them a monetary
guarantee also. He really wanted to go. At the end he
said, "I want to go to Australia. I feel I have a family,
my family; I've got at least 999 members." He certainly
had family. And they would have been very nice to
him; they were very keen on Bill. They were good to
me. However, it was too late.

Q: When did you get married?

CS: Oh, a long time ago. Long, long ago. It was just on forty
years that we had been together. Just within a few
weeks.

Q: You were talking about writing *House of All Nations*.

CS: Yes. After a certain time when I was writing the *House
of All Nations*, I noticed it was turning into French.
And there's a whole passage which would be just the
same in French. . . . I wrote *House of All Nations*
straight off. Well, it shows it. In some parts it looks
just like a precis or something. But that's what I did.
Because sometimes I feel a certain amount of stodginess in writing away solemnly. I feel you have to throw
it off.

Q: You have said that you wrote *The Salzburg Tales* that
way too.

CS: Oh, I wrote that very fast. But there was no stodginess
in that. That just happened to come right. It happens
sometimes. I wrote *Letty Fox: Her Luck* that way too.
After I wrote *For Love Alone*, I thought to myself,
"Well, I'm going to write about quite a different kind
of girl, who's wide awake, or apparently so. Of course,
nobody's wide awake in sex. You always find a person
who gets you somehow. But she was a New York girl I
knew very well. And . . . naturally, the things that I
say she wrote, *I* wrote; she wasn't a writer. I just put
that in. But she went to City College, or some such
place. The groups weren't quite like they are now. Because it was the thirties. But they were very political
in New York City of course. City College especially. I

knew her very well. And she ran into all these . . . she also had her troubles. It can't be helped. It wasn't all from that character. It was partly from my aunt and cousins back in Australia. But the girl was New York City. They liked it, I must say. They liked it in New York City. They recognized it.

But after I'd written *For Love Alone*, which is gloomy and serious, I thought, I must write about another kind of girl. And I also thought, instead of being bogged down in all this stuff, letters and that kind of thing, I must write straight off. I did write it straight off, without any pause whatsoever. That's why it's so bad in some places. But never mind. 'Cause one really shouldn't do that. But I did do it. And I also wrote *House of All Nations* straight off. Didn't stop.

Q: Do you usually revise a lot?

CS: Yes. I should have revised *House of All Nations* too. But when it started to come out again, I just couldn't be bothered. It's a terrible thing. When you go back to a work that was written twenty years, thirty years before, it's not you any more. It's someone else.

For Love Alone—I must explain that that wasn't my title. I'm always embarrassed about that title. . . . I'm also embarrassed by *Dark Places of the Heart*, and that was not my title either. The publishers dreamed up that one. Never mind. They had my title, *Cotter's England*, and they said "It'll never do in the States." I don't know why. But then, alright, I chose another title, which was relevant and they said a book was coming out three months before mine with a very similar title. So they sent me a telegram that some girl in the office had suggested *Dark Places of the Heart*. It's really like some girl's romance. But never mind. Also, *For Love Alone* was another accident.

Q: What was your title for that?

CS: I've forgotten. Something to do with love letters. There actually was a book at that time called *Love Letters*. But that wasn't my exact title. But a friend of mine, a very dear fellow, friend of Bill and me, asked if he could do the jacket. So we were very pleased. He

was that kind of artist and he did a quite nice jacket of
a girl naked down to the waist, leaning out—not exactly the Damoiselle from Heaven, but there was a
suggestion of stars behind her. And he lettered in
"For Love Alone" which was . . . Oh, I know where he
got it. On the preface, on the frontispiece, there was a
quote from a calypso that was going around at that
time about King Edward VIII, and Mrs. Simpson. It
was a calypso I saw in New York City. There was the
king sitting on his throne with "How to be a good
king" in large letters, you'll see it way in the back. And
then Mrs. Simpson, who's a chorus girl, dressed as a
ballet girl, waltzed across the stage and knocked it
over and then they sang the song, "Twas for love, love
alone, King Edward left his throne." I had this calypso
in the beginning and that's where he got the idea. He
thought it was the title. Alright. Never mind. So I
couldn't tell him it was the wrong title. I just couldn't.
Cause, we were very fond of him. So it went in.

Q: Was *The Salzburg Tales* the first book you wrote?

CS: No, *Seven Poor Men of Sydney* was the first, but, I
       didn't actually offer it to anybody. But Bill did. We
       were in Paris and he took it to Sylvia Beach. She was a
       woman whose father was a Protestant minister in
       Paris. They were American; she was brought up in
       Paris and ran a bookstore called *Shakespeare & Co.* It
       became famous because she introduced to letters
       James Joyce and a few other people. Good quality,
       high quality. So Bill, without my telling it, without
       telling me, took it to Sylvia Beach. "Yes, it's good" she
       said, and showed it to various people. I didn't offer it
       to anybody. It reached a very enterprising publisher
       called Peter Davies. He was the godson of Barrie, Sir
       James Barrie. Do you know about him?

Q: Peter Pan?

CS: That's right. Now, this publisher was himself Peter
       Pan. He had been the one that Sir James met in Ken-
       sington Gardens. A charming, delightful-looking boy.
       Barrie became fascinated by him. Possible elements
       of . . . I don't . . . all this. . . . He based Peter Pan—

"I won't grow up"—on Peter Davies. A charming man, really charming. He was a very enterprising man. Prejudiced. He liked Australians for some reason. But he came over to Paris with his partner, James Grant. Bill and I were working in the bank then. Rue de la Paix 18. We sometimes went to lunch around the corner to Philippe's which is quite a famous place. But it was just around the corner from us. Once or twice we went there. And Peter Davies—he'd come over, with his partner, James Grant. We went into Philippe's, Bill and I. Right there in the corner it was, my manuscript. I had had book binding in Paris. I had bound the manuscript. But I didn't know that you aren't supposed to bind manuscripts. The editor can't turn it over. And there it was, my bound manuscript, on the table. Well, he said, "I like this one. Can you write another one?" So I said "yes." So I went home and wrote *The Salzburg Tales* right off like that. In the meantime I had been of course to Salzburg. Right off. That's what I want to do now. Write one right off. So nice. That's the real way one should write a book. He said, "I don't want to publish a book of short stories first, they don't sell." So I thought, "No, this is too far, I'm not going along this road." Alright, he published it. Well, it was actually a successful first, it really was. And then he went ahead with it and published the second book which is really the first one. And I wrote it because—I really don't know why—an instinct. I didn't mean to publish it.

Q: You speak of the underweave of the *House of All Nations* being more French than English. What do you mean by the "underweave" of a language?

CS: There's a rhythm of the thing, of the interlocking concepts. In America the basic pattern is different from the English pattern. There're some marvelous American writers of course, I'm not saying that. But the underneath weave of the language is totally different from English. Whereas the underneath weave of English is not too different from French. It's very easy to translate from English to French. The concepts are the same. But the concepts in America are completely

different. For example, the political concepts. They're
bound to affect the weave of a language, the basic
thoughts. And in America, they have a different idea
of how to spend their lives, how to get on in life.
They've got a business idea. Just as with Italian and
Spanish. You can translate. You can put one thing
into another but the underthoughts are not the same.
The Spanish are so emotional. They're marvelous
people. The underweave is different. Just as in German. German's not in the least related to English, although they always teach you that in school. You'd
have to be a philologist to explain all that, but it's absolutely true. The basic weave in English is unshak-
able. Shakespeare formed the language. It's not true
in the States.

Q: I wonder about your projects, things you've set out to
learn. You've mentioned puppets and bookbinding
and languages. Are there others?

CS: Not many. Language is a natural instinct with a writer.
You like to know what people are really saying instead
of translations. For example, a couple of writers that
I know quite well, if I look at a translation into English, it isn't the same. Language has its own perfume,
music. That's the real reason. And then when I'm
with people I don't like to be a blockhead or a
wooden figure. I like to know what they're saying.
And bookbinding. It was Bill who suggested that.
When I first came to Paris, there wasn't much to do,
and some foreign girls were learning bookbinding
and so he sent me to this place, Rue des Grands
Augustins. They were mostly Danish girls. Big, larky,
lively beautiful girls. It was marvelously interesting.
I met one funny Frenchman, quite old. His view was
that the revolution was coming and if he didn't have
something to do with his hands they would execute
him. Shoot him or something. So he was learning
bookbinding. That was all. But no, I'm not a great
. . . I'm not good at a lot of things.

Q: You said you were just rereading *The Puzzleheaded
Girl?*

CS: Yes. Oddly enough, I never reread my work, but I
      was reading last night because, some months ago, I
      met three psychoanalysts by accident. I don't like
      psychoanalysts. They bore me. I think they're wrong.
      They made some contribution, but not the whole
      contribution to all psychological theory which most
      people seem to think. Anyhow, I went to see a man
      who wrote to me, who has become a friend, though
      I've only seen him this once. But his wife is a psycho-
      analyst and they invited two psychoanalytic friends,
      the wife of whom wished to ask me about *The Man
      Who Loved Children*, what else! I wrote to him
      finally, my last letter: "I have written twelve books,"
      you see. I didn't say I get fed up with hearing about
      The Man Who Loved Children, but there *are* other
      books. And I am a psychologist myself in a way, you
      know. So anyhow, he wrote me back (he's a most sen-
      sitive, kindly man) that the other psychoanalyst's
      wife was reading for the second time *The Puzzlehead
      Girl* and she can't grasp it, you see.

Q: Do you think Freudians in particular are wrong, or
      all psychologists in general?

CS: I think the Freudians are old-fashioned, I really do.
      'Cause Freud was old-fashioned.

Q: Are there other psychologists you like better than
      Freud?

CS: Well, there are the classic psychologists. . . . In his
      time, Freud, Jung, and Adler, of course there were
      these three. They all had some distressing theory
      which makes people miserable. But Freud became
      popular simply because of this sex business. Every-
      body was thrilled. Especially those silly women,
      women in Vienna who were thrilled to bits about
      their sex life. His account of psychology—I know he
      has a few good things—really doesn't resemble any-
      body's mental life. Until they're taken over by their
      Freudian. And then they accept it, you know. No, but
      long before that there were all the classic psycholo-
      gists who had plenty to say about normal psychology,
      and frankly, . . . going back to the ancients, the

Greeks and so forth, they're wonderful at psychology.
The playwrights. (You don't have novelists in those
days.) They're wonderful at psychology, *normal* psychology. Freud is really for the abnormal, the unbalanced, but because of his lovely sexual line he was
taken over by everybody. We're not all abnormal.
We're just normal people. But of course he has this
marvelous selling line.

Q: One thing I think brilliant about him is that he did
       pay attention to the importance of fantasies and the
       unconscious.

CS: Yes, this is true. This is the great contribution of
       Freud. Before that people thought dreams showed
       you were crazy or were completely disembodied
       ideas floating through your brain. We'd do better to
       get rid of them. But Freud did instill a respect for
       dreams. In fact he raised them on a pedestal. People
       began to take them as a serious part of their mental
       life. And so they are. And now of course they say
       they're absolutely necessary to mental life. He estab-
       lished that. Quite interesting. Yes, of course he stud-
       ied in France first of all with the school of Nancy,
       which was very interested in all kinds of abnormal
       psychology, and hence bodily psychology. They're
       very interesting. I used to read them a lot, Nancy,
       when I was a girl. I was very interested. Just—not for
       any reason, I was interested. I didn't agree with all
       they said.

Q: One reason I like your writing is that in it I often
       have the feeling that fantasy is very real.

CS: I'm very pleased to hear that. My friend that I was
       with the other night, he was very kind to me. He
       went over all this stuff he thinks I'll be asked in the
       overseas broadcast Thursday. And he thought of it
       from another angle. Then he asked me about a cer-
       tain writer in Australia. "What are you going to say
       about him?" And I said, something, and he said,
       "Well, you could say that he's a fantasy writer and
       you're a quotidian writer." Quotidian, day-to-day. So
       I didn't say anything. I really mustn't say anything.

But I've been brooding over this. Thank you very much. I've been feeling bad about this "quotidian." And I thought I should have asked him—Well, you can't ask a person how many books have you read, can you? What can you do?

Q: The reality of fantasy for you is striking, especially in *For Love Alone*.

CS: The girl in *For Love Alone*, it was me of course, everybody knows that, started off dreaming quite young. When I was about fourteen, I read George Henry Lewes, you know the husband of George Eliot. He wrote a life of Goethe, immense big volumes. It's fascinating. Beautifully written. Really not boring. How when he was small Goethe did this, that and the other, made jokes, calculated this and that, later became what he was—the great hero of his time. But it's a fascinating book. And it spoke about the German University, "Göttingen. This inspired me so much I wanted to go to Germany, to a university. That was the very first dream I had. And then it all built up. But it really began on this little fantasy.

Q: A fantasy which bore fruits, though not the expected ones.

CS: I think they *all* do. A very good writer, Julian Green, had a beautiful theory, which I believe is true, that we're all deeply formed, our fantasy and probably our life, especially writers, but probably all other people too, by some fairy story that we read or was read to us in childhood.

      I asked Bill, because Bill was an economist. He wrote novels later, but he was essentially an economist. I said, "What story impressed you most when you were a boy?" And he though a bit and told me two. One was *How the Sea Became Salt*, the story of the salt industry. This must have appealed to a grain in him that was economist. That was one. And the other was a very peculiar one. I know he had this dreadful feeling all of his life. A story he read when he was a boy about someone waking up in one of those lost cities in South America. Don't even know who built it. And there was nobody there. It was moonlight and the jungle had invaded the city. And that was all. He woke up all alone in this moonlit city. Dreadful story. And I know that this invaded his psyche.

I thought to myself, "What one formed me perhaps?" There was "*Der Treue Heinrich*," True Harry. It's a bit of a story that's got attached to Grimms' "The Frog Prince." When the frog prince is transformed to a prince by all those goings on and the carriage arrived for him from his kingdom and *der treue Heinrich* is standing behind, as they roll along there's a loud crack. The prince says, "Is the carriage cracking?" "No," says True Harry. "I bound four bands around my heart to prevent it breaking when you were taken away and changed by a witch into a frog. That's the first band breaking." I thought that was marvelous. And the other thing that impressed me, oddly enough, is also a story of fidelity. In the Sydney Art Museum there's a huge canvas. It's called "The Sons of Clovis." It's probably not very good at all, but when I was a child it impressed me. The sons of Clovis, so that they wouldn't inherit, I think is the idea, were hamstrung and set on a barge and sent down the river. I used to look and look at those two boys. It gave me a great feeling of loyalty. That was the impression I got. These two going down the river forever. Tied. Hamstrung. They can't move. I don't know why, but that got me. I still think of "The Sons of Clovis." Not as I did then, of course. In both of them there's the feeling of loyalty. That's a very great feeling with me. Loyalty to people.

I thought I'd ask people what their fantasy was. But people don't really seem to remember. They're ashamed probably of some story they read that affected them. Or they don't really remember. It's been overlaid. But I think that's a thing worth asking people. Because these things deeply form you.

I love to read Grimm. Bill got me Grimm in German, an old edition. I'm very fond of it.

Q: Did you read a lot of Dickens at some time?

CS: Yes, yes. Dickens was in the family. My grandfather—
I wrote this in an article—was a freethinker, atheist
(freethinker's polite) and he belonged to the Odd Fellows, a freemason sect that broke off from the
Church of England. And he left here when he was a
boy of eighteen, went off to Australia, in a little box-
like thing. It was a nice article. I lent it to someone
who never sent it back. Never mind. He knew all
about building houses. He was a carpenter. And he
joined the Independent Order of Odd Fellows, which
isn't like the Elks. They are more artistic, I think.
Well, they were just fellows getting together of
course. But I once or twice heard him. They had
Dickens evenings, it was a Dickens lodge he began, he
belonged to. And in this article, I pointed out, I said
that *Great Expectations* came out I think about two
years before he left for Australia. I'm sure it affected
him deeply. Do you know *Great Expectations?* The
criminal, the runaway convict, Magwitch, goes to
Australia, makes a fortune in sheep and keeps a boy
at home. You know. Well, he was a great one for
Dickens. I don't know that this really affected him.
But when he was alive the family was full of Dickens.
As I say, we went to a lodge meeting once or twice
when he was acting. He had a bit of the actor in him.
The reciter. He wasn't a swashbuckler, nothing like
that, but he loved it. So he did something from
Nicholas Nicholby, something from *Barnaby Rudge*,
I think. I'm sure about the *Nicholas Nicholby*. I
forget (I was quite small) about the other ones. Yes,
the family was full of Dickens in those days. Well, I
didn't take him as a model, but I must have been
deeply affected, I suppose, by him. A very dramatic
writer.

Q: I suppose other writers seep into you more than they
are conscious models?

CS: Oh yes, yes, yes. I don't think, I don't have any conscious model at all.

Q: I've wondered if you read D. H. Lawrence. One scene
in *For Love Alone* in particular reminded me very
much of Lawrence.

CS: I never imitated him *at all*, but, when I came to read
        him I liked him very much. He gets under a cloud
        every three months here in England. I don't know
        why. I think because for snobbish reasons, that's my
        real opinion.

Q: When did you start reading him?

CS: In Paris. I was sick in bed and Bill brought me his
        poems. I think *Sons and Lovers* was the first I read. I
        thought that was very good. And some of the short
        stories are very, very good. He's a marvelous man.

Q: What do you think of Lawrence's Australian novel,
        Kangaroo?

CS: He's very bad on Australia. By the time he got there,
        well, all right, that's the way he saw it, but he was an
        invalid. And he talks about the old tired cliché about
        there being no smells there. No scents, odors. The
        scents could knock you over! He was so weak. But he
        probably couldn't smell. And, "Flowers have no
        smell, birds have no song." Their song! It's like Bar-
        tok, or somebody like that! Such songs! But well, all
        right. He's wrong. He didn't like it. It didn't suit him.
        So we must forgive him. We really must because he
        was a genius. But it's nothing like Australia. It's not a
        bit Australia. I mean, I don't worship D. H. Law-
        rence. He has mortal sins. *White Peacock* is tiresome.
        And yet he is a genius.

Q: Who are your favorite current authors?

CS: Well, I'll show you. [She had a list she'd compiled a
        while ago.] I actually read a lot of junk because
        somebody told me it was wonderful. But my favorite
        authors—Yes, here now. Somebody asked me . . .
        I've just got a junk shelf. I can't tell you what it is,
        can I? Actually, it's good for writing . . . necessary.
        . . . Anybody who writes, I have respect for.

Q: I think sometimes people actually prefer to read
        junk.

CS: No, I don't. That isn't true, for me at least. No, I
        don't enjoy reading junk. I do if somebody tells me

to read it, I read it. [She explains, in a low voice, how her downstairs neighbor is always bringing her books to read.] If it's possible I say I like it. That's what I feel. I feel they feel something. You have no right to say it's bad, unless it's so bad it's degrading. And that isn't usually true. For example [the neighbor has been bringing] a series of novels. I gathered that it was about her birthplace. It was, more or less. There's always some reason. These are the authors I really like. I wrote it down, four years ago I think. Günter Grass, you know him? Marvelous. I haven't read absolutely everything, but *The Dog Years*, marvelous. Mervyn Peake, you know him? He's a British writer, eccentric but remarkable. I'll show you some. [*Titus Alone* and *Gormenghast*] Brought up in China. He has an interesting, fascinating style. I saw in the *Times*, I found an advertisement for a Gormenghast Society. Fascinating stuff. Dalton Trumbo. It's called *Johnny Got His Gun*. It's hard to read, I admit, but it's *very* good.

Q: That was the boy who lost all his limbs. . . .

CS: Yes, that's right, became a basket case. Couldn't see, couldn't hear. Very depressing. That's a wonderful man all the same. I met him once in Hollywood, just for a minute, but that isn't the reason. I'm just saying that.

   Last night I was reading *People in Glass Houses*. Do you know Shirley Hazzard? She's also born in Sydney, Australia. Wonderful diction! She worked for the U.N.O. in New York City. She has another book. Very good diction. Good writer. Erskine Caldwell, I like some of his very much. He's a wonderful writer. Carson McCullers, of course, I like her.

Q: Readers often have strange reactions to *The Member of the Wedding*. . . .

CS: They couldn't take it. . . . It's a sad experience, adolescence. In a way you feel that you don't know anything. It's so true. Yes, she's very good. James Thurber, I've got down. I do like him very much. I was reading him again. He's amusing. He expresses himself so well. Geoffrey Household. Do you know him? He is a British writer who does spy stories that are very good. He's really quite entertaining, delectable, very interesting because he writes as if (I don't say he has) he writes as if he's been through all this. Strange stuff. Hiding in ditches. He writes violently too, but he's really very good. Unusual.

Q: Do you like spy stories?

CS: I *hate* them. I absolutely hate them. I mention that about him because it's so unusual. I don't like that sort of thing.

Q: Do you read Doris Lessing at all?

CS: I've met her. I don't like her very much. Her early stories, yes, the early work from South Africa, beautiful. And then she became sort of steeped in Bohemia and I think she . . . am I on the air? . . . I'll not say. I think she could have done better with her considerable talent. That's . . . now, but not the first work, the first work was beautiful.

       Oh, I've got here Bernard Malamud. [*The Fixer*] Yes. And then Carlo Emilo Gadda, do you know him? He wrote that thing *Acquainted with Grief.* . . . He's a remarkable Italian writer. He wrote under Mussolini, and his work shows some of the side effects of oppression. But in a way it hasn't hurt him. And then I've got down here Shirley Ann Grau, do you know of her? She's an American writer, of course, writes about the South. And she's very good. A rather tough writer, but she's good. Well, I've got more of course.

Q: Did you know Randall Jarrell?

CS: Mrs. Jarrell wrote me after his death, and sent me some of his books. Very kind. She said he was always like that, with girl students in his class. (He taught at a girls' college.) He was always like that. It's marvelous, isn't it, marvelous. [Jarrell wrote a highly complimentary analysis of *The Man Who Loved Children*.]

Q: What do you think of the current Women's Libera-
      tion movement?

CS: Look, I don't know much about it. It's very exagger-
      ated. I realize that women, of course, lack many
      rights. Especially working women and mothers who
      are forced to stay at home with their children and
      really must get out and do something, but this is
      basic, I think, for all. I've seen some Women's Libera-
      tion movement literature from America through a
      friend of mine, and it was so eccentric. It's one of
      these amateur programs where they include abso-
      lutely everything: whether the sun should rise and
      set, whether they should have the crêches, whether
      they should have laws protecting gay people (gay's an
      expression for homosexual) and everything and every-
      thing in one roof. They should or should not have
      drugs. Drugs to take by mouth, for fun. It's nonsense.
      It's eccentric. It's not a genuine movement. It's to-
      tally, purely middle class. A waste of time. Eccentric.
      As much as the Suffragette movement was, except
      that it was very important, and essential. And they
      did get through the women's vote in this very back-
      ward country. Very backward.
          Women should have rights. But Women's Lib is
      nonsense. What put me off is throw away their bra.
      What would I do without a bra, I should like to
      know! Unfortunately, it's middle class. This woman
      who got me the materials, who loves people, a very,
      very close friend of mine, she told me very earnestly
      about some friends of hers, some three or four mid-
      dle-class women who had been very good because
      they had tried to get higher pay for some char. One
      char! And of course they all have chars! Talking
      about Women's Lib, the char comes in and does the
      carpet, cleans up. In the Suffragette movement you
      had lots of nonsense of that sort. Doesn't mean they
      were wrong. If a thing has such a strong voice, there's
      a real need behind it. But I wouldn't join in. I
      couldn't. I would hate it.

Q: And yet there seems to be in your books some of the
      same concerns. . . .

CS: No, I had no feeling about women when I wrote. I *am* a woman, therefore I write a certain way about women. No, it wasn't Women's Lib. Any more than I suppose a writer who writes about man's sorrows is writing about men's liberation. It's what he sees, the tragedy of people.

Q: In *For Love Alone*, Teresa expresses some views about the limitations imposed on women.

CS: Ah, yes, she does. I thought about that the other day. She does say something, but it's only about women's sexual position, and that's not meant to be manipulated by law. I mean the girls now are all trotting on the streets running around making love with all and sundry. And I know it's more accepted now. It's a rite for youth. And it used to be that in the very old days, long, long ago. But they are trying out what Teresa is talking about. "Woman's season is so short." And she should be able to try, and she can't. Well, she couldn't in those days because she'd have children right away, that's what she's talking about. Of course, it's true now, very few girls are in a position to do what they want. Very few do go about freely. God bless them. And it's right. But very few are in a position to do it. They're living at home. Or they're living in a bed-sitter alone, with nobody to help them. It's just that they won't become pregnant because there are contraceptives. Still there are an awful lot of tragedies. There're a lot of girls who don't benefit by it.

Q: Beyond sexual freedom women seem to see themselves reflected through men, see themselves as secondary.

CS: Yes, I know. I don't feel myself secondary to men and I never did. And this is what they blame me for, elitism. And it's not because I haven't suffered. That isn't the reason. This is very interesting and this is perhaps the family system. I don't say I'm sure about that. Who can be sure about those things? Perhaps if they were brought up in larger communities it might

disappear. Now, why did I feel it? Because I was the
eldest of the family. I was in a sense the eldest son.
I'm only making use of that expression. I wasn't any
eldest son. I was a daughter, the eldest. But I never
had this feeling of inferiority, because, purely on
animal feeling, there were four boys younger than
me, and I looked after them, helped them. Therefore
I could never feel inferior to them. I didn't bat them
in the eye or anything. I looked after them, rocked
their cradles, washed their bottles, washed their
diapers. (You had to in those days.) But how could I
have a feeling of inferiority? Now that's the reason I
don't have it. And of course we had the women's vote
very early in Australia, long before here. I never had
much feeling of inferiority. I'm well aware that I
can't lift a two hundred pound hammer or something
and I don't want to. There are things men can do and
. . . and even this can be changed. I think it was the
Second World War, in America, they had to use female labor and so they found a way of changing the
heavy old iron and steel equipment into something
more efficient. So women's inferiority is just a question of adjustment. They can do the same jobs.
They've really been wasting men's energy on this
slogging away with those heavy materials.

Q: What about women who are housewives, mothers?

CS: Yes, that needs organization, of course it does. I
      know Henny [the stepmother in *The Man Who
      Loved Children*], a person I knew intimately. She was
      brought up in a real old-fashioned la-di-da way:
      women's accomplishments, drawing, poetry, piano,
      painting, but not at all having children. In fact, she
      thought she was being wasted, so she was. I was very
      surprised at the end of her childbearing period. A
      woman candidate for Member of Parliament came
      round to distribute campaign literature. Henny, who
      had never done any such thing, became so enthusias-
      tic because she thought she was going to be repre-
      sented by a woman. She wasn't a married woman
      either, which was something very unusual. Because

previous to that, Henny had always hated the school-teachers who looked after her children at school. That might be a basic reason why I didn't like school-teaching. She used to insult them: "Old-maid school-teacher, doesn't know anything about it." A very old-fashioned woman.

In this respect, of course, I suppose Women's Lib or some form of Suffragettes must have been bringing a sort of message to lots of women. Frankly, Henny had a horrible life. It wasn't her fault she was brought up that way, to expect servants. That's what she'd had all her life.

But women have too dull a life. The home is an extremely dull institution. And of course they do need help. Who wouldn't need help? I have a woman who comes to help me Thursdays. (Since I had a heart attack, the Doctor told me not to do too much.) She works for a big company, a very old firm. It's very hard work. She's a very bright woman, with a strong political impulse. "Oh," she said shamefaced one day. "What am I but Mrs. Mop!" (Mrs. Mop is what they call chars.) And I said, "Don't say you're Mrs. Mop! We're all Mrs. Mops. All women are Mrs. Mops!" And that's true isn't it? If something goes wrong, you're supposed to mop it up. And there's no harm in that. I think that's good. I think that's right. At the same time you must realize that it's a slavery that goes on forever.

I've always thought women would make marvelous diplomats, because they have this gift, to run a family, run a husband, in a way. What's the harm in it? It's very nice to manage people, to make things happy, or better. I don't mean a revolution, we don't want it. Not really. It's a good thing. I like that.

Q: Isn't it sad when women, after raising a family, want to go back to work but feel helpless and are afraid to go back? They have lost their feeling of competence.

CS: Yes, they do lose competence. My hairdresser told me (not this one who gave me this "mattress" permanent but the previous one) that they have girls who go away to get married and try to come back after two years, but they have lost their skill. Very difficult for them. Well, this has to be remedied. But you see, all these things are not Women's Lib. They're a question of industrial regulation, impact on the trade unions and so forth. Women's Lib are just all up in the air. Nonsensical ideas about sororities. All women living together. What a dreary idea! But some want it, or they think they want it. Women's culture, Women's Lib, I don't know anything about it. It's not a subject that interests me. I can't interest myself in an island full of women. Because I believe that the sexes stimulate each other. You manage him and he manages you. And it's a good thing. It's nice working together. You get something from each other. It's a true fertilization, which is sexual without . . . You don't even have to have sexual relations. It's a beautiful thing, sex. You can make a lot out of it. These girls who are making all the noise are clouding an issue.

I know what they say, trades union men are very hard headed and conservative on these subjects. They have been very bad about it. Women's pay. Joining trade unions. But the way to attack that is not Women's Lib. It should be attacked. It's very bad for women. But, a women's group came up and said, "We're going to harass the trade unions, give them handbills, and preach at them." The Chinese—they used to do at the beginning of the revolution, if a comrade or whoever it was, citizen, lagged, then they would go and talk to him. And if he wouldn't have them, they would set up loudspeakers out in the street and talk to him from the street. They got many people in that way. They would me. I couldn't stand it. Well, that sort of thing. All kinds of things one can do.

Q: In your novel, *For Love Alone*, why was Teresa so blindly enamored of the cruel Jonathan Crow?

CS: She had no experience of men. Not sexually, I mean, not a love affair, that sort of thing. And probably he

was so different from her. We often fall for people
who are enigmas to us. The enigma may be their stupidity or total unsuitability, but to us . . . This is
very common in the love affair, falling for the
enigma, and it's very common with young people who
have a certain amount of ability. But their ability is
in one direction and the other person's ability, if any,
is in a totally other direction. Not to mention the
problem of sex which they don't fully understand
however wide awake they may be. That's all.

Q: What do you mean one direction?

CS: Well, supposing a musician, a young girl who's a
      musician, who's very keen about music. Well, she
      may fall in love with a mathematician, that's close to
      music—but with a geologist, or just a money grubber.
      Or a civil servant who's working at his desk all day.
      Kakia Kakiavitch. Perhaps he's thoroughly stupid.
      But she cannot—but she's attracted by him sexually,
      she cannot grant this. So there's a big mystery, in
      fact, a mist fogs her view.

Q: But even when Jonathan's cruel? . . .

CS: Well, I think by the time he was cruel they were sepa-
      rated by a distance, weren't they, by a big distance?
      [He had already left Australia for England.] There-
      fore there was no daily contact. But, of course,
      cruelty is not disassociated from sex, is it? It's no
      good using the discarded old coinage of "masochism."
      That really doesn't meet the situation because you
      can have quite energetic people getting into this
      situation. It's simply that you don't understand. If a
      person is weak enough, or even courageous enough,
      they think, well, this is just part of the routine. And
      behind it all is not understanding. After all, a lot of
      women get married and they don't understand what's
      required of them. And I don't mean sex. I mean ac-
      commodation to the other person and his problems
      and so on. And they end up thorough miseries. Prob-
      ably never get over it. This is nothing. This is a pre-
      marital situation and it's very common. If a man has
      this fatal attraction for women . . . You know who

he was like physically, except he wasn't anything like as attractive, a famous American actor (actually he was Australian) who did all those swashbuckling roles. And afterwards, and he wrote a diary about all the women he'd slept with—a real horror. But he had the same attraction for women. He had a narrow face, and he was superficially handsome and agile. He got all the women. This is the mystery of sex. There's nothing special about that. If a man has charm, or a woman (it's true of a woman too) she will exercise it whether she wants the other person or not. She can't help exercising it. Any more than a cat can help being a cat.

Q: And Jonathan was like that?

CS: He had a certain number of girls he kept on a string. Quite different types too. All different types. And he, and he led off with this "Pity me" routine. You know, "I come from the slums" and all that kind of thing, and "I had to struggle hard to get here. Had to struggle hard to get my scholarship." He was very rich in detail of his struggles. Motherly hearted women—which I regret to say, can't be helped, we all are—naturally bleed for this kind of struggle. More for the girl, than for her own struggle. They do have a thing about that. When a man finds out the motherhood racket, he's home. And these men often are dependent on their mothers. He was. So as I say, in a sense he knows the way to a woman's heart. Without all that. He's appealing to Mama. "Did you have a hard day at college, Jonathan?" And then his tale of woe. "But I came top of the class, Mother." And so forth. He's used to this racket, this kind of person. How would she know that? She doesn't know that. I know it now, but I didn't know it then.

Q: Your novella, *The Puzzleheaded Girl*, seems to make an abstract statement about the isolation of men and women.

CS: Yes. I didn't write it with that idea, but that's what struck me yesterday when I was reading it. That this is really the state of women, if you want to say. Also

any ignorant youth starting out in life trying to solve
life with its own solutions, not everything that's
handed to it. And she is a little eccentric, of course.
She's a little astray mentally. And this makes her always try to solve it with her own solutions. She never
accepts anything. She's not very bright. She's just eccentric. And possibly a little artistic touch too. I
never knew her, but I heard about her. Again you've
got this thing: that the thing you don't understand is
very attractive to the other sex. Men fell for her because they did not understand her. And some would
throw her over because she was too eccentric. But the
man in the story—Gus DeBrett, a kind-hearted man
obviously, was very puzzled, very touched because
the thing I say about Koiné. You must not, what is
the expression, turn down the suppliant. That's a
thing in Greek literature. The suppliant comes from
the gods. I'm deeply affected by this. I can't go past a
beggar in the streets. If I do I feel dreadful. She was a
suppliant obviously. He could tell that she wasn't
quite normal mentally, but that didn't mean he
thought she was feebleminded or anything. And he
felt instinctively, he eventually says something about
it to his wife I think, he felt that she was one of these
strange cases not exactly sent by the gods, but a suppliant. In Spain—I was in Spain. I saw this—whatever else you may think about Spain, they have this
extraordinary attitude to the feebleminded and the
village idiot and all those people, people who go
about twisted like this [gesticulates]. They feel they
were sent by God to call on your compassion. Bill
wasn't religious, but he had this feeling very deeply.
So when he got there—Bill wasn't a doctor, but you
know a lot of people do have this feeling. . . . She
had this appeal to people who felt like that. For example, the man who married her, who always was devoted to her. It's a mystery. It's a great thing in sex
for really holding people, mystery. She didn't know
she had it. She couldn't. She was mad. She was a real
person. She was the sister of a very famous man, an
artist. I'm not saying who of course. I never met

either of them. You might say all that really happened. But because I didn't know her it became
slightly abstracted. And in fact you might say it's—
what I say at the end. Mari, M-A-R-I, Mari, that's
really me. It's the only me in the book, story. She says
she's really the soul of women that hasn't been
caught. Well, that sort of came to me. When I was finishing the story that that's what it was. Pathetic
really. Because I suppose that's what a lot of people
feel about themselves. Especially some women, who
haven't made it somehow.

Q: Feel what?

CS: That they're dead. That they should have been
caught. That something's all wrong. That they've
been caught but not caught. But I wasn't really
thinking about the fate of women. I don't go about
thinking about the fate of women. It just came out
that way. Because I heard this, I heard it over many
years, from different people. It was one of the first
things I heard from Bill. He mentioned her. He told
me her name and something about her brother. I
mention in the story she was the sister of a famous
artist, don't I? He wasn't a painter, actually. And
over the years I heard little scraps about her.

Q: So you knew her for a long time?

CS: Yes. And that gives it an abstraction too I suppose.
But I wouldn't have liked the girl if I had met her,
you see. It's just as well I didn't.

Q: There are some related characters, who seem to me
sisters: Catherine in *Seven Poor Men of Sydney*.

CS: Catherine is a sort of—larger than life. She's one of
those sort of dramatizations of youth. That was my
first book of course. There was a woman I knew who
was quite like that, called Catherine. She was like
that. She also was slightly eccentric, or thought she
was. She felt she couldn't stand the stress of everyday
life and she'd every now and again go into a lunatic
asylum. They allowed her there. And she liked it

there. And then she'd get fed up and then she'd come out again. She was probably the kind of character you meet in old Bohemia as I would say.

Q: Isn't it one of Doris Lessing's ideas, that you have to dip into madness to find yourself?

CS: I don't know about that! That's not true for me. I should hate to be mad. I'm sure I shall never be mad. Touch wood, of course. Horrible, to lose contact, slip—Oh no, I should hate it. But I don't think I ever will. It's probably that I have a very coarse healthy strain in my family, one side, and I've inherited that. I think I'll be alright.

Q: What about Elvira in *The Beauties and Furies?*

CS: She was a very unhappy . . . A natural pessimist, a melancholic really. But, that's just a sort of fill-in, that book. I wrote it when we went from England to France, and the only character that really appeals to me is Malpurgo. Remember him? He was a real man. A New Yorker. I got very tired of Malpurgo. But I was very impressed in those days. The first man about town I'd ever met. He was a great show off— producing himself.

Q: He seemed to me to be almost a Jacobean villain.

CS: He'd want to be a villain. Yet he did nothing villain- ous. He would have loved to have been a villain, I'm sure. He was a flaunter. He got in on various projects. Made huge money, spent it all. Lived the high life like a sheik or something. He'd have no more money and he'd crawl along. Get another job. Do the same thing over and over again. He had two brilliant sons. He was brilliant in his way; they got the brilliance without the lack of balance. No, one also had a lack of balance. He was a very brilliant boy. Had a mathe- matical scholarship. One was a physicist. He and she between them—the mother was a brilliant Russian woman, a lovely Russian woman. Old Russian, you know, like Chekhov. Like those women you meet in "A Month in the Country" and Turgenev. One of those big-hearted, broad-minded generous women had married this man, and she was very unhappy with him. You can imagine. He wasn't a man to marry. She probably added the solidity that the boys needed. I love her really, but I couldn't bear her coming. Because there was no sex in the marriage. He was a sexless man really, in spite of the two sons. She was a big, generous nature. She had this high-up scratchy voice which every time I heard it reminded me of sexual deprivation. It was too much. It was horrid. She's not in the story. It had nothing to do with her. I didn't meet her then. I met her years and years later. A really lovely woman.

Q: Didn't Malpurgo have an invalid wife in the novel?

CS: Ah, maybe. But he didn't have an invalid wife. He would have liked an invalid wife. It probably would have been better for him. He had a fine, splendid, big-built beautiful Russian wife of the old school. A beauty. A bit heavy by the time I saw her. She had that great Russian outgoing nature, you know, kissing you, embracing you, and carrying on in a true old-fashioned manner. Which I admire, I like it. She wasn't the first one I met. I met another Russian woman in Paris who became a close friend of mine. She also had that nature. She was different of course.

Q: Are all your characters based on people you knew?

CS: Oh yes, you can't invent people, or they're puppets. Sometimes you'll see people writing popular novels that are quite clearly based on real people. They are the best, because the characters carry it along. You don't know the people, but you recognize the human energy, the vigor in it. But as for writing about puppets. Well, puppets are very nice. I like puppets. I have a puppet. But you shouldn't write about them. That's all.

The odd thing about puppets is that if you have a favorite puppet, and every puppeteer has one, this one is your soul. It's like an oracle that speaks to you. When I used to use this puppet all the time—his name was Nello, short for Genello, from the Frères Zemganno, by the Goncourt brothers. The Zemganno brothers are athletes, trapezists. Nello is called after one of them. He's a little clown. He's in pieces now because during the war his knee cap had to be opened up. Went to pieces. Rotted. But he was wonderful. He was a success. Puppets aren't always a success. But there's the accidental success. And he was a success. A string puppet. Wonderful movements. I got to like him so I used to ask him things and he would say the right thing. If I had a dilemma, he'd say, "Well, do this or that." I would listen for a while and he would give the right answer. Of course, it would be me, you know. Very fascinating, isn't it? Of course, it's what they call the unconscious. But I don't call it the unconscious. It's the more sensible part of yourself.

Yes, I used to love that Nello. Bill *loved* him. He used to call him my little brother. I had a routine with Bill. He loved to sit there. "Bill," Nello would say, "I carry a picture of you with me everywhere." And Bill would say, "Do you, Nello? That's very nice." And he would say "Yes" and show his heel. Bill thought it was marvelous.

Q: Where did he come from?

CS: Ah. We used to live on Fourteenth Street in New York, in a place that has been torn down—a huge pyramidal black building. An apartment building. I've seen it since. I went back there the year Bill died to New York City to see it. And Eighteenth Street, we used to walk up and down. There was a sign hanging out with a soldier I think, a grenadier or something, a European soldier, and I think it was animated. At any rate, I was very interested. I started to write a story about that. I sensed there was something. And I said to Bill, "I really can't because I don't know how it's done. So I must learn it." So he was willing. We weren't very rich, but he was willing. He was a very good helper. I went in. There were two Europeans. She was an English girl, who had gone out to Chile with her father, an engineer in Chile, but she was Scotch really. She had married a German puppeteer who had become an exile under Hitler. He told a fascinating story how he escaped across the Basle front. He wasn't Jewish. He was a German liberal. Big, tall fellow, he looks like a puppet himself, like a woodcut man. His father had been a toy maker who made a marvelous [toy of] pyramidal discs—that they had in Germany. They had the twelve apostles. It goes up and up and up. As each child is born you add a disc. They're beautiful toys, from Europe. But he became a puppeteer. Under Hitler, he had to fly. So he came to the German frontier here, at Basle, Switzerland. They wouldn't let him in. The man at the front here said to him, "Well, how many of you are there?" He said, "Seventeen." Wasn't that nice? They let him in. He showed them that puppets were people much more than puppets. So they let him in. So they came to Switzerland. Then he got to the U.S.A. eventually.

Q: Didn't you have a story in *The Salzburg Tales* about a puppeteer?

CS: Yes. That's odd because I didn't know anything about it then. Ah, yes. Because in Salzburg there is a famous little puppet theatre, about the trolls who also live there in the mines. And it's something about Beltswirker—or something about that. Famous. And that was the first time I really saw puppets. That's why.

Q: How was it for you and Bill, two writers living together. Did your writing affect each other's?

CS: Our writing didn't affect each other but of course our interrelationship did. It's taken me all this time, five years, to get over his death, because there's a fabric, a structure, you see, built up between each other. You're not doing it consciously, but it's there naturally. And it broke down, it all flew away, rotted away, blew away. And I had to begin like an imbecile who doesn't know anything. And I didn't do it consciously. It's only now I'm doing it a bit consciously, to build up something else. That's what affects you.

We could never have collaborated. We thought too
differently. But yes, his death did stop me writing,
that's true of course. But it was that other thing, you
see.

Q: Do you write regularly?

CS: No, I tried it but, that's just typing, just turning
pages. It's much better to do one good page, rich, fine
page which you mean, once a fortnight, than to type
every day. I'm not writing to schedule, after all. I'm
not doing a detective novel for a contract. I don't
have to. Why should I? I believe in writing with
energy and saying what you mean at the moment. Of
course, it may not be what you mean in ten years . . .
saying what you mean. Being yourself in that respect.

Q: What is writing to you?

CS: I know it's wrong to say you write for yourself, but I
do, by instinct. I do basically write for myself. That's
what I can do, so it's moral. I do have a certain
amount of experience. I have a few ideas. I'm not
moral when I'm not writing. When I'm writing—it
doesn't matter what I'm writing—I'm a thoroughly
moral being. That's what I really feel. I'm in tune
with everything. Everything's going properly. That's
moral, to me.

Notes

1. ALWAYS ORIGINAL: THE SHAPE OF A CAREER

1. *New York Times*, Sunday 14 November 1976.
2. When the *New York Times Book Review*, in its June 3, 1979, issue, asked well-known writers for works they thought belonged on a list of the hundred most important books of Western literature, Lillian Hellman included *The Man Who Loved Children* as one of "the books I like best among those published in my time." (p. 5). Denis Donoghue includes it on his list of "highly wrought elaborately composed" works that are candidates for immortality (p. 13).
3. *Styles of Radical Will* (New York: Dell, 1966), p. 36.
4. José Yglesias, "Marking Off a Chunk of England" (review of *Dark Places of the Heart*), *Nation*, 24 October 1966, p. 421.
5. *New York Times Book Review*, 11 May 1975.
6. José Yglesias, "Marking Off a Chunk of England."
7. "Domestic Manners" (review of *The Man Who Loved Children*), *New York Review of Books*, 17 June 1975, p. 14.
8. "Marx as Muse" (Review of *The Man Who Loved Children*), *Nation*, 5 April 1965, pp. 368–370.
9. "The International Symposium on the Short Story," Christina Stead (England), *Kenyon Review*, 30: 4 (1968), p. 446.
10. *Twentieth Century Authors—A Biographical Dictionary of Modern Literature*, ed. Stanley J. Kunitz and Howard Haycraft (New York: H. W. Wilson Co., 1942).

11. Christina Stead, "A Waker and Dreamer," *Overland* 53 (1972), p. 33.

12. Interview with Christina Stead by Joan Lidoff. June, 1973. All subsequent references, to "Interview" are to this one, reprinted here on pages 180–220.

13. "A Waker and Dreamer," *Overland*, p. 35.

14. Interview.

15. William Blake had also just arrived in London in 1928 to be the Managing Director of a firm of grain merchants which his friend A. Hurst was just starting. Stead's account of their first meeting at her job interview echoes her description of the first encounter of Teresa and James Quick in *For Love Alone*, and that of Honor Lawrence and Gus Debrett in "The Puzzle-headed Girl":

"I had been saving up for four or five years. I was a skeleton when I came [to London]. You should have seen me! . . . I must have looked like a dead duck. . . . Bill told me years afterwards that I looked so shy and at the same time serious. But I think the clincher was—I was carrying a book of Bertrand Russell. And I think that got him. So he engaged me. And, in fact, for life. And I thought he looked nice too. Very nice. I thought he looked marvelous. So pure. What girls think! But I wasn't wrong, really." (Christina Stead: Interview.)

Blake was born on July 28, 1894, in St. Louis, Missouri. The son of Gustavus Maximilian and Rosa Sachs Blech, he had his last name legally changed to Blake in his boyhood (*Contemporary Authors*, vol. 5-6, p. 47). His mother was a German Jewish immigrant (from whom Stead learned Yiddish later when she lived with them) and his father an army general. The extent of Blake's formal education was a few special courses at Columbia University, but his career began on Wall Street when he was fourteen, and took him eventually all over Europe. He was the editor of the *Magazine of Wall Street* in New York; the Managing Director of the London Scottish Banking Corporation (starting in 1928) and the Investment Manager of Grain Union S.A. Antwerp, Belgium. He also read French and German learned works for British and American publishers (*Contemporary Authors*). In the introduction to his book, *Elements of Marxian Economic Theory and Its Criticism* (1939, also published as *An American Looks at Karl Marx*) Blake gives this account of his career:

"My title to speak of Marxian political economy comes from the world of economic practice. For thirty years as a statistician, economist, financial editor, banker and grain merchant, I have found the study of political economy in my evenings in a running commentary on the employments of the day.

"I came to economics from the stock exchange and banking: naturally I concentrated on money and taxation. Marxian economic theory, rooted in production relations, was the antipodes of my profession and my interests. It had the attraction of all opposites. I began with several essays on the theory of rent in 1912 and have been incurable since."

He wrote romantic and historical novels: *The World Is Mine, the Story of a Modern Monte Cristo* (1938), *The Painter and the Lady* (1939), *The Copperheads* (1941), and *The Angel* (1951). He has other books, *Understanding the Americans* (1954) and *An Intelligent American's Guide to the Peace* (ed. Sumner Welles, 1945), for which he prepared the research; and several translations from the German, done in the late 1950s.

Blake died at the age of 74 of cancer. His obituaries cite him as an author, editor, economist, and the husband of Christina Stead (Obituaries: *London Times*, February 9, 1968; *New York Times*, February 21, 1968; *Antiquarian Bookman*, March 4–11, 1968).

When asked in our interview in 1973 whether her writing and Blake's had affected each other's, Christina Stead replied:

"Our writing didn't affect each other but of course our interrelationship did. It's taken me all this time, five years, to get over his death because there's a fabric, a structure, you see, built up between each other.

You're not doing it consciously, but it's there naturally. And it broke down, it all flew away, rotted away, blew away. And I had to begin like an imbecile who doesn't know anything. And I didn't do it consciously. It's only now I'm doing it a bit consciously, to build up something else. That's what affects you. We could never have collaborated. We thought too differently. But yes, his death did stop me writing, that's true, of course. But it was that other thing, you see."

16. Christina Stead, "A Writer's Friends," *Southerly*, 28: 3 (1968), p. 168.

17. These were: *Modern Women in Love*, ed. Christina Stead and William Blake, 1945; *Great Stories of the South Sea Islands*, 1955; and these translations of Fernand Gignon, *Colour of Asia*, 1955; Jean Giltène, *The Candid Killer*, 1956; and Auguste Piccard, *In Balloon and Bathyscaphe*, 1956.

18. "U.N.O., 1945," *Southerly*, 22: 4 (1962).

19. Interview.

20. "A Writer's Friends," p. 168.

21. *Twentieth Century Authors*.

22. Interview, June 1973. Stead, like Doris Lessing, is one of a generation of women writers who managed considerable accomplishments without the support of a coherent feminist movement, and who decline to identify themselves as feminists. In part, Stead is reluctant to identify herself with any movement; in part she is reacting to exaggerated media images of feminism. And she does genuinely oppose any form of feminist separatism. In spite of her disclaimers, however, and of her own habit of singular action, Stead's feminism cannot be dismissed. Her acute political perceptions are undeniably rooted in feminine experience. Her political analyses are feminist in essence if not in name.

Stead is opposed to sexual separatism. "I hate any sort of segregation," she writes in a letter to *Partisan Review* in 1979 (271-274). She believes in "women's natural affection for men" (273) and in the importance of sexual and intimate love between men and women: "one of the best and most momentous things

in life, love of a man." (273) Many feminists would
agree with her. But further, Stead is unsympathetic to
the need for separate forms to enable women to define and express their own visions. Having crafted
hers by herself, she feels none of the urge for collective support that motivates today's feminists, although,
as with everything, she is willing to grant, if there is a
real need, "it must be taken care of." (274)

Nevertheless, her writing abounds with perceptions that precede but agree with feminist social analyses: she grants the harms of women's lack of economic
independence. She sees the constrictions the nuclear
family imposes on women, and acknowledges "the problems of suburban loneliness and the man-dominated
family." (272) "Women tied to the home . . . sacrifice
willingly their entire adult lives," she writes, (271) and
describes, what her novels show, "the outbursts of
domestic misery which spring from the common unhappy marriage where the wife is the husband's only
serf." (272)

In a most interesting contribution to a *Vogue* article on "Woman's Intuition," Stead articulates the
subtle analyses of women's lives that she does in fact
share with feminism. ["Woman's Intuition," Eileen
Simpson (four interviews), *Vogue (Australia)*, 15 Sept.
1971, pp. 60, 61, 130]. She attacks the myth of women's
special intuition, only to assert that all of us operate
by a host of intuitions, and then to concede that since
men and women have different experiences of life,
their intuitions are probably somewhat different.
Nevertheless, it is what is behind the myth that is
most interesting. Stead writes: "All this is based on a
simple-hearted belief in a truth, a good and bad, to
which local conditions, sickness, temperament, hypocrisy are irrelevant. There is a truth and there must
be someone who knows, some bright-eyes who can
take us through the confusion; and so we go to the
crystal gazer and even lose sleep over a teacup sibyl.
There is a truth if we could spot it: there must be a
litmus paper for people. This natural longing leads
to fictions and interesting daydreams, and probably
blinds us to the real nature of intuition.

"About women's insight, there is a sort of folk-lore we inherit. Many women and more men believe in women's peculiar gifts of divination: our husbands, brothers, lovers, sons believe it; more male writers than female refer to it; a sort of shorthand for saying 'she was truly feminine, more sensitive, and so saw it all differently,' a careless gallantry. It is something, we infer, left out of male makeup. Women have bene-fited and suffered from this, which is related to the sex taboos and mysteries; to the white goddesses; to the wicked hag of the gingerbread house; 'the noonday witch'; Goethe's 'eternal feminine which leads us for-ward' (a nauseating sentimentality, but related to the concept of Penelope, Solveig, Deirdre, and how many other legends); to matriolatry, and the lover's dream.

"Some of this enchantment, foul and fair, comes from our early days when the women in the home, so weak and ailing, often moneyless, powerless, often anxious, disturbed, wretched, with no status to speak of, no trade union, yet had the awful power of hunger and suck, gave life and held off death, set out her law, defied *their* law for our sakes, a magic woman shelter-ing these small creatures, ourselves, obliged to live in the country of the giants. Mothers and fathers can and do maim and kill; and children have their moments of fear with even the kindest of parents. But the man's power is evident; the woman's is stranger. Behind the concept of woman's strangeness is the idea that a woman may do anything—she is below society, not bound by its law, unpredictable—an attribute given to every member of the league of the unfortunate. To make a small payment for their disability, we endow the slave, the woman, with unusual interior vision.

"But that woman's intuition may be a fable, a pretty package handed to the socially disabled, some-thing to hold off the evil eye, does not mean there is no intuition; it does not even mean there is no femi-nine intuition (pp. 61 and 130)."

If she is concerned, primarily, with our shared humanity, she also, always, understands the particular feminine shapes of that human experience.

23. "A Writer's Friends," p. 165. *Cotter's England* is the English title for *Dark Places of the Heart*.

24. "International Symposium," *Kenyon Review*, pp. 449–450.

25. Dorothy Green, "Chaos or a Dancing Star? Christina Stead's 'Seven Poor Men of Sydney,'" *Meanjin Quarterly* 27: 2 (1968), p. 151.

2. FAMILY FICTIONS: *THE MAN WHO LOVED CHILDREN*

1. Clifton Fadiman, *New Yorker*, 19 October 1940, p. 104.

2. "The Moral Design of *The Man Who Loved Children*," *Critical Review* (Melbourne), No. 14 (1971), pp. 38–61.

3. Stead transposed her family history from Sydney, capital of Australia, where her father, David Stead was an ichthyologist in government service, to Washington, D.C., where Sam Pollit too works for the government. Stead was living in the United States when she wrote this novel, and spent several months in Washington and Baltimore absorbing details of setting. (She says she adjusted the flora and fauna to compensate for the differences in salinity in the Chesapeake Bay and Sydney Harbor.) There are numerous small details, however, like eleven o'clock tea and some of Sam's slang that betray the author's own background. Had the story been set factually in Australia, "it would have been a bit too naked," she told interviewer Ann Whitehead. [*Australian Literary Studies*, 6: 3 (May 1974), p. 242]

4. "Domestic Manners," *New York Review of Books*, 17 June 1965, p. 14.

5. For studies of the grotesque, see Wolfgang Kayser, *The Grotesque in Art and Literature*, trans. Weisstein and Ulrich (New York: McGraw-Hill, 1963); Lee Byron Jennings, *The Ludicrous Demon: Aspects of the Grotesque in German Post-Romantic Prose* (University of California Publications in Modern Philology, v. 71; Berkeley: University of California Press, 1963); Arthur

Clayborough, *The Grotesque in English Literature* (Oxford: Clarendon Press, 1965).

Freud's interpretation of the disturbing nature of the process by which grotesque imagery works is that it takes us back to an earlier state in the development of thought, in which the distinction between imagination and reality is effaced. The uncanny, he says, recalls our primitive inability to distinguish between wish and act, between the inner world of our fears and desires and the outer world of pragmatic action and reaction. See "The Uncanny," *The Standard Edition of the Complete Psychological Works of Sigmund Freud*, trans. and ed. James Strachey (London: Hogarth Press, 1955), vol. 17 (1917–19).

6. *Purity and Danger: An Analysis of Concepts of Pollution and Taboo* (New York: Praeger, 1966).

7. *A Very Easy Death*, trans. Patrick O'Brien (London: Deutsch, 1965; rpt. N.Y., Warner, 1973), p. 51.

8. Interview.

9. James Walt, "An Australian Novelist Looks at America," *UNISA* 4 (November 1969), p. 38.

10. "A Waker and Dreamer," *Overland* 53 (1972), p. 33. Stead, who often describes life as shaped by fantasy, explains her grandfather's emigration from England as influenced by a fantasy taken from Dickens: "Dickens in 1861 brought out *Great Expectations*, in which the transported convict Magwitch makes a fortune in sheep in Australia and secretly supports a boy in England. In 1864, Samuel, age eighteen, made himself a small toolbox . . . and with it under his arm stepped aboard a sailing ship for Sydney, leaving behind him parents and numerous brothers and sisters."

11. Interview.

12. As Dorothy Van Ghent points out for Dickens. "On *Great Expectations*," in *The English Novel: Form and Function* (New York: Rinehart, 1953.)

13. See Edmund Wilson, "Dickens: The Two Scrooges," in *The Wound and the Bow* (Cambridge: Houghton-Mifflin, 1941, pp. 1–104), and George Orwell, "Charles Dickens," in *Dickens, Dali and Others* (New York: Harcourt Brace Jovanovich, 1946).

14. Van Ghent, *The English Novel*, p. 127.
15. See Harvey Peter Sucksmith, *The Narrative Art of Charles Dickens. The Rhetoric of Sympathy and Irony in His Novels* (Oxford: Clarendon Press, 1970), p. 132.

3. *FOR LOVE ALONE:* A WOMAN HERO

1. (New York: Harcourt, Brace, 1944). All references are to this edition.
2. Although it perhaps fits precisely only its first, German exemplar, Goethe's *Wilhelm Meister*, the term *bildungsroman* has been used to describe a common form of the realistic novel. The *bildungsroman* concerns itself with the spiritual development of a sensitive or talented young man. Often an orphan, both deprived and free of anchorage by the support and limitations of family, the hero leaves a constricted, provincial setting to venture into the wider world. Naïve, he suffers trials which educate him morally and spiritually. The *bildungsroman* portrays and criticizes the specific social world in which the hero struggles to survive and mature. Modern novels often define a society that does not support the fully developed individual spirit which is nevertheless its ideal.

It is also typical for the *bildungsroman* to have a male protagonist. When women are used as central characters, as they begin to be in nineteenth-century English fiction, they express the even greater initial and terminal constrictions within which women operate in society. Cf. G. B. Tennyson, "The *Bildungsroman* in Nineteenth-Century English Literature," *Comparative Literature Conference, first.* (University of Southern California, 1967); *Medieval epic to the "epic theater" of Brecht*, ed. Rosario Armato and John Spalek (Los Angeles: University of Southern California Press, 1968), pp. 135–146; Marianne Hirsch, "The Novel of Formation as Genre: Between Great Expectations and Lost Illusions," *Genre*, 12, 3 (Fall 1979), pp. 293–311; and Annis Pratt, "Women and Nature in

Modern Fiction," *Contemporary Literature* 13: 4 (Autumn 1972), pp. 476–490.

3. Christina Stead says this title was not hers but her publisher's.

4. While the journey of the romance hero follows a pattern similar to that in the *bildungsroman*, the romance is allegorical rather than realistic. In romances, the hero operates not in the context of a specific, realistic social world, but in a symbolic domain, whose features are projections of his own psychological world. See Joseph Campbell, *The Hero with a Thousand Faces* (Princeton: Princeton University Press, 1949); also Northrop Frye, *The Anatomy of Criticism* (Princeton: Princeton University Press, 1957).

5. In her "Prelude" to *Middlemarch*, Eliot longed wistfully for a modern St. Theresa whose "passionate, ideal nature demanded an epic life," whose flame "fed from within, soared after some illimitable satisfaction" (1872, New York: New American Library, 1964, p. vii). But she despaired of the possibility of such a woman's existing. Today's Theresas, she writes, are foundresses of nothing, whose love and yearning for good are dispersed in daily hindrances "instead of centring in some long recognizable deed." She believed a modern hero, especially a modern woman hero, impossible. Stead has created the modern St. Theresa George Eliot despaired of, but only by making different assumptions about both heroism and femininity. Lacking faith in a transcendent system of values, the twentieth century has defined heroism largely as an existential quest to create the meaning of being human. Modern man is ambivalent about his aggressive role in the world; the possibility of heroic action has largely given way to a struggle for self-knowledge. As often as not, our heroes are explorers who emerge from inward journeys with an increased capacity for perception and awareness.

St. Teresa of Avila (1515–1582) to whom Eliot alludes, and whose work Stead had read, was a Carmelite nun who, with St. John of the Cross, originated a system of mystical teaching. Transcending her youthful enchantment with reading and writing romances, and a desire to be a martyr, for which she and her brother attempted to run away from home, at twenty she joined a convent. Her later conversion experiences are well-known. She felt raptures in which she experienced a mystical marriage with God, and continued susceptible to interior speeches. The Bernini altarpiece, "The Ecstasy of St. Teresa" and her famous description of having her heart pierced repeatedly with an angel's golden arrow, the sweet pain of which left her on fire with love of God, emphasize the sensuality of her mysticism.

Though committed to the contemplative life, St. Teresa also led an active life of considerable influence. Founder of convents of reformed Carmelite nuns, she devoted herself to convent reform, traveling, writing, and speaking. Her introspective writings include her spiritual *Autobiography* and the *Interior Castle* (which Teresa Hawkins's novel-in-progress, "Seven Houses of Love" imitates), which talks of the need to travel through the seven mansions of a soul in a quest for self-knowledge that culminates in a spiritual marriage with God.

St. Teresa was a powerful personality; a person of strong inner life, whose religious doctrine grew from her own mystic experiences, and a woman of wit, intelligence, courage and vigor, as well as empathy and tenderness, who fought for what she believed in with great strength of will. The self-aware intensity of her inner life and the purposefulness and accomplishments of her active life must have appealed to both George Eliot and Christina Stead as a model of feminine strength.

See Butler's *Lives of the Saints*, ed. Herbert Thurston and Donald Attwater (New York: P. J. Kennedy and Sons, 1956), Vol. IV, Oct., Nov., Dec.: October 15, pp. 111–121.

6. In *Cunning Exiles*, ed. Don Anderson and Stephen Knight (Sydney: Angus and Robertson, 1974), p. 13.

7. "The Prison of Womanhood," *Comparative Literature* 25: 4 (Fall 1973), pp. 336–351.

8. *Twenty Australian Novelists* (Sydney: Angus and Robertson, 1947), p. 196.

9. "Women in Love," *Nation* 28 (October 1944), pp. 535–536.

10. "Amor, Amor, Amor," *New Republic*, 13 November 1944, p. 633.

11. In his introduction to *Emma* [Jane Austen, 1816 (Boston: Riverside Press, 1957)], Lionel Trilling acknowledges this form of discrimination against women:

> "There is a great power of charm in self-love, although to be sure, the charm is an ambiguous one. We resent and resist it, yet we are drawn by it, if only it goes with a little grace or creative power. . . . We understand self-love to be part of the moral life of all men; in men of genius we expect it to appear in unusual intensity and we take it to be an essential element of their power. . . . But we distinguish between our response to the self-love of women. No woman could have won the forgiveness that has been so willingly given (after due condemnation) to the self-regard of, say, Yeats and Shaw."

12. *Sincerity and Authenticity* (Cambridge: Harvard University Press, 1971), p. 99.

13. Cited by Ellen Rose, "The Eriksonian Bildungsroman: An Approach Through Doris Lessing," *Hartford Studies in Literature*, 7: 1 (1975), p. 5.

4. NO MORE HEROES: THE DEVELOPMENT OF A VOICE AND A VISION

1. In a book review of Louis Aragon, *The Century Was Young*, *New Masses* 47, 20 January 1942, pp. 23–25.

2. Interview, *Australian Women's Weekly*, 9 March 1935. Quoted by R. G. Geering in *Christina Stead*.

3. Interview, *Australian Women's Weekly*, Ibid.

4. Ibid.

5. Randall Jarrell, Introduction, *The Man Who Loved Children*, 1965.

6. Denis Donoghue (review of *The Puzzleheaded Girl*), *New York Review of Books*, 28 September 1967, p. 8.

7. José Yglesias, *Nation*, 24 (October 1966), p. 421.

8. Dorothy Green, "Chaos or a Dancing Star? Christina Stead's 'Seven Poor Men of Sydney,'" *Meanjin Quarterly* 27: 2 (1968), p. 161.

9. Michael Wilding, "Christina Stead's Australian Novels," *Southerly*, 1967, p. 23.

10. Graham Burns develops this idea in "The Moral Design of *The Man Who Loved Children*," *Critical Review* (Melbourne) 14 (1971).

11. Denis Donoghue, *New York Review of Books*, 28 September 1967, p. 8.

12. "The Puzzleheaded Critics" (review of *The Puzzleheaded Girl*), *Nation*, 1 January 1968, pp. 21–22.

13. Clifton Fadiman, *Reading I've Liked* (New York: Simon & Schuster, 1941), p. 546.

14. C. T. Samuels, "The Puzzling Miss Stead," *New Republic*, 9 September 1967, p. 31.

15. "Framing Father" (review of *The Man Who Loved Children*), *New Republic* 104: 61, 13 January 1941.

16. "Domestic Manners," *New York Review of Books*, 17 June 1965, p. 14.

17. Throughout Stead's fiction, characters are united by no one nationality, age, profession or class, but only by a common isolation. Aliens by birth or temperament, they all stand outside the social mainstream wherever they are. Stead's is never a fiction "well-rooted in some spot of native land," as George Eliot wished life and fiction to be [*Daniel Deronda*, p. 50 (1876, Penguin 1967)], but neither does Stead "divorce experience from [its] social basis." [Jack Lindsay, "Vision of the Twenties," *Southerly*, 13: 2 (1952), p. 70] She is able to capture the texture of the integration of personal, social, and political values and systems wherever she is.

18. "International Symposium on the Short Story. Christina Stead (England)," *Kenyon Review* 30: 4 (1968) pp. 448–489.

19. Interview.

20. *Twentieth Century Authors.*

21. Interview.

22. Stead continues this anecdote: "The odd thing about puppets is that if you have a favorite . . . this one is

your soul. It's like an oracle that speaks to you." In New York, she had a string puppet, called Nello. "I got to like him so I used to ask him things and he would say the right thing. If I had a dilemma he'd say, 'Well, do this or that.' And I would listen for a while and he would give the right answer. Of course it would be me, you know. . . . It's what they call the unconscious. But I don't call it the unconscious. It's the more sensible part of yourself." Interview.

23. "International Symposium," *Kenyon Review*, pp. 444–450.

24. Stead may have gotten this from the German poet Schiller who wrote, "Deeper meaning resides in the fairytales told to me in my childhood than in the truth that is taught by life." Quoted by Bruno Bettleheim, another believer, in "The Uses of Enchantment," *New Yorker*, 8 December 1975.

25. "Fairy Child," *Harvard Advocate*, 106: 2–3 (Winter 1973), p. 56.

26. Although Stead claims that loyalty is the virtue she prizes most, her fantasy of the friendship of Roland and Oliver is a heroic vision of two noble men acting apart from society rather than of a close-knit unit of daily life. The heroic motif is the idealized polarity of the grotesque version that appears in her fiction and also in another of her favorite anecdotes. Stead tells of a favorite picture she would see as a child in the Sydney Art Museum: called "Sons of Clovis," it is one of her early and persistent images of loyalty. In *Seven Poor Men of Sydney*, one of the characters, Michael, dreams of that picture: "An old-fashioned picture of the sons of Clovis, hamstrung, deathly pale, floating bound on a barge down a ghastly grey river." This picture is taken by Michael and his crippled friend Kol "for a picture of themselves." That grotesque vision of crippled loyalty seems to be the one families in her fiction promote.

27. In "A Writer's Friends," p. 165, Stead describes how she had collaborated with her art teacher at Sydney Teachers' College to do a book of short stories, which they offered "to a well-known publishing house in

Sydney which, in the spirit of colonial enterprise said they would take some if a British firm did it first." The stories were not published. Stead took the rejected manuscript with her when she left Australia, but it was lost in a Paris hotel room. However, when she started writing *The Salzburg Tales*, she "remembered three of the stories . . . "On the Road," "Morpeth Tower," and "The Triskelion," and put them in (rewritten from memory). All three of these tales are intense expressions of an adolescent girl's fantasies.

28. Sigmund Freud, *The Standard Edition of the Complete Psychological Works of Sigmund Freud*, trans. and ed. James Strachey (London: Hogarth Press, 1955), vol. 9 (1906–1908), pp. 237–241.

29. Or: "All these things are appurtenances of passion itself [and accompany] any interest that draws the frail, sick and wicked human heart."

30. Though more extreme, this heroine's trials are not unlike Teresa's in *For Love Alone*. An earlier and more violent rendering of Teresa Hawkins's story appears in these *Tales* as "The Russian Heart." Maria leaves her peasant home and husband for the city and Ivan Soklow, a sterile pedagogue, whom she mistakenly thinks epitomizes the heights of both love and intellectual glory. Releasing the hatred she feels for Jonathan in *For Love Alone* in a violent fantasy in this tale, Stead punishes the fraudulent, lascivious old scholar by having him decapitated by a window that falls on his neck. Her anger, however, is accompanied by grotesque, masochistic anxieties. Maria relates a dream:

"I went to sleep and dreamed that a barge boy stood in front of me. . . . He gave me the [barge] donkey, which was very small and skinny and had a ragged beard like Ivan Soklow, and took in exchange my two children. Then he cut their heads off and filled a little puddle with blood, and I sat inanely holding the donkey by the tale. 'Here you are, Maria,' he said, and gave me back two apples which I put in my dress. Then he took the donkey by the tail and drew it away from me, brandishing a thick corded whip. The farther he went, the larger grew the donkey, until he swelled so much that I thought my head would split with looking at him, and he swallowed me entirely, and I fell and fell, and presently fell into the pool of blood, where I saw my two children drowned at the bottom, but stiff and smiling, like dolls. 'Ivan,' I cried, but they opened their mouths and yapped, Wap, wap, wap: then they shut their eyes and smiled slyly and sillily at each other, turning to each other, and closing together so that there was nothing left but a loaf of bread."

Not only in these gothic tales, but in all Stead's writing, heroines find that they cannot be feminine, assertive, creative, and independent all at the same time. The tensions that put these components of maturity at odds with one another are both personal and social; their psychic roots are exposed in *The Salzburg Tales*.

31. (New York: Doubleday, 1976), chapter 5.

32. Both this tangled undergrowth and its poisonous spiders are typical of Stead's sexual imagery. Marie in "The Russian Heart" sees two lovers on the road as spiders with eight legs; a tarantula is dropping onto their heads; she speaks of her own "gluey arachnid, tentacular fingers." In "On the Road," a story of forsworn Lesbian attraction, two women take a symbolic journey up a "red, isolated mountain, barren, waterless, with head cleft, and low foothills crouched in woods" where they are beset by a "rough and bestial" storm. The imagery of "Sappho," a tale of ultimately narcissistic homosexual love, includes "forests and lakes . . . dark like the secret locks of young women" and the unusual menstrual metaphor, "a groan [that] bursts from the belly of the sea, black as blood." In "Silk Shirt," a man afraid of passion is trapped in "a thicket [of] strange, smooth tendrils, like female hair."

33. Another tale full of such images is "Gaspard," where the first stirrings of sexual attraction are more queasy than passionate; a pregnancy is echoed in these images: "autumn itself flowed through the trees, savage, flattering, overripe, full of corrupt purples and blues, perfect and preternatural as the exotic orchid."

34. *Washington Post Book World*, 31 December 1972, p. 3.

Quoted in *Adrienne Rich's Poetry*, ed. Barbara and
Albert Gelpi (New York: Norton, 1975), p. xii.

35. The cosmic disharmony of the grotesque suggests an
extension of personal feelings of fragmentation, pain
and internalized denigration. While there are many
sources for such feelings, one is social subordination.
Traditionally bound by images of nurturing maternal
benevolence, women have been denied outlets of aggression, and have been made the bearers of a competi-
tive culture's discarded values of feeling, introspection, and self-effacement. Stead's Domestic Gothic
style draws on the virtues as well as the damages of
that position. It utilizes the permissible access to fantasy and feeling of a constricted subculture to express
the angers and frustrations of being thus confined.

Other women writers have shared this mode of
expression. In *Literary Women*, Ellen Moers starts
tracing a feminine gothic style with Mary Shelley,
Emily Brontë, and Christina Rosetti. Carson McCullers
and Flannery O'Connor practice variants of the Domestic Gothic; contemporary poets (one thinks especially of Sylvia Plath and Anne Sexton) share it too.
But the Gothic and grotesque are not exclusively feminine modes. Writers like Dickens and Kafka share this
angry way of perceiving helplessness and pain. Hu-
mankind, in the existential twentieth century, is often
imagined at a loss in a valueless world, distressed by
human nature that is animal as well as cultivated,
irrational as well as humane. Assertion is not always
distinguished from aggression and is at best ambiva-
lently regarded. One does not have to explain a grotesque style by saying that it expresses the vision of an
oppressed subculture; it derives too from individual
experience of psychic stress and physical pain and
from modes of perception determined by personal
family histories. But the family is a social institution
as well as a private experience, and some of the perceptions formed by it follow social patterns which
many people share. In *The Man Who Loved Children*,
Stead represents this Domestic Gothic vision as one
created from the constraints and strengths of women's
life in the family.

36. Dorothy Green, "Chaos or a Dancing Star? Christina

Stead's 'Seven Poor Men of Sydney,'" *Meanjin Quarterly* 272 (1968), pp. 150–161.

37. Stead, "A Writer's Friends," *Southerly* 28: 3 (1968), p. 168.

38. Ann Whitehead, "Christina Stead: An Interview," *Australian Literary Studies*, 6: 3 (May 1974), p. 238.

39. Harold Straus, *New York Times*, 12 June 1938.

40. Interview.

41. *Sydney Daily Telegraph*, 25 October 1947. Quoted by R. G. Geering, *Christina Stead*, 1969.

42. Interview.

43. *Times Literary Supplement*, 8 September 1978.

44. The Oneida community was one of the most spectacular of the many utopian experiments in nineteenth-century America. Founded by John Humphrey Noyes, it flourished for thirty years, from 1847–1879 at Oneida, New York. Holding property, raising children, and doing work in common, the community also practiced a system of "complex marriage" in which each was married to all the others. Noyes believed that selfishness could be cured by this extended family system. He also held both religion and socialism simultaneously necessary. See *Encyclopedia Britannica*, 1972.

45. See "Marx as Muse," [Review of *The Man Who Loved Children*] *Nation*, 5 April 1965, pp. 368–70.

46. The first chapter of this novel was published as "U.N.O., 1945," part of the unfinished *I'm Dying Laughing* in *Southerly* 22: 4 (1962).

47. Interview. From 1952 to 1962 nothing saw print; only four short stories appeared between 1962 and 1966.

48. Stead combined "The Hotel-Keeper's Story," *Southerly* 13: 2 (1952) and "The Woman in the Bed," *Meanjin Quarterly*, 27: 4 (1968).

49. Stead's original title for the novel was *Mrs. Trollope and Madame Blaise*. Interview.

50. "Father and Children," *New York Review of Books*, 26 June 1975, pp. 13–15, p. 14.

51. See "An Iced Cake with Cherries," *Meanjin Quarterly* 29: 4 (Summer 1970), and other manipulative invalids and old women, like Letty's Grandmother Fox.

52. See the tour de force scene, "The Stuffed Carp" in *House of All Nations* and similar dinners of the pup-

peteers in *The People with the Dogs* or the family
dinners of *The Man Who Loved Children.*

53. *New Yorker,* 18 August 1975, p. 80.

54. That reviewer C. T. Samuels observed as well in *The
Puzzleheaded Girl* in "The Puzzling Miss Stead," *New
Republic,* 157: 30–31, 9 September 1967.

55. Interview. An especially acute review of the novel:
Stephen Koch in *Saturday Review,* May 31, 1975,
writes that *The Little Hotel* "deals in acidulous miniature with the very large subject of Europe's social
transformations following World War II. The resi-
dents of Monsieur and Madame Bonnard's impecu-
nious little Swiss residential hotel are baffled, touching, contemptible relics of European colonial ad-
ministration and the homeless, compromised leisure
class it once sustained. Filled with a quaintness based
more on absurdity than on charm, they are not attractive people. Besotted with their political paranoia
and genteel racism, they numbly live through their
heartbreaking, insufferable rituals, clinging to dwin-
dling bank accounts, which, instead of providing
them with freedom, lock them all the more tightly
into small and hopeless lives. The book describes
these lives with a focus that is almost disorienting in
its precision."

56. "The Woman in the Bed," *Meanjin Quarterly,* 27: 4
(December 1968), 430–52, and "An Iced Cake with
Cherries," *Meanjin Quarterly,* 29: 4 (Summer 1970),
434–441. Also printed as "A Nice Cake," *Partisan Review* 30: 1 (1972), 86–95.

57. (London: F. Muller, 1954), p. 30.

58. See Stead in a recent interview, talking about her own
childhood: "When I was about fifteen, I thought there
was only one true writer in the world who told the
truth about families, and that was Strindberg. I read
many stories about good fathers and mothers and little
girls running to their mothers' laps, and I thought it
was all lies, all nonsense, like we have commercials
now on TV. I thought they were commercials . . .
some kind of story they sold people." Interview.

59. "The Writers Take Sides," *Left Review* 1 (1935), p. 456.
This motif appears in Stead's earliest and latest fic-

tion. "The Amenities" in *The Salzburg Tales* parodies
its romantic heroine, Sarah, but midway through gives
up its ironic distance to assume Sarah's point of view,
as she expresses this same sentiment: When her husband finds her "wrapped in a Medea-like melancholy"
and gently questions her, Sarah replies to him,

"My body is well, but my mind is never well, for I understand things that we must not understand if we are
to live happily; even love—at the bottom of the greatest passion is a feeling of horror and an icy and hopeless boredom: under the flitting, delusive flame is the
jet of marsh-gas. . . . I love you. . . . and what is a
curious thing with a person drawn by so many cross-
currents as myself, I love you with the simplest
woman's love, a peasant's love; but the deeper my feelings, the more oppressed I am by this feeling."

Sarah is preoccupied with "that lonely part of the soul
which even a husband cannot reach, the simple and
childlike part which is the heritage of the child in
us women. Yes, that is the tragedy of married life, that
with the person to whom you are the most attached, you
still feel yourself, at times a complete stranger. . . .
What is sadder than the eternal difference, the eternal
misunderstanding between the sexes?"

     Sarah's feeling of essential loneliness prefigures
the feeling Teresa has just at the point when she expects the culminating satisfaction of her relationship
with James Quick. When they begin to live together,
she tries to confide in him with utter frankness, but
finds that her revelations distress him, so she is unable to be completely at one with him. She is deeply
disappointed, though she later comes to accept the
distance between them and even delight in the play of
their two personalities against each other. Nevertheless, this refrain of isolation echoes all through Stead's
work.

60. Charles Thomas Samuels, "The Puzzling Miss Stead,"
    New Republic, 9 September 1967, p. 31.

61. "Chaos or a Dancing Star?' Christina Stead's 'Seven
    Poor Men of Sydney,'" *Meanjin Quarterly*, 27 (1968),
    p. 151.

5. THE OPTIMISM OF CREATION

1. Alice Moris, *New York Times Book Review.*
2. "The Puzzling Miss Stead," *New Republic*, 157:30–31 (9 September 1967).
3. "The Puzzleheaded Critics," *Nation*, 1 January 1968, p. 21.
4. "Christina Stead's New Realism," p. 13. In *Cunning Exiles*, ed. Don Anderson and Stephen Knight (Sydney: Angus and Robertson, 1974).
5. Interview.
6. "Love Is Where You Find It," review of *Letty Fox, Saturday Review*, 12 October 1946, p. 40.
7. "The Writers Take Sides," *Left Review* 1 (1935), p. 456.

Bibliography

A. PRIMARY SOURCES

1. Fiction

The Salzburg Tales. London: Peter Davies, 1934; New York: D. Appleton-Century, 1934.

Seven Poor Men of Sydney. London: Peter Davies, 1934; New York: D. Appleton-Century, 1935.

The Beauties and Furies. London: Peter Davies, 1936; New York: D. Appleton-Century, 1936.

House of All Nations. London: Peter Davies, 1938; New York: Simon and Schuster, 1938.

The Man Who Loved Children. New York: Simon and Schuster, 1940; London: Peter Davies, 1941.

For Love Alone. New York: Harcourt, Brace, 1944; London: Peter Davies, 1945.

Letty Fox: Her Luck. New York: Harcourt, Brace, 1946; London: Peter Davies, 1947.

A Little Tea, A Little Chat. New York: Harcourt, Brace, 1948.

The People with the Dogs. Boston: Little, Brown, 1952.

Dark Places of the Heart. New York: Holt, Rinehart and Winston, 1966; [*Cotter's England*] London: Secker and Warburg, 1967.

The Puzzleheaded Girl, Four Novellas: New York: Holt, Rinehart and Winston, 1967; London: Secker and Warburg, 1968.

The Little Hotel: A Novel. London: Angus and Robertson,
    1973; New York: Holt, Rinehart and Winston, 1975.
Miss Herbert (The Suburban Wife). New York: Random
    House, 1976.
A Christina Stead Reader. New York: Random House, 1979.

2.   Anthologies and Translations

*Modern Women in Love: Sixty Twentieth-Century Master-
    pieces of Fiction.* ed. Christina Stead and William
    Blake. New York: Dryden Press, 1945.
Great Stories of the South Sea Islands, selected with a for-
    ward by Christina Stead. London: Muller, 1955.
Gignon, Fernand. *Colour of Asia.* London: Muller, 1955.
Giltène, Jean. *The Candid Killer.* London: Muller, 1956.
Piccard, Auguste. *In Balloon and Bathyscaphe.* London:
    Cassell, 1956.

3.   Individual Short Stories

"O, If I Could But Shiver!" in *The Fairies Return; or, New
    Tales for Old, by Several Hands.* London: Peter Davies,
    1934, pp. 289–310.
"The Hotel-Keeper's Story." *Southerly* 13: 2 (1952), pp. 74–82.
"A Household." *Southerly* 22: 4 (1962), pp. 213–234.
"U.N.O. 1945." *Southerly* 22: 4 (1962), pp. 235–253.
"The Huntress." *Saturday Evening Post,* 23 October 1965,
    pp. 76–89.
"The Puzzleheaded Girl." *Kenyon Review* 27: 3 (1965), pp.
    399–456. Also in *Australian Letters* 7: 2 (March 1966),
    pp. 26–62.
"George." *Paris Review* 10 (Winter 1967), pp. 12–48.
"The Woman in the Bed." *Meanjin Quarterly* 27: 4 (De-
    cember 1968), pp. 430–452.
"An Iced Cake with Cherries." *Meanjin Quarterly* 29: 4
    (Summer 1970), pp. 434–441. Also printed as "A Nice
    Cake." *Partisan Review* 39: 1 (1972), pp. 86–95.
"The Azhdanov Tailors." *Commentary* 52: 1 (July 1971), pp.
    55–58.

"Street Idyll." *Sun* (Melbourne), 5 January 1972, p. 25. (rpt. in *Festival, and Other Stories*, ed. B. Buckley and J. Hamilton. North Pomfret, Vermont: David & Charles, 1975.)

"The Milk Run." *New Yorker*, 9 December 1972, pp. 43–47; also in *Sun* (Melbourne), 3 January 1975, pp. 24–25.

"The Captain's House." *Sun* (Melbourne), 15 January 1973, p. 24. (rpt. in *Festival, and Other Stories*, ed. B. Buckley and J. Hamilton. David & Charles, 1975.)

"The Boy." *Meanjin Quarterly* 32: 1 (Autumn 1973), pp. 23–33.

"Fairy Child." *Harvard Advocate* 106: 2-3 (Winter 1973), pp. 56–58.

"I Live in You." *Sun* (Melbourne), 30 December 1973, p. 19.

"A View of the Homestead." *Paris Review* 14 (Spring 1974), pp. 124–130.

"Uncle Morgan at the Nats." *Partisan Review* 43: 1 (1976), pp. 60–67.

4. *Articles and Reviews*

"The Writers Take Sides." *Left Review* 1: 11 (August 1935), pp. 453–462.

"The Impartial Young Man," review of *Inhale and Exhale* by William Saroyan. *New Masses* 18, 17 March 1936, pp. 25–26.

Review of *The Century Was Young* by Louis Aragon. *New Masses* 42, 20 January 1942, pp. 23–25.

"Pro and Con on Aragon." *New Masses*, 42, 17 February 1942, pp. 23–24.

Review of *Lost Haven* by Kylie Tennant. *New York Times Book Review*, 7 April 1946, p. 8.

Review of *Cousin from Fiji* by Norman Lindsay. *New York Times Book Review*, 7 April 1946, p. 8.

Review of *Sun on the Hills* by Margaret Trist. *New York Times Book Review*, 7 April 1946, p. 10.

Review of *Nowhere Was Somewhere* by Arthur E. Morgan. *New York Times Book Review*, 11 August 1946, p. 29.

"[The International Symposium on the Short Story, Part 1:] England." *Kenyon Review* 30: 4 (1968), pp. 444–450.

"A Writer's Friends." *Southerly* 28: 3 (1968), pp. 163–168.
"About Woman's Insight, There Is a Sort of Folklore We Inherit," in "Women's Intuition," ed. Eileen Simpson. *Vogue* (America) 158: 5, 15 September 1971, pp. 61, 130.
"A Waker and Dreamer." *Overland* 53 (Spring 1972), pp. 33–37.
"1954: Days of the Roomers." *Overland* 62 (1975), pp. 30–31.

5. *Interviews*

Beston, John. "An Interview with Christina Stead." *World Literature Written in English* 15: 1 (April 1976), pp. 87–95.
Lidoff, Joan. "Christina Stead: An Interview." *Aphra* 6: 3 & 4 (Spring–Summer 1976), pp. 39–64.
———. An Interview with Christina Stead. Surbiton, England. June, 1973. Reprinted here, pages 180–220.
Raskin, Jonah. "Christina Stead in Washington Square." *London Magazine* 9: 11 (February 1970), pp. 70–77.
Whitehead, Ann. "Christina Stead: An Interview." *Australian Literary Studies* 6: 3 (May 1974), pp. 230–248. (Interview recorded 18 July 1973).

B. SELECTED SECONDARY WORKS

Baer, Barbara. "Castaways of History." *Nation*, 26 April 1975, pp. 501–503.
Beston, John. "A Brief Biography of Christina Stead." *World Literature Written in English* 15: 1 (April 1976), pp. 79–86.
Beston, Rose Marie. "A Christina Stead Bibliography." *World Literature Written in English* 15: 1 (April 1976), pp. 96–103.
Blake, William James [Blech]. *The Copperheads.* New York: Dial Press, 1941.
———. *Elements of Marxian Economic Theory and Its Criticism* [Also published as *An American Looks at Karl Marx*]. New York: Cordon Co., 1939.

———. *Understanding the Americans.* London: Muller, 1954.

———. *Obituaries. London Times,* 9 February 1968.
New York Times, 21 February 1968.
Antiquarian Bookman, 4–11 March 1968.

Brickell, Herschell. "Some Rare Tales." [Review of *The Salzburg Tales*] *North American Review* 238 (December 1934) p. 576.

Boyers, Robert. "The Family Novel." *Salmagundi,* 26 (Spring 1974), pp. 3–25.

Burns, Graham. "The Moral Design of *The Man Who Loved Children.*" *Critical Review* (Melbourne) 14 (1971), pp. 36–61.

Calisher, Hortense. [Review of *The Little Hotel*] *The New York Times Book Review,* 11 May 1975, p. 6.

Cassill, R. V. [Review of *The Puzzleheaded Girl*] *Book World, Washington Post,* 10 September 1967, p. 3.

Contemporary Authors: The International Bio-Biographical Guide to Contemporary Authors and Their Works, ed. Clare D. Kinsman. Detroit: Gale Research Co., begun 1962. vol. 15–16 (1966).

Donoghue, Denis. [Review of *The Puzzleheaded Girl*] *New York Review of Books,* 28 September 1967, p. 8.

Eldershaw, M. Barnard. *Essays in Australian Fiction.* Melbourne: Melbourne University Press, 1938, pp. 158–181.

Fadiman, Clifton. *Reading I've Liked.* New York: Simon & Schuster, 1941, pp. 521–522.

———. [Review of *The Man Who Loved Children*] *New Yorker,* 19 October 1940, p. 104.

Farber, Marjorie. "Amor, Amor, Amor." [Review of *For Love Alone*] *New Republic,* 13 November 1944, pp. 632–634.

Foote, Audrey. "Pensioned Off" [Review of *The Little Hotel*] *Book World, Washington Post,* 1 June 1975, pp. 1–2.

Gardiner, Judith Kegan. Christina Stead: "Dark Places of the Heart" [Review of *Miss Herbert (The Suburban Wife)*] *The North American Review,* Spring 1977, pp. 67–71.

Gardner, Frederick H. "The Puzzleheaded Critics." [Review

of *The Puzzleheaded Girl*] *Nation*, 1 January 1968, pp. 21–22.

Geering, R. G. *Christina Stead.* Twayne World Author Series. New York: Twayne, 1969.

———. "Christina Stead in the 1960's." *Southerly*, 28: 1 (1968), pp. 26–36.

Gold, Michael. [Review of *House of All Nations*] *Daily Worker*, 8 September 1938.

Green, Dorothy. "Chaos or a Dancing Star? Christina Stead's 'Seven Poor Men of Sydney.'" *Meanjin Quarterly* 27: 2 (1968), pp. 150–161.

Hardwick, Elizabeth. "The Neglected Novels of Christina Stead," in *A View of My Own: Essays in Literature and Society.* London: Heinemann, 1964, pp. 41–48.

Jarrell, Randall. "An Unread Book." Introduction to *The Man Who Loved Children* and rpt. *The Third Book of Criticism* (New York: Farrar, Straus, Giroux, 1969).

Katz, Alfred. "Some Psychological Themes in a Novel by Christina Stead." *Literature and Psychology*, 15 (Fall 1965), pp. 210–215.

deKay, Drake. "Another Decameron." [Review of *The Salzburg Tales*] *New York Times Book Review*, 21 October 1934, p. 7.

Koch, Stephen. [Review of *The Little Hotel*] *Saturday Review*, 31 May 1975, p. 28.

Lidoff, Joan. "The Female Ego: Christina Stead's Heroines." *New Boston Review*, January 1977, pp. 19–20.

———. "Home Is Where the Heart Is: The Fiction of Christina Stead." *Southerly*, December 1978, pp. 363–375.

———. "Domestic Gothic: The Imagery of Anger. Christina Stead's *The Man Who Loved Children*." *Studies in the Novel*, Summer 1979, pp. 201–215.

Lindsay, Jack. "Vision of the Twenties." *Southerly* 13: 2 (1952), pp. 62–71.

McCarthy, Mary. "Framing Father." [Review of *The Man Who Loved Children*] *New Republic* 13 (January 1941), p. 61.

McGrory, Mary. [Review of *Letty Fox: Her Luck*] *New York Times*, 6 October 1946, p. 24.

Moers, Ellen. *Literary Women. The Great Writers.* New York: Doubleday & Co., 1976.

Ricks, Christopher. "Domestic Manners." [Review of *The Man Who Loved Children*] *New York Review of Books*, 17 June 1965, pp. 14–15.

———. "Fathers and Children." [Review of *The Little Hotel*] *The New York Review of Books*, 26 June 1975, pp. 13–15.

Roderick, Colin. *An Introduction to Australian Fiction*. Sydney: Angus and Robertson, 1950, pp. 132–138.

———. *Twenty Australian Novelists*. Sydney: Angus and Robertson, 1947, pp. 190–215.

Samuels, Charles Thomas. "The Puzzling Miss Stead." [Review of *The Puzzleheaded Girl*] *New Republic*, 9 September 1967, pp. 30–31.

Showalter, Elaine. *A Literature of Their Own*. Princeton: Princeton University Press, 1977.

Smith, Harrison. "Love Is Where You Find It." [Review of *Letty Fox*] *Saturday Review*, 12 October 1946, p. 40.

Sontag, Susan. *Styles of Radical Will*. New York: Farrar, Straus & Giroux, 1969.

Southerly 38: 4 (December 1978). An issue devoted to Christina Stead.

Stewart, Douglas. *The Flesh and the Spirit, An Outlook on Literature*. Sydney: Angus and Robertson, 1948, pp. 235–238.

Straus, Harold. "A Novel of Frenzied Finance." [Review of *House of All Nations*] *New York Times Book Review*, 12 June 1938, p. 2.

Sturm, Terry. "Christina Stead's New Realism," in *Cunning Exiles*, ed. Don Anderson and Stephen Knight. Sydney: Angus and Robertson, 1974, pp. 9–35.

Times Literary Supplement. [Review of *For Love Alone*] 13 October 1945, p. 485.

Trilling, Diana. "Women in Love." [Review of *For Love Alone*] *Nation* 28 (October 1944), pp. 535–536.

Trilling, Lionel. *Sincerity and Authenticity. The Charles Eliot Norton Lecture, 1969–70*. Cambridge: Harvard University Press, 1972.

Twentieth Century Authors. A Biographical Dictionary of Modern Literature, ed. Stanley Jasspon Kunitz and Howard Haycraft. New York: Wilson, 1942.

Updike, John. [Review of *The Little Hotel*] *New Yorker*, 18 August 1975, p. 180.

————. [Review f *Miss Herbert*] *New Yorker*, 9 August 1976, pp. 74–77.

Walt, James. "An Australian Novelist Looks at Americans." *UNISA* 4 (November 1969), pp. 34–39. [Bulletin of the Department of English, University of South Africa]

Who's Who in Australia. Melbourne: Herald and Weekly Times, begun 1922.

Wilding, Michael. "Christina Stead's Australian Novels. *Southerly* 27: 1 (1967), pp. 20–33.

————. [Review of *Dark Places of the Heart*] *London Magazine* (November 1967), pp. 98–100.

————. [Review of *The Puzzleheaded Girl*] *London Magazine* (June 1968), pp. 112–113.

Wilson Bulletin for Librarians. "Christina Stead" 13: 4 (December 1938), p. 234.

Yglesias, José. "Marking off a Chunk of England." [Review of *Dark Places of the Heart*] *Nation* 24 (October 1966), pp. 420–421.

————. "Marx as Muse." [Review of *The Man Who Loved Children*] *Nation*, 5 April 1965, pp. 368–370.

Index